144904

La
Stupenda

La Stupenda

a biography of
JOAN SUTHERLAND

BRIAN ADAMS

Hutchinson of Australia

HUTCHINSON GROUP (Australia) Pty Ltd
30-32 Cremorne Street, Richmond, Victoria, 3121

Melbourne Sydney London
Auckland Johannesburg
and agencies throughout the world

First published 1980
Reprinted 1980, 1982, 1983, 1984
© Brian Adams 1980
Designed by Derrick I. Stone Design
Printed in Hong Kong

National Library of Australia
Cataloguing in Publication Data:
Adams, Brian.
La Stupenda.

Index
Bibliography
ISBN 0 09 137410 3

1. Sutherland, Dame Joan, 1926-. 2. Opera—Biography.
3. Singers—Biography. I. Title
782.1'092'4

Contents

For Joan and Richard

Preface

The idea for this book evolved from a television documentary I wrote and directed called 'Joan Sutherland: A Life On The Move', itself the realization of an ambition I had held since Sutherland and Bonynge returned to Australia in 1965 for the Sutherland-Williamson opera season which turned into almost a national occasion. I had returned that year after working in British television and took an apartment at the back of a mansion in the Melbourne suburb of Toorak. A few months later the house was occupied by the Bonynges and their staff and very soon my bathroom became a sounding board for the most glorious coloratura strains rising through the pipes from below. We never met, and soon after their arrival I moved to Sydney from where I wrote suggesting the making of a documentary about their tour. There was no reply and the idea lapsed.

In 1974 I was compiling a feature to celebrate the centenary of J.C. Williamson Theatres, one of the oldest and most celebrated theatrical enterprises in the world, and as a part of the show I sought reminiscences from many celebrities who had been associated with 'the Firm', as it is affectionately known. I filmed with Dame Sybil Thorndike, Sir Ralph Richardson, Dame Anna Neagle, Yehudi Menuhin, Sir Robert Helpmann, Cyril Ritchard, Dame Judith Anderson and many others. But there was one name missing from the list — Joan Sutherland, whose 1965 performances with Williamson's made her a 'must', but once again my efforts drew a blank. I began to think she was a most reluctant prima donna.

In early 1978, having just finished a film about the Australian painter Sidney Nolan, I was thinking about my next subject and one day after a particularly languid lunch in the height of Sydney's sybaritic summer, I sat down and typed a rather formal and pretentious letter to Joan Sutherland at the Sydney Opera House where she was rehearsing *The Merry Widow*. On reflection I certainly wouldn't have sent it in that form if my sobriety at the time had been complete. Part of it read,

It is part of our commitment to present the leading Australians who are work-ing in an international context to the widest television audience in order to enhance our national image.
    Would you consider discussing this proposal in the near future?

A few days later the telephone rang and a friendly voice at the other end said, 'Hello, this is Joan Sutherland. I'd like to talk about this film idea.' Needless to say I was surprised. After avoid-ing television for anything but perfomances, Sutherland and Bonynge were happy to proceed with a documentary portrait about their life and work. While they were in London for *Maria Stuarda* at Covent Garden they saw my Nolan film on BBC Tele-vision. They were in the process of buying one of his paintings and the film endorsed their choice when Lord Clark's narration referred to their very picture from Nolan's series about Australia's North-West and its mining industry. They also thought that Nolan himself had been treated sympathetically in the film.

And so thirteen years after my first attempts to make a film about Sutherland I faced the challenge of shooting sequences with them in London, New York, Switzerland, Japan, Korea and Australia over a period of twelve months. We got to know each other well because of the close proximity demanded by making such a documentary portrait. By the end of that time I realized there was a much bigger story to be told than I could possibly encompass in an eighty-minute film and this book is the result. I subsequently returned to their home in Switzerland and visited London and New York for research and my grateful thanks for those who assisted me in my quest for information are given in the list of acknowledgements. My most heartfelt thanks must go to the many newspaper and magazine music critics who have been witness to Sutherland's performances over a span of more than thirty years and who are the main contemporary sources of artistic interpretation of her many operatic roles, recordings and concert appearances. I have quoted extensively from their reviews.

When quoting the titles of operas and naming arias I have used the style printed in the official programmes of the opera houses

and organizations producing the production. The same procedure has been adopted for recordings, recitals and concerts. A
comprehensive discography, list of first performances and bibliography appear at the end of the book.

Acknowledgements

Research material has come from many sources in Europe, the United States of America and Australia, from people and organizations who have played a significant role in Sutherland's career or had merely a fleeting encounter with it. All of their impressions and comments have been invaluable in building up my mosaic of information.

The principal source has been the Bonynge Archive at Chalet Monet, Les Avants, Switzerland. The orderly scrapbooks of press cuttings, magazine articles and opera programmes, together with picture files, have been carefully supervised over the years by Anne Roughley, Richard Bonynge's aunt. For details about William Sutherland and his youngest daughter's early years I am indebted to Mrs Ailsa Hargraves of Sydney.

Personal recollections and impressions came from many people: principally Terry McEwen, President of London Records, New York; Russell Braddon of London, whose excellent biography of Sutherland published in 1962 is an essential source of information about her early life; and Sister Marie Bernarde of Mary White College, University of New England, Armidale, New South Wales, whose generous offer of access to her own research made my task immeasurably easier.

My thanks for assistance go to the Covent Garden Archive, London; the Metropolitan Opera Archive, New York; the Decca Record Company, London (Graham Turnbull and David Rickerby); the Australian Opera (Moffatt Oxenbould); E.M.I. Australia, Sydney (Patricia Byrne); Mobil Oil Australia Limited, Melbourne (Rex Thomson); the City of Sydney Cultural Council (Barbara Firth); Norman Ayrton, London; Franco Zeffirelli, Los Angeles; Marilyn Horne, New York; Ruthli Brendlé, Chester Carone and Gertie Stelzel of Les Avants, Switzerland; Elizabeth Betson, London; Sandro Sequi, Rome; Reiner Moritz, Munich; and Michael Giffin, Sydney.

Chapter One

I feel a loyalty to the public. They pay a great deal of money to hear me sing and I certainly do not want to displease them.

In mid-1979 the Lincoln Center for the Performing Arts in New York celebrated its twentieth anniversary of presenting the biggest, the best and the most expensive events in the world of arts. The most public feature of the occasion was a vast screen masking the facade of the Metropolitan Opera House and forming the background for a sound-and-light display. On the screen three principal elements of the Center's activities were seen — music, ballet and opera. A huge panel showed the American Leonard Bernstein conducting, another depicted the Russian Mikhail Baryshnikov dancing, and the third represented the Australian soprano Dame Joan Sutherland in full voice.

The celebrations held a double meaning for Sutherland because 1979 was also the twentieth anniversary of her rise to international fame, not in New York, but across the Atlantic at London's Royal Opera House, Covent Garden.

At the same time in southern Europe another event was taking place that re-emphasized the power of opera to capture wide attention for an art form that has been regarded by some as a late twentieth century anachronism, an élitist remnant of the past.

In Athens it was a typical summer Sunday; the sky apparently blue overhead but, when seen laterally from the heights of the Acropolis or Mount Lycabettus, a persistent screen of yellow-brown smog was evident filtering the city's famous translucency. The tourist season had started earlier than usual; in fact, with Greece becoming increasingly popular as an inexpensive holiday destination for Europeans and one of the last affordable countries in Europe for Americans and Australians with their declining dollar-values, the seasons each year were tending to begin earlier and end later. The only threat to a continuing increase of visitors was the looming energy crisis that had not yet curtailed private traffic on Sundays, forced an abandonment of the city's traditional siesta, or closed the nightclubs and bars of the Plaka at the unthinkably early hour of 2 a.m. The temperature was a comfortable 29 degrees, hotels were refusing bookings unless they were for a minimum stay of a week, and the Syntagma Square area was crowded with the rich and impecunious alike, thronging the foyers of the Grand Bretagne and the King George, jostling with the legions of pack-carriers to change traveller's cheques and pick up the latest ferry schedules for the islands at the National Tourist Office, or just sitting in the cafés outside American Express watching other tourists saunter by.

A few kilometres away at Hellenikon Airport, a screaming succession of jets, chartered and scheduled, were landing and disgorging their travellers eager to experience one of the world's most exciting cities to the senses yet intensely uncomfortable in its chaotic and chronic ill-planning.

One flight was given priority and avoided the usual tourist traumas of currency declarations, Customs control and lost luggage. It was direct from Paris, provided by the French government, and its passengers brought very little luggage. One of them, the Greek pianist Vaso Devedzi, carried with him the reason for the special journey: a simple wooden casket holding the ashes of Maria Callas.

For two decades Greeks, who are not often singled out for their outstanding operatic achievements, had basked in the brilliance of Callas's fame. It was a reminder perhaps of the glories of their ancient heritage made immediate by a constant publicity that was, however, more often associated with affairs of the heart and displays of temperament than an outstanding singing career. Now she had returned to the land of her origins, but not of her birth; that was far away in New York where concurrently the Sutherland voice was trilling out in Lincoln Center's sound-and-light show.

Maria Callas had died eighteen months earlier at the age of fifty-three, a dazzling career snuffed out by declining health and crumpled convictions. Her ashes were kept in a Paris cemetery until an attempt was made to abduct them. It was unsuccessful, but close friends, such as Devedzi, realized that something must be done to spare the remains from further abuses. It had been Callas's hope that her ashes be scattered on the Aegean Sea and now they were about to carry out the diva's final wish. Also on the two and a half hour flight were the deputy mayor of Paris, a representative of the public notary who had read the will and needed to see that its instructions were carried out, Callas's sister, and two of the singer's maids who were with her when she died. At the airport they were greeted by the Greek Minister for Science and Culture as well as the Defence Minister.

In classical times, Greeks referred to the Aegean as 'the road'. It was the meeting-point for east and west, and on its unpredictable waters myth, legend and history became inextricably mingled. Most modern Greeks, wherever they live in their own far-flung land or abroad, regard themselves as an island people, and Callas's final request was adding to the many legends of heroines and heroes whose fate was linked with the ebb and flow of that ancient sea.

The strange cortège drove from the airport in the hazy sunshine to Piraeus and then boarded a navy torpedo boat to set out in the direction of the island of Aegina some twenty-five kilometres away. Engines were cut, and within sight of the beautiful Doric temple of Aphaia built in the fifth century BC, they became becalmed as the ship's foghorn sounded and a trumpeter played an eerie lament in counterpoint. The Science and Culture Minister lifted the blue and white Greek flag from the casket, opened its lid, and scattered the grey powdery ashes onto the dark blue waters. A hail of roses, gardenias and carnations followed from the rest of the motley party on board, which included the mayor of Athens, a Greek opera and theatre producer, and the Chief of the Navy.

If there was any doubt that the stars of grand opera — the prima donnas and leading tenors — were superfluous in the closing decades of the century, this surreal ceremony on the Saronic Gulf — as unbelievable as any operatic plot — would be enough to dispel most reservations. In fact, the whole history of opera's leading singers has been studded with similar incidents and, although contemporary reactions may be more blasé in an era of insubstantial show-business stardom, there remains an absorbing curiosity about them. Since the eighteenth century the public has expected

13

its operatic heroines to play out their roles off stage as well as on, and a singer such as Callas strikes a particular chord of curiosity for a vastly wider audience than those who ever enter an opera house.

Callas's successor at the pinnacle of operatic fame was Joan Sutherland, whose star was already in the ascendant as Callas's was slipping. For Callas, only three years older, it seemed inevitable that she should be a living legend; it was a role that apparently complemented her personality and life-style. She fulfilled the popular concept of a prima donna — or was forced to adopt it by the ceaseless glare of publicity which reported and distorted every move. For Sutherland such an image was to sit less comfortably, even reluctantly. Where Callas's life was depicted as eternally eventful, Sutherland's is often reported and distorted because of its lack of incident. Yet she has become the embodiment of a continuing tradition of great singing and her story is all the more remarkable for the new dimensions she brings to the role.

While Callas's ashes and floral tributes were drifting away on the currents of the Aegean, Sutherland was in her native Sydney, beside the Pacific Ocean, preparing to receive from the Governor-General one of the highest awards the community can bestow. In Queen Elizabeth's New Year Honours it was announced Sutherland would be elevated to a Dame Commander of the British Empire for services to the performing arts. It was not at all unexpected, for this was the logical progression from the C.B.E. she had received long ago in 1961. In fact, with the inevitability of the award, the only doubt was when it would be announced.

For twenty years she had reigned as one of the world's great sopranos and, in a tradition extending back to 1919 when Nellie Melba was similarly recognized, Australian singers have left their echoes on the international opera scene and several have been duly decorated by the monarch. Sutherland's characteristic remark was, 'I'm glad it happened before I got too old'.

It also came as no great surprise that when the announcement was made she was in Amsterdam singing *Norma*. For nearly thirty years her life has been on the move, from airport to hotel, hotel to recording studio, recording studio to opera house, opera house to official reception — with relatively few periods of relaxation in between. This consistency and devotion to her art and her audiences, coupled with a unique voice, has gained her great esteem. Sutherland has performed in all the major opera houses of the world and made an impressive number of recordings, so outstanding in their quality and originality that her immortality is already assured.

Not so fortunate were the prima donnas of old. Their voices can be assessed only by contemporary description, or from records that are often scratchy semblances of voices lost in a fog of distance and the inadequacy of technology. In opera's so-called Golden Age, toward the end of the nineteenth century, a diva would make a regal progress from one city to another. Performances were punctuated by leisurely sea voyages, long railroad trips and dusty carriage rides, with at least a personal maid in attendance, if not a large entourage of helpers. These days, with audiences larger than ever before and commitments increasingly demanding, the prima donna has been forced to become more pragmatic, knowing the international flight schedules and aircraft seating plans almost as well as her repertoire.

Joan Sutherland is one of the busiest of an élite group of singers who consistently attract capacity audiences all over the world. Together with her husband and mentor, the conductor Richard Bonynge, she divides her time between home in Switzerland, a house in Australia and a daunting schedule of opera roles, recitals, recording sessions and public appearances. The Bonynge partnership is one of the most formidable in the history of opera and has grown into a big business.

With all of this behind her, and a career for as long as she wants to continue, she might be excused for displaying the hauteur and stormy temperament synonymous with the position. In fact, the apparent lack of such characteristics has been interpreted by some critics as an absence of emotion — both in her private and professional life — lacking the passion always associated with Callas. Sutherland's Scottish background does, however, occasionally lead her into a directness — some call it a bluntness — that compels her to say exactly what she thinks. There is also a latent temper that can erupt in moments of extreme tension, but subsides equally quickly like the passing of a Sydney summer storm.

The combination of Scottish background and Australian upbringing has moulded a personality which is at once endearing and difficult to understand. Most divas bask in constant praise and preen themselves on compliments — expecting them to be continually forthcoming, whether justified or not. Sutherland, in a typically Australian way, shrinks from excessive praise and is much more at home handing out good-natured insults than flattering herself. She doesn't suffer fools or foolishness gladly. This has sometimes led to friction with the press — particularly in Australia, where a continuing ambivalent relationship veered in the direction of affection with the announcement of the damehood and its subsequent status of a living national monument. It was a brief change of heart. Personality clashes within the Board of the Australian Opera, for whom she frequently performs, and where Bonynge is musical director, once again turned the newspapers, who devote an inordinate amount of space to opera's infighting, to question Sutherland's true worth in a typically Australian attempt to cut down her international reputation to a manageable provincial size.

In the face of all this, Sutherland, who is a large resilient woman, tends to make fun of herself and pretends not to notice what is being written about her. It certainly makes no difference at all to the audiences who continue to flock to every one of her performances. She finds it difficult, even with so much attention, to understand how fame came her way and remained. She is still at heart the resourceful Australian housewife and mother she never had time to be, loving to sew curtains, arranging the flowers, cooking, and 'generally pottering around the house', as she puts it. She happened also to possess an outstanding voice and developed an extraordinary stage presence, making it clear that domestic duties would not feature prominently in her life. Instead, it would be a rigid and cloistered existence. As she said, 'You can't smoke, you can drink hardly anything. I drink only a little wine with my meals — and that's a habit I've picked up from mixing so much with Italians.'

The story of the overweight girl from Sydney's eastern suburbs; a secretary with a burning devotion to singing, who eventually became Dame Joan, has many elements of fantasy. But the world of opera is unpredictable and, for its perfomers, egalitarian. A particular combination of circumstance, incident, influence and determination moulded Sutherland into an international celebrity, winning for her the accolades of 'La Stupenda' and 'The

Voice of the Century', and 'Joyce Wonderland' from her colleagues in the Australian Opera.

The career that Sutherland and Bonynge have fashioned for themselves is akin to a daring trapeze act in the circus — without a safety net. The bel canto operas, in which they excel, mean principally about 125 formula works by Rossini, Bellini and Donizetti, requiring great singing for their continuity and survival; there is little other reason for the existence of the tragedies, but perhaps more for the comedies. They had been almost forgotten when the world had time to turn to opera again after the Second World War. Maria Callas, who was not ideally suited for this challenging repertory, made a great impact and attracted a large public to them by the force of her personality. Sutherland was better equipped vocally to carry on the tradition and do justice to the stylistic intentions of the composers. Most important, she had Bonynge who really knew about the traditions.

In this age of musical curiosity, recordings are quickly covering the entire spectrum of composition, but on stage the financial restraints imposed by rapidly rising costs may limit the future of bel canto. Fortunately, as with Callas, Sutherland has a repertoire with a wider breadth than Rossini, Bellini and Donizetti. But since her rise to international stardom in 1959 there have been few other singers emerging with the prodigious vocal powers to suggest that opera's future will see as extensive an exploration into the delights of the eighteenth and early nineteenth century Italian repertoire as has happened during the Sutherland years.

Chapter Two

I used to copy my mother doing her scales and exercises and this formed the basis of my technique. But she thought it wrong to train the voice too young.

'The capitalists are the mass of the people', declared the Australian Prime Minister Stanley Melbourne Bruce, suggesting that few were underprivileged in his nation during those more gullible years of the century. On the sunburnt surface his smoothly mendacious views seemed to have some validity; only 6 per cent of the population were out of work, an ethos of the Good Life pervaded the cities and the air was heavy with hedonism backed by the prospect of prosperity that would grow exponentially into a limitless future. The pursuit of pleasure was the message for those who could afford it — and many could if they earned above the weekly basic wage of £4 10s. Even those of meagre means, it was assumed, need only look out on Sydney Harbour most days of the year and see the sun sparkling on its blue waters, to know that their world was not such a bad place. On the wharves, however, where the water was oily and grey there was a growing threat of union unrest. In Melbourne a petty Chicago-style gangster called Squizzy Taylor was receiving considerable newspaper space for his exploits as he led a gang of thugs in the Fitzroy slums, but it was communism, not Taylor, that was really the Public Enemy Number One. In an attempt to rationalize industrial relations and deal with left-wing disruptives, the government passed a new Crimes Act making it a criminal offence to participate in strikes during a declared state of emergency. There were thought to be undesirables who might try to enter the country to ferment anarchy, and to guard against them another bill was passed in the federal parliament which could exclude any-one who did not subscribe to the principles and ideals for which Australia stood.

The problem was, in that year of 1926, few principles and ideals were clearly defined as an era of materialism threatened to slide into militantism. It was barely a quarter of a century since the self-administering states joined together into a commonwealth, and whatever patriotic fervour was uppermost in 1901 had been dispersed by the intervention of a world war which had seen so many Australians rally to the flag for King and mother country only to remain buried in some foreign field on the far side of the globe. Distance from its Anglo-Saxon roots, a small and widely-scattered population, and delicate vulnerability to world economic fluctuations made the nation in the first quarter of this century a perplexing paradise. Prime Minister Bruce's words could have brought little cheer to the rural unemployed, or to the poor crammed into their inner-city slums, or to the soldier-settlers far out in the backblocks trying to tame vast tracts of land handed to them as a reward for military service.

The news from abroad was hardly cheering either, particularly when it concerned Britain's crippling general strike and the widespread political uncertainties in Europe, but there were some local diversions to take the mind off serious events. Anna Pavlova was receiving great ovations during her tour and a young man from Mount Gambier in South Australia named Robert Helpmann, who had a surprising obsession with dance, was invited to join her company as a student. There was also a visit by the stately English contralto, Dame Clara Butt, who, it was claimed, had been advised by Melba to 'sing 'em muck' on her concert tour. The noted Russian bass, Feodor Chaliapin, sang to Australian audiences as he knew best and enthralled those whose main experience of music-making was either at home around the piano or in suburban music clubs. The first Miss Australia quest was launched, Sydney's first electric train service began, the foxtrot became the rage, and the newspapers were full of society news and advertisements for the new women's fashions which gave promise of youth at any age with their flat chests, long waists and short skirts. Wireless broadcasting moved out of its pioneering stage, the cinema was still silent but vastly popular, and a wide

19

range of electric consumer goods — toasters, irons and vacuum-cleaners — filled the stores. In federal politics the coalition of Bruce and Dr Earle Page — Nationalist and Country Party — was firmly entrenched, guiding the affairs of the nation and looking forward to an imminent move into Parliament House in the new capital of Canberra where it was hoped a focus of attention for Australians might give rise to a binding nationalism.

Meanwhile, at a rambling house overlooking Sydney Harbour about six miles from the centre of the city, William McDonald Sutherland, aged fifty-four, had completed his morning swim below the garden of his residence, Patonga, at number six Wolseley Road, Point Piper. He sat in the shade of the verandah and read about the affairs of the world in the *Sydney Morning Herald* and noted that the crowd of 118,877 who cheered Spearfelt past the post in Australia's premier horse race, the Melbourne Cup, had placed a record amount of money in bets and his religious hackles were raised in protest.

William Sutherland was born on 11 November 1871 on the far north coast of Scotland which faces out to the Orkneys and Shetlands, a sparsely populated region of fast-running streams and rocky crags. The area between Cape Wrath and Dunnet Head, where the influence of the warm Gulf Stream currents coaxes roses to bloom in December, contains the fishing village of Portskerra where he was born and spent his childhood days. His father held interests in several vessels of the fishing fleet which provided the principal industry on the coast but William's inclination was toward a different career and as soon as he was old enough to move away from home he entered the mercery trade in the nearby town of Thurso, where he served an apprenticeship before working in Glasgow, Edinburgh and London. His wanderings took him much further in 1892 when at the age of twenty-one he decided to try his luck in Australia and arrived in Sydney right in the middle of a luckless economic downturn that needed no more tailors. Unable to get a job, he went to join an uncle who ran a general store at Crookwell, a small rural centre in the Goulburn district of New South Wales where he stayed for four years and during that time married his cousin, Clara Ethel McDonald. They went to New Zealand for two years and returned to Sydney just as work conditions were improving and William found employment with the tailoring firm of Loader and Willock in King Street. He

20

remained with them for several years before joining the staff of the fashionable department store of David Jones to become a cutter in their tailoring section. In 1910 he and a fellow employee combined to establish their own business under the name of Sutherland and Gamble until William Sutherland eventually set up on his own and nurtured a large clientele among the legal and medical men of Macquarie Street.

The Sutherlands' was a solid Scots partnership and he maintained a strong interest in nationalist affairs, becoming a councillor of the Highland Society in 1906 and later, chairman of the Highland Gathering Committee, a member of the board of Sydney's Scottish Hospital, an elder of the city's principal Presbyterian church and also a Freemason. William Sutherland was a respected figure in Sydney society, a handsome, principled man esteemed for his religious convictions, appreciated for his impulsiveness and admired for a business acumen which eventually led to the presidency of the Master Tailors' Association and membership of the Trades Advisory Committee of the Technical College. He always cut an impressive and colourful figure in his full Scottish dress at the Highland gatherings on New Year's Day. By the

William Sutherland on arrival in Australia
William Sutherland in later life at the Sydney Highland Games

21

mid-1920s he preferred to spend more of his time at the substantial balconied home facing the harbour in one of Sydney's best suburbs, looking after his family and reflecting on his Highland background with a fervency that only an expatriate can summon and make more vivid with the passing of the years. He remembered with a glowing nostalgia the struggles of the Portskerra men with the unpredictable sea and their simple, childlike faith in the natural order of things. His imagination rambled among the historic parts of his beloved shire, throughout Caithness and its remote highland beauty back to the years when as a young man he competed in the Highland games: putting the shot, pole vaulting and tossing the caber.

As he read his newspaper on this bright November morning he mused that life had been fair to him on this side of the world. There were the four children of his first marriage: Heather, Ailsa, Nancye and James, ranging in age from nine to twenty-three. After his wife Clara had died suddenly during the influenza epidemic of 1919, William Sutherland had married another fine woman, Muriel Alston, who had given him a beautiful daughter, Barbara, and now a second child was about to be born into the comfortable twin-family circle that remained unruffled by most of life's vicissitudes and promised a secure future for the new infant.

The baby was another girl, a large child weighing 11½ pounds, with a flawless skin, blue eyes and an amiable disposition. Joan, as she was christened, soon became a favourite with the others; the grown-up girls constantly made a fuss over her as did her adoring young brother. But it was Mr Sutherland, the Presbyterian martinet, who did most of the spoiling and they often wondered how the newest arrival could twist him around her chubby little fingers. There was a room at Patonga named 'The Pump Room', for no obvious reason, where the other children had taken their meals until they reached the age of seven or eight. But the two girls of the second family seemed to be specially favoured because they ate with their parents as soon as they were able to sit at the table in a high chair.

William Sutherland was a gregarious man and had friends in several walks of life who were often invited home to Wolseley Road; many Scotsmen in particular seemed to find their way there. During the War the British cruiser *Orama* arrived in the harbour with a crew largely made up of Scots. They had been away from home for more than a year and many of them were sought out by Mr Sutherland and entertained with welcoming hospitality by himself and others of the local community. In 1929 at the time of the Royal Easter Show he had as his guests the mayor of Auckland and his son; they had come across from New Zealand to show their pedigree cattle and were invited home to dinner. The children were prompted to be on their best behaviour and speak only if spoken to. 'Joanie', as she was affectionately known, was aged three and sat in a high chair beside her father at the dinner table, a model of polite composure. There was a lull in the conversation between courses and everyone was startled to hear a sudden loud belch from the youngest Sutherland. 'Go to your room this instant', her father ordered as the others tried to stifle their giggles without success. Joan wriggled out of her chair and made her way to the door of the dining room, stopped and turned around to the guests. ' 'Scuse me gentlemens and ladies', she carefully enunciated, 'but I was really not 'specting that. It took me by s'prise.' William Sutherland relented amid the laughter and she was immediately reinstated at the table.

At this early age Joan was introduced to the delights of swimming in the harbour with Barbara and Jim. A small beach was conveniently situated at the bottom of a flight of steps leading from the garden to the foreshore. By now the economic storms had built up in far-away America and culminated in the Wall Street Crash. Its thunder would soon reverberate around the world but, as yet, in Australia life went on much as before. At Patonga they had a 'daily' — a woman named Mrs Fisher but known to all as 'The Fish'. She was efficient at her daily chores and Joan often followed her around the house on her work, but she had one great flaw — she couldn't sing in tune. It was a fact that grated on the young girl even at the age of four. Joan had learned the song 'Take a Pair of Sparkling Eyes' from her mother and in turn tried to teach it to Mrs Fisher. It turned out to be a hopeless task and in frustration at the out-of-tune sounds she was hearing, the young girl finally burst out with, 'Oh! Take a pair of wiggly worms and frow 'em in the dirt. I'll never teach you to sing in a thousand years!' One day 'The Fish' was down on her knees wiping the kitchen floor with a sweat cloth and Joan sat behind her copying her action — but with a handful of tripe taken from the ice

Left: Joan Sutherland 1927
Right: Barbara Sutherland 1927
Below: Joan swimming at Point Piper, 1930

box; to the child it looked just like a floor cloth. It resulted in a standard joke of the Sutherland family whenever father sat down to one of his favourite meals. 'Is this tripe fresh?', he would ask, 'or has my Joanie been using it to mop the kitchen floor again?'

Pets were not much in evidence in the household. There had been a mongrel dog with the name of Heinz — his pedigree seemed to include at least fifty-seven varieties of canine breeds — but his life was a short one because he drowned in the harbour. After the unfortunate Heinz came Timothy, a tortoise. 'The Fish' found it hard to believe that he was the reason for the disappearance of the master's pyjama cords. It was a mystery that deepened over a couple of weeks until one day Joan was seen in the garden tugging on a long rope of pyjama cords which wound around two trees, through a rose bush and down into a hole from which a hibernating Timothy was being extracted, the cords attached to his shell. She picked him up, climbed into the lower branches of a pepper tree and serenaded the reluctant tortoise.

Patonga was a house with music, both from Muriel Sutherland who had such an exceptional mezzo soprano voice that she might have become a professional singer, and from Pansy the Pink Portable which doubled as the instrument for playing records of Melba, Caruso and Harry Lauder in the main part of the house, and for hearing borrowed jazz records by the grown-up children in the seclusion of the boatshed at the bottom of the garden, safe from their father's ears. William Sutherland had little singing voice and disapproved of jazz. 'He couldn't even sing the National Anthem', Sutherland remembers today, but he appreciated good music, the melodies of his native land and he sang hymns in a lusty fashion each Sunday in church. Harry Lauder, the popular Scottish comedian and singer, had presented his famous walking stick to William Sutherland during his tour of Australia in 1914 and the children used it as a plaything for many years. The Sutherlands kept open house at Patonga because father thought it was a way he could know whose company his children were keeping. There was a large age difference between the first and second families and young Joan was taught to call the older children's friends 'Uncle' Peter, 'Aunty' Leonie, 'Aunty' Grace and so on. At this time Heather was studying architecture at Sydney University, Ailsa was on the staff of the University Dental Hospital, Nancye was working in the office of a firm of solicitors in the city and Jim

25

was still at school. Their circle of friends grew ever larger and Joan's collection of 'aunts' and 'uncles' increased to the point where Ailsa had to plead with her father to let both Barbara and Joan drop the prefix or, as she pointed out, 'People will be under the impression that Grandpa must have kept a harem and sired an uncountable number of sons and daughters'.

William Sutherland was a keen gardener and Joan developed a love of flowers that would last all her life. She was eager to know the names of the blooms and her real uncle, Tom Alston, and his sister Bloss, who lived in the nearby suburb of Woollahra, often bore the brunt of her questioning. After spending a weekend with them she would return home and greet her father with the enthusiastic information, 'Daddy, I saw a beautiful How-So-Far in Uncle Tom's garden today. He has some lovely tall Aggies Pants and next week he says he'll give me some Asthmas and Double Pneumonias'. The mangled botanical information referred, in fact, to Watsonias, Agapanthus, Asters and Double Anemones.

In 1929, following the lead set by Britain, Australians elected a federal Labor government headed by James Henry Scullin. For both Scullin in Canberra and Ramsay MacDonald at Westminster the problems of administration over the next few years would be immense. In Australia, however, the 'economic slump' as it was known, seemed at first to be only transitory and the rapid decline in rural exports which was leading to a downturn in the economy would, it was thought, soon be reversed. But by the early 1930s more than a fifth of the nation's workforce was without jobs and there were no unemployment or relief schemes to aid them. Hardship began to permeate all sections of society and the depression was played out against a background of intense parochialism and isolation fuelled by the Customs Department which operated one of the most oppressive censorship systems for books, plays and films in the world. However, few could be worried about that; finding a job and getting a square meal each day was now of paramount importance for the majority.

William Sutherland's principles of his domestic life carried over into his business affairs and he firmly believed that if a man took pride in his work it would be unnecessary to advertise. He was convinced that one satisfied customer would always bring another to him. Although the depression was reducing orders he refused to put inferior materials into his garments. All the twine, silk linings, serges, tweeds and broadcloth were the finest he could obtain from England and Scotland and they had to be paid for in advance, although more and more of his clients were delaying settlement of their accounts. Money became very tight but life at Patonga appeared to go on much as before with harmonious family relations fortified by regular Sunday church visits and musical evenings.

A special day was planned for Joan's sixth birthday on 7 November 1932 with a party and presents that would include a new green bathing costume. William Sutherland went down for his customary early harbour swim. He was feeling a little off-colour and looked forward to a refreshing dip to clear the cobwebs away. Afterwards he took his towel and dried himself while climbing back up the steps as he had done on so many other occasions over the years. Halfway up, a searing pain racked his chest and he fought for breath. He clutched at the handrail, dropped the towel and managed to drag himself to the top before collapsing on the lawn. Neighbours saw what happened, rushed to his aid and carried him into the house. Mrs Sutherland was called and she ran to her husband's side but it was too late; he was already dead after suffering a severe heart attack. William McDonald Sutherland died at the age of sixty, just four days short of his own birthday.

The funeral was hastily organized for the next day, a speed made possible by his long service as an elder of St Stephen's Church. Word quickly spread around Sydney that he had passed away and the church was crowded for the service on the afternoon of Tuesday 8 November conducted by the Rev. Hugh Paton who summed-up the bereaved family's feelings in his address. 'We feel in a sort of daze', he said, 'it has all been so sudden. On Sunday, he was here, his bright hearty self. Monday morning found him in his usual health, and yet an hour afterwards he had gone. We do not seem able to think that we shall see his face no more.' As Muriel Sutherland, the three eldest daughters and son sat grim-faced, wondering about this sudden twist of fate, the organist played 'The Scottish Lament'. Then the funeral cortège left Philip Street for Waverley Cemetery and there the Highland Society pipers, which William Sutherland had helped to form in 1909, played his coffin to the graveside with 'Lochaber No More' and after the final words of the burial service a lone piper sounded 'The Flowers of the Forest', its notes blowing away on the cool southerly change that swept across the exposed cemetery overlooking the white-capped Pacific Ocean. It was the harbinger of a change of fortune in the lives of the Sutherlands.

William Sutherland had died intestate with a considerable sum of money owing to him from unpaid accounts and there was little hope of recovery. Patonga, which was mortgaged, had to be sold, but in the depth of the depression there were few buyers with ready cash and it went for a small amount. The family split up. Muriel Sutherland took her two daughters back to her old home in Woollahra to live with Tom Alston and his sister. Heather, Ailsa, Nancye and Jim moved into a waterfront apartment in Point Piper and a cousin joined them to help spread the expenses. What had been a closely-knit group now drifted apart; the others were too preoccupied with earning enough money to keep their new home together to see very much of Barbara, Joan and their step-mother.

The former life with its pleasant proprieties of family and friends around the dinner table and its wide vistas of water and sky, gave way to a more confined and boisterous existence in the Alston home in Queen Street, Woollahra, a faded near-city suburb of spacious terraces on the edge of the working-class lanes and alleys of Paddington and close to the open spaces of Centennial Park. Joan was now separated from her favourite Heather and began to grow much closer to her sister Barbara, who suffered from occasional and inexplicable fits.

Their mother's sister, Annie Ethel, was known to everyone as Bloss. She shared with the other Alstons the ownership of several houses in Paddington and Surry Hills, as well as the Woollahra home, but they were rundown and difficult to let during the depression. Tom didn't work, claiming to spend his time looking after the Alston properties but he was almost always to be found in the garden behind the house tending the flowers. His love of the soil carried over into the earthy ditties he sang around the place and which Joan was soon imitating; Edwardian music hall songs such as 'My Old Woman's an Awful Boozer'. Mrs Sutherland was not beyond joining in these numbers and between them, her own operatic repertory and the gramophone records brought to the house by a cousin who was known to the children as 'Uncle' John, the six-year-old Joan was experiencing a wide spectrum of music. The recorded voices of Amelita Galli-Curci, Dame Nellie Melba,

'Count' John McCormack, Frieda Hempel, Enrico Caruso and Lawrence Tibbett were an integral part of the girl's musical upbringing and the sanctity of singing held a wide licence.

In 1934 she was enrolled in St Catherine's Church of England School for Girls in the Sydney suburb of Waverley, the oldest girls' school in Australia, and settled down to an unremarkable academic progress that saw her participating in most activities but being made aware of her size when she longed to play feminine roles in the end-of-term plays, and suffering from chronic sinus inflammation which meant regular visits to a doctor for treatment. Joan wanted to sing in the school choir but was told her voice was too loud and drowned out the rest of the singers. She began to lead a more solitary life and became increasingly involved with music. Her mother's vocalises by Garcia and Marchesi were fascinating and she would sing along to opera records when 'Uncle' John brought them around. Mrs Sutherland managed to pay for piano lessons at home and showed a lively interest in Joan's musical progress. Her other daughter and her moods were a mystery and Barbara, in her highly-strung state, turned more to Joan for solace and companionship. Joan's piano teacher was the daughter of the composer Augustus W. Juncker and many years later one of his songs, 'I Was Dreaming' from the operetta *Ma Mie Rosetta* was recorded by Sutherland for her album 'Songs My Mother Taught Me'. It had previously been made popular by Australia's leading musical comedy singer, Gladys Moncrieff.

Sutherland remembers,

I grew up quite happily in Sydney. I was never a very sporty sort of person, although at school we were forced into it because it was the Australian way of life. I wasn't an outdoors person but certain things we had to do at school I had to suffer. I was more interested in musical life and was taken by Mother to children's concerts when I was younger and to orchestral concerts later on. There was a marvellous feeling of community in Sydney and we had a feeling of pride in the beaches and the outdoor living so it was a very free-and-easy way of growing up.

The next-door neighbour, Norman Smith, seemed to embody the height of glamour and sophistication. He had a dinghy with an outboard motor and occasionally took Joan out on the harbour. 'I cultivated Norman and his dinghy', she recalls. 'His family struck me as very rich and successful!'

A continuing and constant factor in Joan's life was her mother's daily singing practice. Its regularity and devotion made it almost a religion, a temporary release from what was to Muriel Sutherland a confusing and unrelenting world. 'I grew up in an atmosphere of the way she sang', Sutherland recollects, 'things like the Page's aria from *Les Huguenots* and the Brindisi from *Lucrezia Borgia*. They were strangely out of gear in the 1930s because it was a period when everybody seemed to be singing Puccini and Wagner.' Mrs Sutherland was once a pupil of Burns Walker who had studied with Marchesi — Melba's teacher. 'Grandfather was a stern but kindly man and would have sent mother to Europe for study', says Sutherland. 'She, on the other hand, was more interested in being with her friends and going with them on motor trips or to the races. She said she was too nervous to embark on a singing career.'

The easing of the depression was the cue for Australia to emerge from its former provincialism and become more aware of the world at large. Its foreign policy, however, was still largely that of Britain and although there were internal pressures for appeasement with Germany, Italy and Japan as the international war clouds gathered and replaced the clearing economy, it was inevitable that the nation would follow the mother country's lead in any hostilities. On 3 September 1939 in London Neville Chamberlain declared a state of war with Germany and an hour later his Australian counterpart, Robert Gordon Menzies, announced that his country was also involved. Soon, troops would be on their way to Europe, the Middle East and Africa, but it was to America that an ill-prepared and virtually defenceless Australia would turn for support.

The 1930s had seen a rapid change of circumstances on the other side of the Sutherland family. Nancye married in 1933, Jim lived with his sisters until he was seventeen and then worked for a shipping firm while studying accountancy, and Heather finished her degree, married a fellow architect and went to live in Canberra. Ailsa continued to work in the city and took part in amateur theatricals, appearing on one occasion with a young man called Peter Finch who played a one-legged, non-speaking pirate in a production of J.M. Barrie's *Peter Pan*. At the outbreak of the war Joan had vague thoughts about being a singer one day and her mother allowed her to appear on a children's radio programme on a couple of occasions, but Mrs Sutherland had strong views about early voice training and was adamant that her daughter should not take any formal lessons until she was at least eighteen.

Following the stoical streak displayed by her mother and with a practicality that would be demonstrated throughout her life, Sutherland decided to take courses in shorthand and typing and dressmaking and then in 1942 at the age of sixteen she left St Catherine's. The family had all been saddened to learn of Jim's disappearance on military service in Malaya and it was with relief they heard he was a prisoner of the Japanese. Joan helped the war effort by knitting scarves and balaclava helmets for the troops, making camouflage nets and working in service canteens.

The Australians at home had a relatively easy war except for the inconvenience of petrol rationing, a shortage of beer and cigarettes, power cuts and some rationing of food and clothing from mid-1942. Wages were pegged, taxation was high but there was

Schooldays at St Catherine's, 1941

31

work for all and, with luck, and trust in General MacArthur's statement on his arrival in Melbourne that 'my faith in our ultimate victory is invincible', the Americans would save the country from Japanese attack. The fear of invasion was uppermost in many people's minds; blackouts were enforced at night and air raid drills were held in factories and schools. Australia's vulnerability was brought home vividly to Sydney-siders on the night of 31 May 1942 when three Japanese midget submarines approached the city; two of them penetrated the boom at the Heads, made their way up the harbour and attacked an American cruiser with torpedoes, missing their target but hitting an Australian naval vessel instead and killing nineteen men. A week later the eastern suburbs were shelled from the sea by a submarine. Far away at the tropical top end of the continent, the city of Darwin was bombed and the small defence garrison beat a hasty retreat into the scrub. The Japanese also bombed the north-west, but the attacks on Wyndham, Broome and other coastal settlements and shipping, remote from the vast majority of the population, were kept quiet by the government to avoid panic in the community. These incidents, however, formed the extent of Australians' direct domestic contact with the war.

A year before the hostilities ended, Joan took her first job, as a typist with the Council for Scientific and Industrial Research at the University of Sydney. She copied endless reports concerned mostly with radiophysics but it was a task that neither challenged her typing speed nor put any demand on her newly-acquired shorthand skills and she soon moved into the world of commerce to work for a firm of rural suppliers, forsaking the frontiers of science for the more down-to-earth requirements of the man on the land. It hardly seemed destined to lead her in the direction of singing in the Town Hall and perhaps travelling overseas one day when the world returned to normal.

Eventually the war ran its long course. On 15 August 1945 Prime Minister Chifley broadcast from Canberra that Japan had surrendered to the Allies, sparking off victory celebrations throughout the country and the prospect of a speedy return of the Australian troops and the prisoners of war — Jim Sutherland among them.

La Stupenda at home in Les Avants

Joan did her daily work typing orders for the supply of rabbit traps, fencing materials and fertilizer for the farmers and in the evenings visited as many musical events and theatres as possible. There was a selection of Gilbert and Sullivan light operas, British drawing-room comedies and revivals of musicals often starring Australia's favourite singer Gladys Moncrieff or the team of Madge Elliott and Cyril Ritchard. The revivals included *The Merry Widow* and *Gay Rosalinda* and there was a new production of Ivor Novello's *The Dancing Years*. One day while looking through the newspaper for the theatre and music attractions, Joan's eye was attracted by a small advertisement that made her pulse beat faster; it was the offer of free singing lessons for 'an untrained or semi-trained young singer' who could win a competition sponsored by the singing teachers John and Aida Dickens. It was an attempt by them to become better known in Sydney and to attract a number of students who might stay on paying fees as a result of entering their contest. The offer of two years' free tuition attracted forty young hopefuls and they were summoned to a city studio to be taken through their paces. Mrs Sutherland brought along her daughter who had decided to sing one of her mother's favourites, 'Softly Awakes My Heart' from Saint-Saëns's *Samson and Delilah*. Aida Dickens played the piano expertly as her tall husband stood by listening. They had a good background in music; on his side of the family the connections with the art went back at least as far as his grandfather, Otto Vogt, who had been a church organist in Melbourne and at one time taught the instrument to a young tomboy called Helen Porter Mitchell, who was to become Melba. Aida Summers played the piano professionally in Melbourne and was also interested in singing techniques. She married John Dickens in 1940 and they decided to move to Sydney and live in a warmer climate after he had been discharged from the army as medically unfit.

To him, the Sutherland girl's appearance was hardly impressive as she sang; her size, the frizzy hair, poorly-applied lipstick and shapeless dress combined to suggest she should be rejected out of hand, but he noted that the Saint-Saëns aria was being sung most impressively, in fact, it was a far better performance than any of the other applicants. It needed only a short discussion before the

Rodelinda at Holland Festival 1973

Dickens decided to give the scholarship to Joan Sutherland.

It seemed rather late, approaching the age of twenty, to start a serious singing career without previous formal voice training, but the long experience of listening to her mother as well as copying singers as different as Flagstad and Galli-Curci on records, had given Joan an excellent grounding on which to build. Mrs Sutherland had resisted any attempts by her daughter to take singing lessons before this time and she came to the Dickens with an excellent but virtually untrained voice. They quickly sensed, however, that she was singing in the wrong register; there was a rich and powerful middle ground but she was reluctant to attempt the higher notes. Lesson by lesson they gradually extended her voice upward by frequent repetition of higher scales. After so many years of singing naturally, but not thinking critically or analytically about her own voice production, these upward stretchings came as quite a shock to Joan and she resisted them. She was backed up by her mother who was sure that her daughter was a mezzo, like herself, and had no need to change. To everyone's surprise, and after a great deal of hard work in the studio and at home, she was prepared to move up from a hesitant G at the top of the stave to a very reluctant top C.

The Dickens continued to develop the Sutherland voice and they were also aware of the need to coax this compliant but rather awkward young lady out of her self-conscious teenage cocoon into a degree of assurance if she was to achieve the potential her voice promised. They suggested she study languages, including French which had been such a mystery at St Catherine's. They also saw the need for some drama training that would help in movement and deportment so that their pupil might have a better chance of winning some of the singing competitions in the Sydney area and perhaps tackle the most prestigious of them, the *Sun* Aria. Sutherland enrolled in a drama school known as the Rathbone Academy of Dramatic Art run by an Englishwoman named Judy Rathbone Lawless who specialized in elocution and was not unaware of the coincidence that allowed her to use the same initials — RADA — as the Royal Academy of Dramatic Art in London. There were drama lessons twice a week with long, seemingly pointless sessions of enunciation followed by tuition in movement. Joan doubted that anything was being gained from all the effort; she would rather have spent the time singing, but her diction improved, even if there was still the residue of a marked Australian accent.

All this activity began to put a strain on her working life and she changed her job again for a similar position with a firm of country suppliers and wholesale grocers whose principal, 'Pop' Clyde, took a keen interest in her singing ambitions and allowed time off to study and prepare for a growing number of engagements, including singing with the Affiliated Music Clubs of New South Wales who ran a series of recital concerts in the metropolitan area of Sydney, usually in suburban halls, and also in country centres. She was preparing to sing at the Killara Club on Sydney's upper north shore when Barbara, with whom she had developed a great intimacy and understanding, one day left the house without telling anyone where she was going and failed to return. She was possessed by inner tensions and reasoned that life was no longer worthwhile. She was an attractive woman, well-liked by everyone, including an American who had fallen in love with her. But Barbara knew that her unpredictable epileptic state could never allow a normal relationship in marriage and she was numbed by the realization that her life seemed to offer very little but a continuing series of personal disappointments. Barbara took the green and cream bus on a lonely thirty-minute journey along New South Head Road past Edgecliff, Double Bay, Point Piper, Rose Bay, and Vaucluse to its terminus at Watson's Bay, a sleepy suburb nestling under South Head at the entrance to Sydney Harbour. She climbed up the path that leads to a windy ledge of rock on the top of the towering cliffs facing the restless Pacific and threw herself off 'The Gap', as Sydney's notorious suicide site is known.

A telephone call from Mrs Sutherland summoned Joan home from work. They were confused and perplexed as to why Barbara would do such a thing, although Joan quietly understood the pressures that had built up in her sister's mind until they became too intense to live with; but that understanding did not make the acceptance any easier. 'I'll never sing again', was the immediate reaction. Ailsa was one of the first of the family to rush over to Queen Street. She comforted her half-sister and told her she must continue with her singing because that was what Barbara would have wished. Joan finally agreed to perform at the Killara concert on the understanding that none of the family was present, and she sang as a quiet, personal requiem for her beloved sister.

The big goals for a singer in Sydney immediately after the war were to win the *Sun* Aria competition, the finals of the ABC's vocal and concerto competition or one of the events in the City of Sydney Eisteddfod. The Dickens had their sights set on each of these for their prize pupil but first she joined a group that gave choral concerts under the direction of the conductor Henry Krips, whose elder brother, Josef, had been such a force as a conductor at the Vienna State Opera before he was dimissed by the Nazis in 1938. The group was called 'The Singers of Australia' and in August 1947 she got her biggest chance so far by singing Dido in a Singers' concert performance of Purcell's *Dido and Aeneas*. This resulted in Sutherland's first, fleeting press notices: 'Of the soloists who sang with feeling and insight', wrote the *Sun* critic, 'especially notable were Joan Sutherland, Shirley Wallwork, Noel Melvin and Ronald Dowd'. The September edition of *Tempo* magazine described Sutherland as 'a vocally somewhat lightwinged Dido with promising material'. In the same year she won the women's section of the ABC's contest in the City of Sydney Eisteddfod and this led to regular broadcasting engagements.

A young pianist called Richard Bonynge, for whom many were predicting a brilliant career, sometimes appeared on the same programme as Sutherland for the Music Clubs. He was studying at the New South Wales Conservatorium of Music and also had the ambition to further his career overseas and, like Sutherland, was competing in the local contests. In May 1948 she appeared as a finalist for the first time in the ABC's Vocal and Concerto Competitions singing Elizabeth's Greeting from *Tannhäuser* by Wagner. Eugene Goossens conducted the Sydney Symphony Orchestra but the winner was a nineteen-year-old pianist who played Mendelssohn's first concerto. In 1948 she was also a semi-finalist in the *Sun* Aria competition, but failed to reach the final eight singers selected by the former Wagnerian soprano, Florence Austral.

The year 1949 was a better one for achievement. Sutherland resigned from her job to give full-time attention to singing and said at the time she enjoyed Wagner better than any other composer but hoped to have enough experience to sing *lieder* one day 'with the artistry it deserves'. Richard Bonynge won the principal pianoforte awards at the Eisteddfod, and at the Conservatorium he obtained both his teacher's and his performer's diplomas. One of his teachers was Lindley Evans, who had been

Melba's accompanist in her later performing years. He was a strong influence in fostering Bonynge's appreciation of the voice as well as his growing love of eighteenth and early nineteenth century opera. Bonynge, then nineteen, observed that Sutherland made a big, impressive sound but lacked the refinement and delicacy he considered to be essential attributes of a good singer. He noticed her platform manner but gave little thought to what her future might be — after all, he had won a scholarship to the Royal College of Music in London and was now on the threshold of his own career. There was a farewell concert for Bonynge at the Conservatorium and Sutherland was one of the artists taking part. He remembered afterwards, 'I thought she had a marvellous natural voice, but it didn't move me in any way and I wasn't particularly struck by it'. He also recalls what musical life was like in Sydney in the late 1940s before he left.

It was symphonically interesting because we had Eugene Goossens as head of the Conservatorium and conductor of the Sydney Symphony, which was a very fine orchestra. I attended concerts sometimes three times a week. Regular chamber music recitals began about 1946 but operatically there was very little. We had an Italian touring company in the late 1940s and that was the only opera I saw apart from productions at the Conservatorium, some of which I took part in. I prepared *Falstaff* and *The Marriage of Figaro* while I was there, otherwise it was Gilbert and Sullivan and I saw practically the whole repertory performed by a wonderful company we had which included members of the D'Oyly Carte Company who were caught in Sydney during the war. That was my real initiation into the theatre.

Sutherland was not particularly concerned with analyzing her own voice, although almost everyone else was now calling it a dramatic soprano. She sang at every opportunity and in every style, around the bathroom, in the kitchen, out in the garden, in the Dickens's studio, at the ABC and on the rickety stages of suburban halls. Her only desire was to sing and she was delighted, and not a little surprised, that more and more people were letting her carry out her wishes and paying for it. She had firmed her thoughts about going overseas if she could gather enough money together and the most immediate opportunities for this were in the *Sun* Aria with its first prize of £300 and a new competition sponsored by an oil company which was offering £1000 for its winner. She entered them both.

Australians sometimes regard the arts in terms of contest, and in painting, sculpture, literature and singing, a competitive element often adds the flavour of a sporting occasion. The Vacuum Oil Company saw the publicity value of sponsoring a competition to find the most promising operatic singer in Australia after obtaining good results from backing some recitals and outdoor operatic concerts in Melbourne. Some of the preliminary rounds, together with the semi-finals and the grand final were broadcast on a commercial radio network and the most accomplished singers were to be offered engagements to join a touring group called 'The Stars of Mobil Quest'. It was corporate sponsorship of a high level, giving the company prestige advertising and fees to the participants and the prospect of gaining wider attention. The final of the first Mobil Quest was held in the Melbourne Town Hall on Thursday 15 September in an atmosphere of keen rivalry. There were the added tensions of a live broadcast, a large audience and the formality of a celebrity announcer on stage in front of the fifty-piece orchestra conducted by Hector Crawford. Nearly two thousand singers entered for the Quest and now the six finalists were about to go through their paces. Sutherland had survived the preliminaries and felt reasonably confident but, as in a horse race where barrier positions are chosen, the order of singing was selected and her name came first. It meant that she had to give a particularly brilliant performance in each of her arias in the two halves of the programme to score better than the other five competitors. Her selections were Elsa's Dream from *Lohengrin* and '*Ritorna vincitor*' from *Aida*. It was not one of her best nights and in the final placings Sutherland came fourth, receiving a cheque for £50, but there was always next year and the *Sun* Aria was only a few weeks away.

Sydney proved to be a happier location for her. She won the *Sun* Aria by a single point and the adjudicator, Harold Williams, said she had a fine soprano voice and should do well in opera. The third prize of £50 went to June Gough who, as June Bronhill, went on to a notable singing career in Europe.

'Uncle' John, who had first introduced the young Sutherland to some of the greatest voices in opera through his gramophone records, continued to show an interest in her musical development. He knew she wanted to go to Europe and to help her he offered to match the prize of £1000 if she could win the 1950 Mobil Quest. His tanning business and property interests had amassed him a comfortable sum over the years but he was not a man known for his largesse. 'I have a few quid', he said, 'and I'm a bit of a gambler, but I don't throw my money around to anybody. I don't know if she'll turn out to be great, but I know she'll try.' And try she did, although she was lucky to escape elimination during the qualifying heats when she missed an entry toward the end of an aria and the orchestra finished it alone. The judges referred to this lapse but declared her the winner 'because of vocal superiority'. Sutherland found herself again on stage in the final at the Melbourne Town Hall and this time she was very apprehensive with her future at stake. 'I thought I had no chance of winning', she remembered, 'so I tucked a four-leaf clover into my glove. I made myself think of that lucky clover.' It was a long evening. She sang *Voi Io sapete, O Mamma* from *Cavalleria Rusticana* and *Dich teure Halle* from *Tannhäuser*. At the end there was an agonizing ten minutes before the winners were announced and then in the best traditions of sporting suspense the top places were given in reverse order — fourth, third, second. It was Sutherland's name that was held to the last. She had won the coveted prize and could book a passage to England for herself and her mother.

Following her success in the grand final she had her first taste of extensive touring with a series of Mobil recitals in towns and cities right across the Australian continent. She went to Brisbane, Canberra, Sydney, Newcastle, Kalgoorlie, Perth, Adelaide, Launceston and Hobart: they were distances that would make subsequent travels in Europe and America seem modest by comparison. The Vacuum Oil Company were proud of their new star and arranged further concerts for her with 'Music for the People' outdoors in the Melbourne Botanical Gardens and 'Carols by Candlelight' with the South Australian Symphony Orchestra conducted by Henry Krips in Adelaide's Elder Park. Sutherland then returned home for a performance of Handel's *Messiah* with the Sydney Symphony Orchestra. By now her press reviews were beginning to mount up. The *Sydney Morning Herald* critic wrote of her *Messiah*, 'Joan Sutherland, who began by using her fresh and clear soprano voice with style and beauty, seemed to lose confidence in the 'He Shall Speak Peace' number, and did not quite recover her artistic poise afterwards'. The *Sun* thought she sang 'with greatest clarity and strength, managing the florid vocal writing of 'Rejoice Greatly, O Daughter of Zion' and the calm thankfulness of 'I Know that my Redeemer Liveth', with equal ease'. The *Daily Telegraph* wrote, 'The soprano, Joan Sutherland, has a really beautiful voice, which she uses with intelligence and musicality'.

All these engagements, together with the Music Clubs recitals and the continuing study with the Dickens, who had offered her free tuition for as long as she wanted it, quickly turned Sutherland into one of the country's most experienced singers and her resolve to further her career in Europe was assisted by Vacuum Oil and Associated Newspapers, the sponsors of Mobil Quest and the *Sun Aria*, who combined to present a farewell benefit concert for her in the Sydney Town Hall on Friday 20 April 1951. It was advertised as 'A programme of popular appeal — Proceeds in aid of Miss Sutherland's overseas studies'. The concert was a generous tribute to the impact she had made on the musical life of Australia in such a short time. Her fellow artists included the singers Ronald Dowd, Frank Lisle and Florence Taylor, pianist Marie van Hove, violinist Brenton Langbein and the accompanists Adrian Holland and Aida Summers (as she was billed). Sutherland performed twice in each of the two parts of the concert with songs by Marcello, Peri, Arne, Cyril Scott, C. Armstrong Gibbs, Thomas Dunhill, Delius, Schubert, Liszt and Wolf. Her two operatic arias, which give an indication of her voice quality and repertoire at the time, were '*Pace, pace mio Dio*' from Verdi's *La Forza del Destino* and Isolde's *Liebestod* from *Tristan und Isolde* by Wagner. The evening was a critical and financial success and she received £350 from the proceeds. An 'appreciation' from Sutherland printed in the concert programme thanked the many people who had contributed to her success and paid a special tribute to her mother's influence on her career. It ended with some sentiments that held more than a hint of prophecy, 'I hope the most tangible gesture of appreciation to all who have helped me will lie in the fulfilment of my ambition to win a place alongside those many Australian singers who have won recognition for our country in the opera houses and on the concert platforms of the world'.

Departure day was set for 10 July but she wasn't ready to leave yet because there was the invitation to sing in her first full-scale opera. Sutherland had already appeared in concert performances of *Dido and Aeneas* in 1947 and *Samson* in 1950, but Eugene Goossens invited her to appear in his own work *Judith* on a double

After Farewell Concert at Sydney Town Hall
A kiss from Mrs Sutherland

41

bill with Puccini's *Gianni Schicchi* at the New South Wales Conservatorium during June, barely a month before leaving. The one-act work to a libretto by Arnold Bennett was completed in 1927 and given its first performance at Covent Garden in June 1929 with the composer conducting and the Finnish Soprano, Aino Ackté, in the title role. Goossens and Bennett planned to collaborate on a one-act comic opera as a companion piece to *Judith* but Bennett's death in 1931 put paid to that. The story is taken from the Book of Judith and tells how the city of Bethulia is beseiged in the time of Nebuchadnezzar by an army under the command of General Holofernes. He falls in love with Judith who, being a good patriot as well as a Jewish widow, takes advantage of his infatuation to decapitate him and save the day for Bethulia. There were six performances in the season and Sutherland sang the title role in four of them, alternating with another soprano.

Studio portrait, Sydney 1951

Judith was an unimaginative and hesitant production with skimpy sets and costumes, although it was strong musically with Goossens conducting a sixty-piece orchestra made up mostly from his Sydney Symphony. Sutherland's embryonic stagecraft was extended to its limit on the first night when, concentrating on playing the part of the seductress with all the conviction she could

42

muster, she faced a moment of high farce in the decapitation scene, which seems to be *de rigueur* in most operas on a biblical theme. After she had carried out the deed and proudly displayed the detached papier-maché head of Holofernes to precipitate the tide of revolt against his invading Ammonite army, the unfortunate leader was seen to slip off his deathbed and miraculously become re-capitated. The curtain fell only to rise on the sight of Sutherland helping him up from the boards. They froze and the curtain was quickly dropped again. Two days later, the first press review of a Sutherland opera performance was printed in the *Sydney Morning Herald*. It read,

> The declamatory vocal writing was handled freshly and well by Joan Sutherland's dramatic soprano, although a more severely 'biblical' sense of Old Testament character could have helped her and others. Poor stage direction, exaggerated by the cramping scenery, left Miss Sutherland and others wondering what to do between the registration of various high points of emotion specified in the text.

The performance was hardly a fitting finale for Sutherland's exit from Australia but Goossens recognized in her singing a quality that was outstanding by local standards and he offered to give her a letter of introduction to ease her entry into the British musical world where his name held influence. She gratefully accepted the letter and added it to a list of London landladies who were sympathetic to singers.

Sutherland and her mother left a changing Australia as their liner, the *Maloja*, made its way down Sydney Harbour en route for Europe. That continent was now sending many of its war-wearied citizens to the far side of the world seeking peace and security and bringing with them the possessions, skills and cultures of the old world to vitalize the new. These 'New Australians' pouring off the ships by the thousands in Fremantle, Port Adelaide, Port Melbourne and Sydney would change the face of the nation within a decade by manning vast development schemes in the remote areas and altering the life of the cities with new cosmopolitan styles of eating and drinking. As the ship reached the Heads and began to plough into the Pacific's swells, Sutherland's thoughts were already far ahead at her destination 12,000 miles and a month away. A practical streak showed through, however, as the coast receded. 'I'll brush up on my shorthand on the way', she admitted, 'it will probably come in useful if my money runs out'.

43

Chapter Three

I can't remember when I didn't want to sing at Covent Garden. Whether it was because of Melba I'm not sure. We had many recordings of Melba and Caruso, and other singers of their time, and they all seemed to be associated with Covent Garden.

After coming from a Sydney winter — which can often be more like an English summer — then experiencing the languors of the Red Sea followed by the exhilaration of the Mediterranean with its blustery mistral and meltemi winds, London in August was no great climatic shock for Mrs Sutherland and her daughter when they arrived in August 1951. In all other ways the difference was enormous.

The national mood had been given a government injection of gaiety after the grey austerity years of the war and its aftermath — 'A Tonic to the Nation', it was officially styled. The Festival of Britain permeated all levels of life and leisure, but particularly in the capital where the spectacular South Bank Exhibition, built on a dereliction of rotting wharves and crumbling factories, became the vision of a brave new Anglo-Saxon world, and the design pattern for its planned new towns. The Pleasure Gardens at nearby Battersea Park provided a fair-ground escapism offering a foretaste of the long-awaited better life. Their most popular attractions included a Mississippi showboat, Oscar the Octopus, and spectacular fireworks displays at dusk. The British were urged to be cheerful and this mood was reflected in a feeling of facelift that was everywhere. Just about anything that could be brightened with red, white or blue paint was duly covered and the exhibition buildings on the South Bank incorporated much glass among the reinforced concrete, as if to emphasize the official light and bright mood. Behind this fulfilment of concerted efforts by government, industry and the arts, lay something of a failure. Preparations had begun in 1947 when it was confidently expected that Britain's economy would be improving and there would be something to celebrate. But it was not so. When the Festival opened in May with a bold flourish, it was to a nation still suffering the chronic economic consequences of military victory five years previously. The Great Exhibition, that proud symbol of Britain's pre-eminence during the glories of the Victorian era, had taken place in 1851, and so the Festival was conveniently linked to the centenary of that occasion. The event, however, did provide its prescribed national tonic, and in October 1951, the Archbishop of Canterbury, Geoffrey Fisher, would declare at the closing ceremony that it had been 'a good thing for us all'.

None of this was of much concern to those who flocked to marvel at the new technology within the vast Dome of Discovery, or gaze up in wonderment at the Skylon, a slim rocket-like structure thrusting one hundred metres into the sky and said by some wag to have, like Britain, no visible means of support. The crowds packed the concerts in the Royal Festival Hall, the only permanent structure on the South Bank, and justification enough for the whole Festival, because it changed the taste and pattern of music appreciation in London almost overnight.

The Festival was a time for national stock-taking, particularly in the arts. *The Times Literary Supplement* thought it 'an age unpropitious to great art', the cinema seemed to be in one of its continuing crises, and although music and ballet were well attended, British compositions were in little demand. A competition for new operas produced such works as Arthur Benjamin's *A Tale of Two Cities*, *Wat Tyler* by Alan Bush, and Karl Rankl's *Deirdre of the Sorrows*, but they were not given Festival performances.

After the measured provincial life of Sydney, London to Sutherland was the centre of the world and as she joined the throngs of visitors from Britain and abroad who were in the city that golden summer, she wondered if the confidence and enthusiasm she saw all around indicated the normal pace of life — and assumed it did. She stood beneath the rather grubby facade of the Royal Opera House, hemmed in by the bustling Covent Garden fruit and vegetable market on two sides, the dingy Victorian offices on another, and Bow Street Police Station across the road, and was thankful that she had, at least, got this far.

Sutherland had an introduction from her former teacher in Sydney, John Dickens, to Professor Clive Carey at the Royal College of Music. Richard Bonynge, who had won his scholarship in Sydney to study at the College, had become disenchanted with the way his career was going and spent a decreasing amount of his time there in favour of private tuition. He was not very complimentary about the institution when he met up with Sutherland and her mother soon after their arrival. Bonynge had, however, immersed himself in the musical life of London and was revelling in its rich diet of music, opera and ballet. His delight in the past led him to London's antique markets, where many a bargain was available, and he had already bought some Staffordshire figurines and theatrical prints, kindling a life-long obsession with collecting. The day Bonynge arrived in London in 1950, he went straight to Covent Garden to see a performance of Donizetti's *L'Elisir d'Amore* given by the visiting La Scala company. He followed that in quick succession by hearing Sylvia Fisher in *The Flying Dutchman* and Elisabeth Schwarzkopf in *La Traviata*. 'They made a tremendous impression on me', he says, 'I spent all my money going to the theatre'.

His feelings about the Royal College were not enough to deter Sutherland, who made an appointment to see Carey, knowing that he was a man whose tuition had helped to launch many of Britain's best singers, and who, himself, had studied under the great tenor Jean de Reszke. Carey was charming and sympathetic. He read her letters of introduction and listened to her sing, noting a mastery of breath control and difficulty with the higher notes. There was also an ungainly manner and this, combined with a lack of stage experience, suggested that she should study at the College's opera school for at least a year — a recommendation she accepted.

Mrs Sutherland and her daughter moved out of their small hotel and became members of London's bedsitter fraternity at Notting Hill Gate, not far from the West End and conveniently on the underground, but in an uninspiring area of seedy Victorian terraces suffering from the neglect of the war years. Sutherland remembers,

46

We had digs for £3 a week and Richard had everything thrown in for thirty shillings a week. I had a free change of sheets once a fortnight which was supplemented by our own which we had brought from Australia. Food was inexpensive, but there was still rationing and we could add to it with things like rabbit and sausages.

Bonynge introduced her to the world of London's theatre and music. 'We used to sit in the gallery almost every night, at the Old Vic, at the opera and the ballet', she remembers, 'I think we probably had it as good as any students who ever went abroad from Australia'. Sutherland bought a piano for £14, had it lifted with the greatest difficulty up many flights of winding stairs to the fifth-floor bedsitter, and she and Bonynge began working together. At the school she was being introduced to many of the multifarious skills needed to equip a person to be a singer in opera — acting, speech, dance, vocal development. She was embarrassed about her size, her square-jawed plainness and her speaking voice. Sutherland's movements were far from graceful, and she thought the Australian accent was something to be erased. But back in bedsitter-land Bonynge was beginning to work on a different approach to her singing voice and within the privacy of the Sutherlands' London 'home', there began the creation of a unique vocal sound in an atmosphere of uninterrupted and unembarrassed toil.

Bonynge's passion for early nineteenth century romantic opera had increased since his early teens in Sydney. Now he had studied the Italian repertoire more fully and was committed to the works of the great age of bel canto and the singing style demanded by its operas. He detected in Sutherland's voice the potential for such roles, which needed a brilliant and pure high coloratura. He knew her voice had far more flexibility and range than anyone had previously imagined, but he faced no easy task in convincing Sutherland and her mother, who were both of the opinion that his ideas were out of step with the current operatic trends — as indeed they were. He had heard her singing around the bedsitter, quite naturally and freely, and there was a quality which could be developed to help it up into a higher register.

Bonynge's main ability to carry out his scheme was his own perfect pitch — an attribute neither Sutherland nor her mother had. And so he stood Sutherland away from the piano keyboard, where she couldn't see what he was playing, and pitched her vocalises higher. He told her it was a C and, in fact, it would be an E flat. Sutherland fell for the gentle deception and began to sing in a higher register without realizing it. Bonynge says,

When we began working together I began to hear things I hadn't heard before. Naturally I hadn't heard them because she hadn't done them in public. She had a great natural ease in the voice and a flexibility — which she always believed she didn't have. When she was singing spontaneously at home she would do lots of fantastic things that in public she'd never dream of doing.

Bonynge's plan was built upon these observations. 'It followed that what she could do at home she could do in public. So I encouraged her to work along other lines, which, from a selfish point of view, interested me much more because I was fascinated by a different type of music from most of the stuff she studied'. Sutherland says, 'Richard decided — long before I agreed with him — that I was a coloratura. I didn't have perfect pitch and so when I thought I was singing a top C it was really an E above — and then I found I could get an F. I was really astounded.'

The vocal tradition into which Bonynge was leading Sutherland went back nearly three hundred years to the time when there were already separate French and Italian styles of singing. The French, in the operas of Rameau and Lully, placed more importance on declamation, so that to experience one of their performances was to hear an almost endless succession of recitatives. The Italians, on the other hand, personified by the works of Alessandro Scarlatti, concentrated on the sound of the singing voice. But for reasons not connected with music development, what became known as bel canto did not begin until castrati were a vital force in the theatre. There was certainly nothing new about them, for they had been associated with Italian churches since the twelfth century. The Church of Rome, taking its cue from two biblical exhortations — 'I suffer not a woman to teach, nor to usurp authority over man, but to be in silence' (I Timothy 2:12), and 'Let your women keep silence in the churches' (I Corinthians 14:34) — applied the principle to both the church and to the public theatre. The male falsetto — simply a voice with an unnaturally extended top range — was not flexible enough to meet the demands of composers. Spanish falsettos had enjoyed a monopoly of the Sistine Chapel choir but then in 1599 two Italian castrati were introduced, which caused something of an international

Sutherland with her secretary, left, and her mother at Glyndebourne opera season 1956

The Bonynges in New York 1963

In Piazza San Marco, Venice, before *Alcina*, 1961

With the tenor Renato Cioni, Palermo 1961

incident. Soon they took over, however, and the age of castrati had begun, together with the beginnings of bel canto.

Castration was never approved by the Church; in fact a blatant double standard was adopted: the operation if discovered was punishable by excommunication at the very least — or by death, yet they turned a blind eye to it for their own vested interests. The result was a rapid development in singing but at the cost of male mutilation and the taxing of credibility for audiences. Castration did not stop beards from growing, and audiences were asked to accept some grotesque stage conventions in the name of art and entertainment. A number of castrati, however, were very handsome and convincing in female classical roles.

Opera can conveniently be dated from Jacopo Peri's *Euridice*, first produced in Florence in February 1600. It was largely made up of long recitatives and bore little similarity to the type of work that developed in which the aria was predominant. Opera was a courtly entertainment until the opening of a public theatre in Venice in 1637. Women were allowed to appear in some roles because the edicts of Rome were not strictly enforced, but there were moral objections in the community to their appearance and castrati took most of the female roles. With their exceptional singing voices — perhaps superior to anything produced at that time by a woman — they dominated the Italian stage for a hundred years. In England, there had been no such banishment, and Italian opera with castrati flourished there at the same time, but also with a succession of outstanding women singers — among them Cuzzoni, Strada, Faustina and later, Mara and the Englishwoman, Mrs Billington.

There is no way of telling exactly how seventeenth or eighteenth century singing sounded. All the techniques developed by the singers — the arpeggios, portamenti, roulades and skips — although brilliant in themselves, were essentially part of the vocabulary of dramatic expression at a time when they were not expected to act in today's meaning of the term. The standard emotions such as vengeance, bliss, rage, love and fury were all confined within the limits of vocal techniques. It seems likely that if the castrati and the best women singers of the time were in open competition it would be the castrati who would win, with a more brilliant tone and a wider dynamic range. A writer named Raguenet in 1702 gave an insight into castrati singing.

There does not exist in the world a voice of either man or woman so flexible as that of the castrato; it is clean, it is touching, it penetrates to the very soul. They have the throats and sounds of nightingales. They have infinite breath with which they can execute passages of I don't know how many bars; they sustain notes of a prodigious length, at the end of which, by a movement of the throat similar to a nightingale, they make cadential trills of a similar duration. Also, these voices are as loud as they are sweet; as sweet as any woman's but much larger.

Other descriptions of the time refer to the stage presence and expression commanded by the castrati. They performed in theatres much smaller than today's and with orchestral accompaniments considerably lighter, so that it is impossible to assess the actual volume of the voices and whether they could survive in today's conditions. Their vocal prowess and ability are, however, without question. Reference to what composers wrote for these voices confirms Raguenet's flowery prose. Many eighteenth-century manuscripts contain passages that few singers today could manage and consequently the leading castrati — Farinelli, Caffarelli, Marchesi, Guadagni, Crescentini and Velluti, among many others — are a vital part of the development of opera.

It was common practice for the singers of what is now called the bel canto period — the term didn't exist then because 'beautiful singing' was the normal expectation — to study for seven years learning their craft, castrati and women alike: conventions always favoured the treble voice, whether male or female. Their strenuous courses included correcting the smallest deficiencies in the voice and they were not considered ready to face the public until after this training period. Many of the leading singers became teachers when their active stage careers were over and some of their techniques and exercises — their vocalises — were documented. Several have survived in libraries and museums so that researchers can at least have access to the methods, if not the actual sounds, of the past. Most of the leading women singers of the age of bel canto were pupils of castrati or learned their craft from observing their techniques and were judged on the same level. They brought with them a new competitive rivalry that had been unknown previously. During the nineteenth century there was an intense curiosity about the distant and the recent past — the great boom in archaeology and exploration is witness to the former; an interest in the previous century's music is one facet of the latter. There were many editions of eighteenth-century music

50

published and it was also the time when the operas of prolific composers such as Bellini, Donizetti, Rossini and the young Verdi were being written within the bel canto tradition which had become not only a style of voice production but also a musical style as well. With the nineteenth century came the age of the prime donne — Lind, Pasta, Malibran, Grisi — and the leading male singers — Davide, Nourrit, Rubini, Mario. The development of opera was far from static; tastes were changing as composers such as Wagner and Berlioz wrote a new music for a different kind of voice. Orchestras grew in size and singers needed to concentrate primarily on strength of voice and to see beauty of tone and agility of technique as a secondary consideration.

The age of bel canto can never come back — except in a modified form — but much of the current operatic repertoire is due largely to the exploration and re-presenting of many forgotten bel canto operas by Maria Callas and then, building upon that, the enthusiasm and drive that led Bonynge in the early 1950s into believing that Sutherland's voice could be moulded into the bel canto style, while at the same time remaining a vital, flexible instrument, not to be used exclusively for perpetuating an art of the past.

Sutherland continued to resist many of Bonynge's attempts to raise her voice to a higher register because she still didn't believe it would work — and she continued to be backed up by her mother.

I used to listen to my mother sing at home. She had a very beautiful mezzo-soprano. She said she wouldn't let me study singing until I was eighteen, because my voice might be forced or trained in the wrong direction. But she guided me into a mezzo range with scales and breathing. I never dared to try to reach beyond a top C. But I jumped the gun on mother and her plans for me and joined the Bach Choral Society. My voice wasn't heavy enough then for Wagner, but I never realized it until I heard Wagner sung as it should be.

A turning point was singing an aria from Bellini's *I Puritani* for Professor Carey in which she and Bonynge had worked out an authentic period ornamentation and which ended on a high E flat. Carey was surprised at such a delivery from someone he had regarded as a potential dramatic soprano and realized at once it was Bonynge's influence he was hearing.

In the face of all the activity going on around her, Sutherland did not overlook the fact that she was no longer a youngster and needed to make a quick step forward if she was to realize her ambitions. She remembered the letter from Eugene Goossens to the Covent Garden administration and she wrote to the general administrator, David Webster, enclosing Goossens's note which read,

The bearer of this letter has a magnificent dramatic soprano voice and has done excellent work here in concert and operatic appearances. Her voice is in the true 'Austral' tradition, and she made quite a sensation recently in her creation of Judith in my own opera of that name. Her departure for Europe will be a great loss for Australia, for such grand natural voices as hers are all too scarce nowadays.

The reference to an 'Austral' voice gives another clue to the quality of Sutherland's voice at the time. Florence Austral made her mark at Covent Garden, European opera houses and in America during the 1920s and 1930s in a number of Wagnerian roles, and recordings suggest that her voice was dramatically powerful and highly suitable for such parts. She died virtually forgotten and alone at the age of seventy-four near Newcastle, New South Wales. That Goossens and consequently Carey had the same impression about Sutherland, indicates the insight Bonynge had in identifying a voice behind the voice. The letter to Webster brought a prompt offer of an audition. Bonynge agreed to be her accompanist and together they prepared a group of dramatic and coloratura arias that ranged from standard repertoire to bel canto. The audition was not a great success — at least in terms of results — but she was not turned-down out of hand. There was an invitation to try again in six months' time. The report of the Covent Garden musical staff to the general administrator stated, 'She starts with a good ring in her voice, but has very little experience or gifts by nature'.

Meanwhile, Sutherland furthered her collaboration with Bonynge, while attending the opera school at the Royal College. There, she was getting some performing experience and appeared as a Cigarette Girl in Bizet's *Carmen* in March 1952, Mrs Empson in Geoffrey Shaw's opera *All At Sea* two months later and, a larger part, Giorgietta, in Puccini's *Il Tabarro* in July at the annual students' performance. This resulted in her first British press notice by the eminent critic, Arthur Jacobs, 'The most original portrayal came from Joan Sutherland's Giorgietta; here is a soprano of high quality and well-controlled power. Doubtless Clive Carey, director of opera at the College, has assisted Miss Sutherland to develop her considerable stage presence; and one may confidently look forward to hearing more of her.' Carey, who was then sixty-nine, held more than a passing interest in Australian singers because he had been professor of singing at the Elder Conservatorium in Adelaide from 1924 to 1928 and was back there again in 1939. He taught in Melbourne between 1943 and 1945 and was one of the judges for the Sydney Eisteddfod before taking up his post as professor of singing and director of opera at the Royal College of Music.

More than six months passed and there was still no word from Covent Garden, and so Sutherland wrote reminding them of their promise of a second audition. It was arranged, and this time she and Bonynge prepared five arias, culminating in 'Non mi dir' from Mozart's Don Giovanni with the vocal ornamentation common in the past, but which had virtually disappeared by the middle of the twentieth century. She sang with a control and agility that impressed the audition panel more than before; previously they had been preoccupied with her appearance. Further study at the Opera School had managed to smooth that out a little, and now they noticed the brilliant voice. But it was still not enough to get her into Covent Garden. She was asked to audition yet again — this time on the stage of the theatre itself. Sutherland wondered if that next appearance might be the only time her ambition to sing at Covent Garden would turn into reality.

At the third audition they asked her to repeat the 'Non mi dir' that had impressed before. Once again she added the ornamentations and brilliance not common in modern times. She also presented several other arias from the standard repertory in more straightforward interpretation. Afterwards she was thanked politely and she and Bonynge left the theatre and walked out into the bustling, noisy world of Covent Garden market, their scores under their arms, and headed home. A confidential report to Webster read, 'Stylish. Very good diction. Top quite good. Middle very good. Sympathetic. But is she a proposition for this theatre?'

In the early 1950s Covent Garden could afford only four resident sopranos. If they were to take Sutherland, she would need to be completely adaptable, fitting in to many and varied roles demanded by the repertoire. Star quality was not a necessary requirement for such an appointment, but reliability was essential. Unknown to her, there had been representatives of Covent Garden at the student performances at the Royal College and they were aware of her developing abilities. By now, the term had ended and there was still no word about a possible engagement at the Royal Opera House. It was an agonizing time of wondering and waiting. Then, after two months, Mrs Sutherland received a telephone call; her daughter was being offered a contract at Covent Garden. The salary was £10 a week in London, £15 on tour. When Sutherland arrived home she called the Garden and eagerly accepted.

The person directly responsible for the appointment was the general administrator, David Webster, a man whose background had been in the business world, but who had a good eye and ear for new opera talent. He was aware of Sutherland's physical short-comings, but her voice held for him the promise of a future at Covent Garden. He remembered, 'Obviously hearing her in audi-tion one thought that she had possibilities, I think probably nothing more than that, at that particular moment'. Sutherland became a member of the company she had dreamed of joining, but she realized her immense good fortune was only the start of a long process that would keep her as the 'junior' until she could prove herself. She began a period of 'learning the ropes' during long hours at the theatre.

When I first went to Covent Garden they were all so helpful. I had read in books and biographies about feelings of jealousy and tricks being played on new hands. But I felt that everybody was so eager to be helpful and make this new-comer feel at home as quickly as possible. I was very gauche and overweight — and I was very conscious of not being able to make myself any better.

Her debut was to be as the First Lady in Mozart's *The Magic Flute* and she subjected herself to intensive preparation both at the Opera House and at home with Bonynge. The other ladies-in-waiting were Janet Howe, an English singer, and a Canadian, Jean Watson. They, with more experience, were able to calm an extremely nervous Sutherland. And then on Tuesday 28 October 1952, with three equally edgy members of the audience — Mrs Sutherland, Bonynge and sister Ailsa who had come to work in London — she made her debut in a production designed by Oliver Messel and conducted by John Pritchard. It was the 128th performance of the work there, which had first been performed at Covent Garden in May 1833 after its Vienna premiere in 1791.

The Sutherland temperament of not taking things too seriously even on an important occasion such as this was nearly her downfall during the first scene of the opera where Tamino is saved from a serpent by the three attendants of the Queen of the Night. It happened to be the night of one of the densest fogs London had experienced and the choking, clammy vapours penetrated the capital's theatres so that some performances had to be cancelled. The Royal Opera House decided to go ahead with its production and as soon as the curtains parted, the stage lighting was barely able to penetrate the gloom. Ailsa turned to her stepmother, 'Muriel, why do they have the stage so dark, can't they put up the lights or something?' 'Shush', replied Mrs Sutherland, 'the lights *are* on but the smog has even filled the Opera House'. Tamino was prostrate at the feet of the Ladies of the Night and suddenly Sutherland seemed to stumble in her singing. Bonynge turned to Mrs Sutherland and said, 'What happened there?' They both knew the score well. 'I don't know', she whispered, 'Joanie seemed to falter and then go on again'. Afterwards in the dressing-room Sutherland revealed that the thought suddenly struck her how silly it was to have these three ladies hovering over a prostrate Tamino who was, in fact, an invisible man — the fog was making it impossible for any of them to see what was happening at their feet. Her sense of the ridiculous had almost caused her to miss her cues. There were no press notices of the production until a performance nearly three months later when Andrew Porter wrote, 'The Queen of the Night's Ladies, Joan Sutherland, Janet Howe and Jean Watson, although at the start they were not quite together, formed a trio distinctly above the average'.

And then under the guidance of Covent Garden's team of *répétiteurs*, she continued learning other roles, both for actual performance and as understudy. According to Webster,

She developed naturally as people do in a company such as this, giving their whole time to the work and developing part after part. In some of the small parts she was outstanding. For instance, I think she was by a long way the best High Priestess in *Aida* I've ever heard. Some of these small parts, although they may be small in terms of time, are madly important.

Sutherland saw it this way,

I think the Opera House was coming alive again after the Second World War and they wanted any of their artists who were regular members of the company to succeed. There was a general feeling of help from behind the scenes. And there was a great feeling of competition with oneself to make each performance that much better than the one before. It was an atmosphere that was very hard to be found anywhere else in the world afterwards.

As they moved into another winter, the damp and foggy climate of London began to tell on Sutherland's delicate sinuses and ears. Covent Garden's resident laryngologist, James Ivor Griffiths, was helpful and understanding and, although she was only a fledgeling member of the company, he took as much interest in her problems as if she had been a prima donna. There were regular visits when he would drain the blocked nasal cavities and flush out the sinuses with a saline solution, an unpleasant procedure. But Sutherland accepted the discomfort and immediately after treatment, took the underground to her rehearsals at the theatre or home for more study with Bonynge. He was more than ever convinced of her potential to be a great singer, but it needed continuing effort for both of them, and frequent bullying, to convince the reluctant Sutherland that it was worthwhile. 'We fought like cat and dog over it. It really took Richard three years to convince me to stop singing Wagner and start singing the early nineteenth-century operas by Bellini, Rossini and Donizetti.'

This concentration on her career had meant a shift of direction in his own. His personal ambitions to be a concert pianist were being replaced with a new involvement.

I was supposed to be pursuing my career but I found increasingly that I was so much more interested in the music of the theatre. I was surrounded by opera singers all the time and working constantly in that medium and so I found I was putting most of my energies into that, rather than practising the piano. I don't think I would ever have had the patience to sit playing the same repertoire over and over again because the standard of piano playing is so high that you have to be technically phenomenal before anything else. It's just not acceptable to play the piano professionally unless you are quite extraordinary. In the nineteenth century pianists could get away with playing handfuls of wrong notes — but not any more. Anyway, it opened up the theatre to me.

After *The Magic Flute* came the small part in *Aida*. It was noted by the London *Daily Telegraph* that 'Joan Sutherland sang her Priestess solo admirably clearly' in a performance that was conducted by Sir John Barbirolli, and then within the space of a fortnight came a role that would see Sutherland sharing the same stage as Maria Callas in Bellini's *Norma*. She was to sing the part of the maid Clotilda to Callas's title role. The *répétiteurs* who were teaching Sutherland found it hard going because her movements were awkward and her learning of the music was slow. Edward Downes bore the brunt of the efforts for *Norma* and other works and began to lose his patience at the slow progress achieved. At a staff meeting he suggested that perhaps her employment ought to be terminated. David Webster would have none of it and Sutherland got to opening night unaware of what was being said behind her back. Contrary to reputation, Callas was easy to work with, having no prima donna tantrums and Sutherland, when not on stage for her small part, stood in the wings marvelling at the professional ease with which she and Ebe Stignani, who sang Adalgisa, projected their singing and acting.

I stood and watched Callas through my own special peephole and was astonished at the impact both Maria and Stignani made. I remember how Callas worked, she was always indefatigable. You couldn't fault her. The impact of *Norma* and her *Aida* and *Il Trovatore* made me wonder if I had the audacity to continue. I wanted to, but I really thought ten times about it after I saw those performances.

In Callas she saw a dramatic soprano with a large voice singing a coloratura role. This was what she, too, could do. On that night of *Norma*'s first performance, Bonynge was convinced that the road ahead would be a little easier. He recalls,

In the beginning when she was starting to learn the way of the coloratura technique, for a long time she tended to lighten the voice artificially. It was the wrong thing to do. As time progressed that was eliminated and she found that to sing coloratura you in no way need to lighten your voice. Coloratura is a technique and you see it with whatever sort of voice you have. One should be able to sing all the different roles in the repertory with the same kind of voice without having artificially to change the voice to sing either a dramatic or coloratura role.

The Times on 10 November reviewed *Norma*. Their anonymous and tetchy critic thought it 'worthwhile to revive a tedious work not seen in London since 1930' because of the presence of Maria Callas who was described clinically, but accurately, as 'An American soprano of Greek parentage'. There followed a none too enthusiastic summary of the evening and its performers but also: 'Two subsidiary parts were creditably sung by Miss Joan Sutherland and a Maltese tenor, Mr Paul Asciak'. After placing so many national tags on the performers it was a wonder that Sutherland escaped being labelled Australian in what the writer concluded to be 'an historical curiosity'.

An indication of how far Sutherland still had to go in voice development and interpretation came soon after *Norma*, in November 1952, when she displayed her voice in the exacting test of a solo recital. The recognized way for artists to introduce themselves to the British public is to give a recital at London's Wigmore Hall. For one thing, the serious press attends most of the recitals and good notices can help a career. Sutherland made her Wigmore Hall debut soon after her debut at Covent Garden and the perceptive critic of *The Times* realized that she was not just another of the dozens seen and heard every year and promptly forgotten. Under the headline 'Promising Soprano' he wrote,

The name of Miss Joan Sutherland has recently appeared among the cast of *The Magic Flute* and *Norma* at Covent Garden; on Friday she gave a recital at Wigmore Hall in order to afford a more ample view of her capabilities. This young Australian has the voice and the physique to make her a dramatic soprano capable of tackling either heavy Italian or Wagnerian roles. At present she is inclined to spoil her vocal line in the middle and lower registers by throwing her tone back into her mouth, but at the top there is flexibility, power, brilliance, and beauty of tone. She has much yet to learn about style — Gluck, Mozart, Bellini and Liszt are all much of a muchness to her, and are likely to remain so, until she attends to her words. At the moment she is fully occupied with the mechanics of singing, and although her programme ranged widely, she appeared to have given no thought to its interpretation. Attention alike to the significance and articulation of words is now required if she is to become the great singer that on the strength of her voice she might hope one day to be.

Her accompanist was the leading person in this field, the redoubtable Gerald Moore. Bonynge had prepared her for the recital but it was desirable to have a 'name' accompanist for reasons of prestige.

Sutherland's first big role came unexpectedly in late December 1952 when she was woken by the telephone ringing and the request from Covent Garden to take over Amelia in Verdi's *A Masked Ball* that night. All the staff sopranos were ill and the guest singer who was to have appeared, Helene Werth, was ill in Hamburg and couldn't get to London. Sutherland had been studying the role as an understudy, but it was only one of many parts, and she doubted she were up to standard. Covent Garden was reluctant to cancel the performance and Sutherland was the only singer available to take over the role at such short notice.

58

Instinctively she agreed to accept the challenge and secretly wondered if it might lead to her downfall. Edward Downes was in the prompt box and for him, too, it promised to be a night of tension, particularly in the light of his previous experiences with her. But Sutherland had not come this far to make a fool of herself, or anybody else. She was unsure of her stage movements but, on the night, an innate sense of theatre seemed to take over which, helped by Downes's cues, developed into a creditable performance, with a fine reception at the end of it from an audience that included Mrs Sutherland, Bonynge, and a fellow singer who had known her own successes on this stage, Joan Hammond. After the performance Downes was jubilant and congratulated Sutherland on her ability to succeed in such difficult circumstances. He then admitted to her that he'd tried to get her out of the company — and promised never to do such a thing again.

Early the next year she sang the part of Amelia again as a last-minute replacement for an indisposed guest singer during the company's spring tour of the north of England. 'A Special Success for Joan Sutherland', was noted by the *Edinburgh Evening News* adding that, 'She rose magnificently to the strains of a very challenging role'. The long tour had started in February when Britain, and particularly the north, was still gripped by winter. The weather affected many singers and resulted in understudies frequently taking over the leading roles as well as being introduced to new parts in the repertoire. The *Manchester Guardian* review of *A Masked Ball* on 31 March noted,

The part of Amelia was to have been sung by Elfriede Wasserthal...who was ill; it was taken over by Joan Sutherland, who sang pleasantly and accurately, and managed the *Traviata*-like fioriture very comfortably. Her performance last night was not very free nor very big, but it suggested she will grow in the part if given the chance, and has the makings of a first-rate dramatic soprano, if her voice can be properly developed.

In Edinburgh, Sutherland sang the Countess in Mozart's *The Marriage of Figaro* for the first time and then toward the end of the tour in April she filled in yet again in *A Masked Ball* which prompted the *Birmingham Post* to remark about the role of Amelia, 'Last night it was sung by Joan Sutherland at the traditionally short notice; and one hopes for the sake of all concerned that she will prove the exception [to being indisposed by illness] since she was quite excellent'. The tour was good experience, but there was little glamour surviving on £15 a week, much of which seemed to be devoured by hungry gas meters in a constant quest for warmth.

In the early 1950s Covent Garden was building up a resident British company because that is what its government subsidy demanded. 'British' then included singers from the Commonwealth as well, principally Australia, Canada and South Africa. They had a good dramatic soprano, the Australian, Sylvia Fisher; Blanche Turner was a lyric soprano; Adèle Leigh tended to be given the lighter soubrette parts; and there was Sutherland who at first was used as a general-purpose singer and fill-in, but was considered to be a potential dramatic soprano. It was the toughest training ground imaginable, and Sutherland was prepared to see it through. She'd slimmed down considerably to a much more acceptable silhouette and tried several new hairstyles to soften her jawline, but while her size diminished and her looks improved and her vocal powers were increasing, the stage presence continued to be static and ungainly. Covent Garden, however, was beginning to realize the asset they had with their new soprano. She'd proved herself to be an able and willing trouper, both in London and on tour. David Webster's faith in her voice was amply justified, although Lord Harewood, one of the Board of Directors, was not impressed with her as a complete artist. He thought that a concerted attempt should be made to improve her stage techniques and a leading producer, Norman Ayrton, was suggested as a coach. Now, in addition to learning new roles, attending regularly to her ear, nose and throat problems, working with Bonynge and finding time to eat and sleep, there was the added commitment of independent coaching and stagecraft. It was an extremely heavy schedule. Sutherland, through inhibitions going back to her schooldays, had always been reluctant to project her natural personality in public. She loathed attention being drawn to her; disliked making a scene. Now, the same type of challenge that Bonynge was accepting with developing her voice, Ayrton faced with her acting.

Sutherland had a strong conviction that singers should be primarily equipped to sing, and any other stage attributes were incidental. After all, so many of the great sopranos had very shaky reputations as actresses; it was their voices that made them what

60

they were and established the reputations that remained after they had trod the boards for the final time. 'I've been criticized very severely for relating to the vocal line and not being sufficiently dramatic', she agrees, 'but I think that the composer has written the vocal line to the best of his ability to express the feelings he wants. I think it is the sound of singing that people want when they come to the opera. If they want a great dramatic performance they should go to a straight play.'

The Countess in *The Marriage of Figaro*, Covent Garden 1953

In spite of such feelings Sutherland always listened to advice from those she respected, and Ayrton patiently pointed out to her that singers such as Callas had conditioned the public and critics alike to expect a combination of fine singing and exceptional acting — or at least a commanding stage presence. Acting, too, needed as much practice and skill before it could be fitted into an integrated performance. Ayrton, who is a deceptively mild-looking man, is, in fact, rather direct. When Sutherland protested that she could never come to grips with graceful movements, he bluntly suggested, if that was the case, she should not waste any more of his time and go home to Australia and resume her secretarial career. This approach touched a kindred chord in Sutherland and she agreed to continue their twice-weekly lessons, including specific coaching for her most important billing yet, Agathe in a new staging of Weber's *Der Freischütz* — a role that was to be much more her own, not a last-minute fill in, because she headed the second cast for the opera. Sylvia Fisher had the lead in the production.

During the summer months of 1953 she travelled with the Covent Garden company on a tour to Southern Rhodesia to take part in the Rhodes Centenary celebrations. In Bulawayo the company members were greeted as celebrities and the press reported that she particularly liked the city because it was similar to Australian towns. 'How familiar were the jacaranda trees and the gums, the hibiscus and poinsettias.' She said she thought even the houses — or 'bungalows' as she called them — reminded her of the houses in Sydney and of her own home there. Sutherland sang one of her few roles in contemporary opera with Penelope, Lady Rich in Benjamin Britten's *Gloriana*. Back in Britain she sang Frasquita in *Carmen* and, during the spring tour in the north, performances of Agathe in *Der Freischütz*. Sutherland regarded this role, which she was scheduled to sing regularly when the company returned to London, as her biggest test to date. 'I really felt that the outcome of my operatic career depended on this performance', she said. 'It seemed to me that, if I was a success, I could look forward to bigger parts. A great deal depended on it.' Ayrton worked steadily on Sutherland's dramatic technique. He taught her how to glide gracefully across a stage and to fall effectively. She took elementary ballet training with barre work and all the time they sparred and shouted at each other. She also had to

Top left: Frasquita in *Carmen*, Covent Garden 1953

Bottom left: Helmwige in *Die Walküre*, Covent Garden 1953

Right: Agathe in *Der Freischütz*, Covent Garden 1954

accept a considerable amount of verbal fireworks from Bonynge during their own work sessions. She accepted it all, although sometimes tearfully, but one major obstacle remained, the Australian accent. Ayrton pointed out firmly that as everyone was fully aware of her country of origin, why should she bother about it?

The Times critic was at Covent Garden for the London premiere of *Der Freischütz* in May and reported in clipped prose,

Miss Sutherland has been heard in smaller roles, and has taken larger ones, too, in time of need. This, it is believed, is the first major role that has been deliberately allotted to her. Her appearance and behaviour are, to the life, those of the demure, gentle country maiden... The spirit world released some undesirable gremlins in this performance. Miss Sutherland was almost assaulted by an act drop at the end of one scene.

Reports of the performance were flashed across the world and the Sydney *Sun*, one of the city's two afternoon papers, printed, 'The performance was stopped for a number of minutes by applause after each of the two big arias'. After the performance Sutherland's dressing-room was crowded with Australian admirers. She admitted to being 'terribly nervous'. She said, 'I was so scared, I could hardly breathe'. London's *Daily Express* of 14 May, under the heading 'Take a Note — It's a Voice to Watch' commented, 'She is a believable, if somewhat artless actress. Give her time and she should become a valuable addition to Covent Garden's shockingly short list of good sopranos.'

A small but growing band of opera administrators and admirers was beginning to take notice of Sutherland, but if the Covent Garden management now had its way, her career would move steadily in the direction of dramatic soprano roles. *Der Freischütz* was a step along that way and there were plans for her to be introduced gradually into Wagnerian roles. Mrs Sutherland, after spending nearly two years in Britain watching her daughter progress from job-seeking hopeful to up-and-coming soprano at one of the world's major opera houses, decided she must go home to Australia, but would be back at the end of the year. It seemed sensible now to move out of the bedsitter and find somewhere more convenient and congenial for living and working. There was still money untouched from 'Uncle' John's gift after she had won the Mobil Quest in Melbourne, and that went into a seven-year lease on a house nearby in Campden Hill, just down the road from Notting Hill, but a world away in its leafy, tree-lined streets. Into it she moved, with her piano, and Richard Bonynge and life and work continued as before but in more congenial circumstances. Bonynge was preparing for a recital at Wigmore Hall, a professional introduction to London's music world. His heart was not completely in it because, although previously it would have been vital to his career, now his plans and enthusiasms had been replaced by the attractions of the theatre and the development of Sutherland's voice. His life was becoming more and more locked into her career. He was, in the background, masterminding many aspects of her professional life, preparing new parts, commenting on her dress and appearance and all the time working on the voice, extending its range to encompass a bel canto purity that would lead it far away from the

Wagner currently being planned for her by Covent Garden.

Their lives had become so close that a permanent partnership was to be the next step. Bonynge proposed, was accepted and at a simple October ceremony in Kensington Registry Office Clive Carey gave away the bride who was dressed in a red velvet dress with a cardigan neckline and a face-trimming hat of pale grey with a saw-tooth brim. Bonynge wore a double breasted grey suit and sported a large bow tie. There were no other guests, no flowers — except for a bouquet of red carnations sent by David Webster, who was one of the few people to know about the marriage. 'Star's Secret Wedding' was one small headline in the press, which went on to say that Sutherland was rehearsing new operas including Walton's *Troilus and Cressida* and Tippett's *A Midsummer Marriage*. 'They will have no time for a honeymoon.' Mrs Sutherland was on her way back from Australia by ship and they sent a cable to her at Colombo, giving the news. She replied, 'You naughty children. Watch yourselves. Love Mum'.

Ailsa was having a party for some Australian friends at her small flat in Ladbroke Grove that Saturday night and Joan and Richard were invited. Just as she was getting herself ready the phone rang; it was Sutherland. 'Hope you're sitting down, Lal', she said, 'what I'm about to tell you will probably be a bit of a shock. Rick and I have just been married and we'd like to get there before the other guests to tell you all about it.' When the newly-weds arrived, the others had rallied round to make it a celebration, but even Australian ingenuity couldn't find a wedding cake in London on a Saturday night so they had to make do with one of Ailsa's home-made apple tea cakes. There was champagne, however, and it seemed a perfect complement as it was quaffed from a collection of lemon spread, Vegemite and peanut butter glasses. Sutherland was twenty-seven and Bonynge nearly four years younger. Soon after, he played his first London recital at Wigmore Hall on 28 October 1954. The programme included sonatas by Soler, Arne and Liszt, together with other pieces by Schumann, Weber and Lennox Berkeley. A press notice thought he displayed a limited dynamic range 'both of sound and emotions, which inhibits his work at the moment'.

Sutherland tended to shrug off comparisons that were being made between herself and her famous countrywoman, Nellie Melba. She, naturally, wanted to be considered on her own merits and it was certainly foolish to compare the two careers except on the superficial level of common heritage. The Australian press, however, continued to call her 'the new Melba' and surprisingly, their two careers have several points in common, although we can only guess at Melba's true vocal powers from contemporary accounts and recordings made when the medium was in its infancy and she was moving past her prime.

The Bonynges' careers develop, London 1954

Both sopranos were born in Australia of staunch Presbyterian fathers who had emigrated from Scotland to seek a better life in the colonies. David Mitchell, Melba's father, came from Forfarshire, while William Sutherland was born in Caithness. Mitchell was a master builder, and the Scots Church in the centre of Melbourne is one of his more notable constructions in the city. William Sutherland was a master tailor and he built up a flourishing business in Sydney, particularly among the professional men of Macquarie Street. On the Alston side of Sutherland's family

66

both her grandfather and great-grandfather were builders responsible for the medical school at Sydney University, Gladesville Asylum and a portion of Sydney Hospital. Church-going was an essential part of both families' weeks. Both Helen Porter Mitchell (the Melba came much later) and Joan Alston Sutherland sang from an early age, but their personalities were entirely different. Melba was something of a tomboy as a child and later became outgoing but rebellious, entering into an early, disastrous marriage that should have swamped her singing aspirations in a lather of humidity because it took her north to tropical Queensland where her husband, Charles Armstrong, was manager of a sugar plantation and there was little demand for Nellie's singing.

Sutherland was a much quieter, self-contained person, conscious of her size and appearance, but she got as far in the world of singing for the very reasons that Melba succeeded — the sheer drive and willpower to win through. Both went to London to try their luck — Sutherland stayed, Melba went to Paris — but both of them became associated with strong individuals who would set their careers in motion. For Melba it was the celebrated singing teacher, Mathilde Marchesi; for Sutherland, Richard Bonynge. Melba, in the late nineteenth century made her name in Brussels and Paris before Covent Garden adopted her as its favourite soprano, where she sang with Caruso and feuded with Tetrazzini. She was a grand success in New York and at La Scala — where she sang a great *Lucia* and afterward never returned there. 'I am Melba', she stated, 'I shall sing where and when I like, and I shall sing in my own way'. Later in her career she returned home to Australia in triumph for recital tours and seasons of opera with her own company — the Melba-Williamson Grand Opera Company. So was Sutherland destined to do. Melba, like Sutherland, had a reputation for being down-to-earth, but unlike her it was often cloaked in the hauteur of prima donnaship. She never married again, but her affair with the Duc d'Orleans caused a stir in late-Victorian England and probably delayed her damehood because the Queen was not amused by such scandals. In fact, the honour came late in life, when she was already fifty-eight and it was announced, not specifically for singing, but for charitable services during the Great War. Melba became rich through her singing and recording activities and maintained homes at various times in London, Paris and at Lilydale, outside Melbourne. She died in St Vincent's Hospital in Sydney's eastern suburbs at the age of sixty-nine. Sutherland, who was then four and a half, remembers the day vividly, 'I was playing in the garden of our house at Point Piper when our next door neighbour, Dame May Barlow — a Papal Dame who wore a high-collared velvet dress with a beautiful cameo — came up to the fence and cried out, "Joan, run tell your mother that our marvellous songbird, Nellie Melba, has died".'

There would be many parallels drawn between their two careers in the years to come. Melba became a household name, even to those who associated it merely with peaches, toast, or staging interminable farewells — known in Australia as 'doing a Melba'. To mark the impact she made at Covent Garden in her career spanning thirty-eight years, a marble bust was commissioned from her friend the Australian sculptor, Sir Bertram MacKennal, and it stood for many years with a companion bust of Adelina Patti in the main entrance foyer of the Royal Opera House. Sutherland did not see it there, however, when she was a staff singer in the 1950s; it had been taken out for safe storage during the Second World War and was gathering dust in a corridor of the offices and rehearsal rooms across the road.

Chapter Four

I suppose I was born in the wrong century. One hundred and fifty years ago composers wrote operatic roles for specific singers like Pasta, Malibran, Viardot. But no modern composer has ever come up to me and said, 'What can I write for you?'

The five years from 1954 to the end of 1958 were to be pivotal in Sutherland's career. Everything that happened then from her vocal development, health and personal life, to the critical response to performances, would mould her future status as a singer. It was a time of consolidation following the outlines set by David Webster, although Bonynge did not regard Covent Garden as the sole base for his wife's career; there were many more opera houses that would want to hear her voice in the future. Webster recalled, 'I had no doubt she was going to get to the top, and she went fairly quickly. I've known quite a number of singers go to bits through getting there too soon, but I've never known anyone who got there not quite so quickly, who suffered because of it.' Certainly nobody could accuse Sutherland of too much too soon. As she says, 'I studied for years in Australia, then sang concerts for five years before entering opera. Then I spent many years in opera before anyone took notice of me.' Bonynge adds, 'She had something to back her up. It is essential, not only for getting to the top, but also for staying there.'

In the mid 1950s Sutherland was accepted as a loyal and valuable member of the Covent Garden company. While other singers were often indisposed, she never missed a performance through illness, but her outwardly placid nature tended to obscure the talent that was being developed.

I think one must be reasonably placid or I don't see how I could possibly cope with all the trials and tribulations we come up against. I can lose my temper. I can take just so much and then go completely off. But I soon forget about it and I don't bear any grudges. Sometimes you can't feel any sense of rapport between the other artists and the conductor, and if that goes on for too long I just fly off the handle and feel much better afterwards.

An operatic rarity for Covent Garden audiences as well as for Sutherland was a single performance in the title role of Verdi's *Aida* when Joan Hammond, who was to have sung the part, was involved in a car accident. Sutherland had barely twelve hours' notice for what was to be her biggest role to date and much of that time was taken up with hurried wardrobe alterations and fittings. Amongst the audience that night were her sister Ailsa, Clive Carey, now retired from the Royal College of Music, and Douglas Fairbanks Jr with a party of friends. They opened their programmes to find a small white slip of paper inserted bearing the information, 'Owing to the indisposition of Miss Joan Hammond, the role of Aida will be sung by Miss Joan Sutherland'. 'What a pity', remarked one of Fairbanks's guests. 'I always like Hammond in the role of Aida.' He replied, 'If you like we could leave and come again another night. But I think we should wait and see what this Australian can do — she's very brave to take it on at such short notice and I remember reading somewhere that she's rather good.' Fairbanks was wise to persist; Sutherland gave an assured performance and Carey summed-up the evening by noting, 'It really was a great triumph for her'.

Marriage and an intimate working relationship with her husband helped to fashion Sutherland's outlook. Bonynge saw it this way,

Naturally I could help her more than anybody else because I am more used to her and she to me. I don't like her to work with other people because, from a jealous point of view, I like to work with her myself. I don't like her to get other interpretations which are foreign to the way we study. It's the constant work that helps and I think I've learned as much from her as she's learned from me.

Having Bonynge for a husband and mentor — someone who was prepared to construct her career, began to change Sutherland's standing at Covent Garden. It was becoming known that she would take his advice first in most things and it was also acknowledged that he would influence his wife's attitude to the roles she was being asked to accept.

The summer of 1954 had seen *The Ring* cycle performed at the Royal Opera House with Sutherland singing the small parts of Woglinde in *Das Rheingold* and the Woodbird in *Siegfried*. The previous October she had made her first Wagner appearance as one of the Valkyries (Helmwige) in *Die Walküre*. Wagner was not the musical direction they wished to take and it was only with an eye to the future that Bonynge was able to bring himself to coach her in these roles. There would be only one other stage association with Wagner, and that was her Eva in *The Mastersingers* three years later. In direct contrast came a production that was much more to their liking, and an early indication of another direction their careers would take in the future. In November 1954 she sang the part of the consumptive Antonia in Offenbach's *The Tales of Hoffmann* as a replacement for another Australian singer, Elsie Morrison, who had a strained back. Later she would sing all four parts in the operetta, but in early 1955 she was hard at work originating the role of Jennifer in Michael Tippett's new opera *The Midsummer Marriage*. The huge contrast again between Offenbach and Tippett confirmed the constant challenges to a Covent Garden staff singer.

Relaxing Valkyries, Covent Garden 1954

The composer had toiled for seven years on the music and lyrics of his work, which was on the theme of sexual love as it affects two pairs of lovers on both the physical and spiritual planes, and no new opera for a long time had been heralded by so much explanatory prognostication. When Sutherland was announced for the role of Jennifer, Lord Harewood suggested to Tippett, who was still completing the score, that he might write as many coloratura flourishes for her as he wished. Harewood, who was now controller of opera planning, was being pressured by Bonynge for more suitable roles for his wife to sing, but the problem was that Covent Garden's repertory, apart from the occasional new work, was linked to a predictably safe group of productions which the public would support — and for which there was often scenery and costumes available in store. *The Midsummer Marriage* was baffling all those who were involved in it. The meaning of the complex symbolism, not so far removed in spirit from *The Magic Flute*, was not eased by the Czech Otakar Kraus singing in heavily-accented English, and Oralia Dominguez from La Scala, who did not speak the language at all, learning her words parrot-fashion. Sutherland, completely confused by the plot-line, appealed to Tippett for help in understanding it. Additionally there was the problem of contemporary music. She had not been happy singing in Britten's *Gloriana*, commissioned by Covent Garden to celebrate the coronation of the Queen in 1953. The contemporary idiom was as distasteful to her and Bonynge as was the heaviness of Wagner. 'Mr Tippett told me not to worry if I didn't understand his opera', said Sutherland. 'He told me just to sing it as well as I could and leave the audience to work out the significance for themselves.' Her fellow Australian John Lanigan remarked tight-lipped, 'I can only say that I know my part'. Miss Dominguez, whose face was painted blue for the performance, said, 'The music is most interesting but I cannot talk about anything else. I am not even sure why my face is painted blue.' Otakar Kraus admitted that he didn't know what it was all about. 'I thought just for once I would be able to live an opera out. I always die. I die again in this. I drop dead through some supernatural power.' The fifty-year-old composer was not disturbed by the fuss: 'The whole thing seems perfectly simple to me. This is a story of two sets of lovers and their different approach toward marriage. It is a piece of depth and imagination. It is like a crystal ball which you can turn endless ways. My opera means what it says — nothing more.'

The performance of *The Midsummer Marriage* went well enough to a mixed audience reaction which included some booing as well as applause. The critics' consensus was that the work was dramatically weak but there were many musical qualities to praise. The years have mellowed the public's attitude to Michael Tippett. A knighthood and the Order of Merit set the seal of acceptance on his music and time helped to make his works much less impenetrable than they seemed when new, but Sutherland still looks back on that time with disbelief. After *The Midsummer Marriage*, Poulenc was the only other modern opera composer she would tackle, claiming

It's no good putting on operas few people want to see; the public must be pleased. We are entertainers. And unless we entertain, the purpose of our work is defeated. They're not all musicologists sitting out there; most of them don't even read music. We're the ones who are paid to do that, and they pay to listen, and they should bloody well get something they can enjoy.

In spite of the eccentric range of roles chosen for her, Sutherland's career began to gain momentum from the mid 1950s. In October 1955 she sang a rather mature Micaëla in Bizet's *Carmen* and, with a rare show of spirit, disagreed strongly with Rafael

Micaëla in *Carmen*, Covent Garden 1955

Kubelik over the edition to be used. He was musical director of Covent Garden Opera between 1955 and 1958 and insisted on spoken recitative as Bizet had originally intended, but which at Covent Garden had been traditionally sung. Sutherland was notoriously bad at dialogue and ever-conscious of her accent. In spite of the continuing coaching from Norman Ayrton, her speech was the rawest nerve-end remaining and she found it hard to recite lines on stage before the whole company. Eventually Kubelik agreed to compromise, but only after considerable differences of opinion and a walkout during rehearsal by Sutherland which led to Webster's arbitration in the affair and the reinstatement of Micaëla's recitative before her aria. There were also, however, some amusing moments when Sutherland's sense of fun shone through. *Carmen* was sung by a cast made up of Irish, Australian, Czech and American singers. At one performance the Irishman had to ask her about Seville in a line that came out as, 'Ah Micaëla! What are yer doin' in Brazil?' Sutherland broke up completely and it took several moments before they could regain composure and continue with the performance.

Blonde-wigged Micaëla was one of her most repeated roles and offstage as well as on she was now wearing a new hairstyle — bleached blonde. She was also pregnant. The gypsy girl's skirts needed to be increasingly voluminous and every week the wardrobe mistress, Gertie Stelzel, would add more material as the pregnancy extended into the seventh month. Sutherland then took a short break from performance to deliver an eight pound son on 13 February 1956. They called him Adam Carl. A few

A proud mother, 1956

weeks later she was back at work, and had moved to a new apartment in Kensington and engaged a Swiss nanny named Ruthli Brendlé to look after the infant.

At this time Bonynge was in the middle of what was amounting to a row over the direction of Sutherland's career. The big dramatic roles were looming ever larger, Agathe had been a step in that direction and the prospect of bel canto operas for her seemed remote. But Bonynge pressed for them. He was certain there would be a good public response — especially as he knew how far her technique had progressed in that direction, although little of it was being heard. The opinion was based on his show-business premise:

> The audience that goes to a bel canto opera is going to a vocal circus. The critics say that against it, but I say that for it. The singers need to tread the high wires, they are doing vocal gymnastics. If they are big singers and bring it off well, it can be very exciting. And there's always that element of doubt whether they will make it. A singer just may crack on that high E-flat and fall flat on her face.

Bonynge saw bel canto as 'the true art of singing well' and he dearly wanted it to be the next step in Sutherland's development. Discussions began about a possible production of Donizetti's *Lucia di Lammermoor* with her in the title role. The work had a patchy tradition at Covent Garden and the enthusiasm was not overwhelming. Melba had made her London debut in it in 1888 to a half-filled house and, having so little impact, scurried back to the safer scene of her successes in Brussels and Paris before she returned the following year to a triumph in Gounod's *Roméo et Juliette* with Jean and Edouard de Reszke. Toti dal Monte sang *Lucia* for a single performance in 1925 and then Covent Garden took it off. The work's reputation with British opera lovers rested almost entirely on a recent recording by Maria Callas. Members of the Board were not convinced that the cost of a new production and Sutherland singing the taxing title role were a proposition for Covent Garden. Charpentier's *Louise* was suggested as a less-expensive alternative — a compromise, because the properties were already in existence from a production that had originated before the First World War. Bonynge had a look at the battered sets and tatty costumes and vetoed the idea, holding out for *Lucia*. David Webster was prepared to take a chance and insist that it should go ahead. He had, after all, been right about Sutherland so far; his faith in her had never faltered and there was every reason to believe that it could be the work that would introduce her to prima donna heights. He recalled, 'Quite a few people connected with the place didn't think that she could do *Lucia*. To them the idea of putting on a huge production for her was rash and definitely too risky. That is something I never felt.'

A special English libretto was planned for the opera; to be commissioned from Christopher Hassall, and in the meantime Bonynge and Sutherland began working on the score in its original Italian, going over every phrase for meaning and interpretation and working out the techniques used by the singers in Donizetti's day. Bonynge prepared a literal translation of the Italian text so that the libretto would be easier to understand. Sutherland was reading as much as possible that was relevant to the opera's background, including Sir Walter Scott's novel *The Bride of Lammermoor* on which it was based. 'From the opera alone you cannot completely understand and get inside the character', she said. At first, the enormity of the challenge seemed daunting. Lucia is on stage for much of the opera and, in addition, a wide range of acting is required for the role. This time of intense learning, sandwiched between her regular performances and concert engagements, was one of considerable nervous tension and physical exhaustion. Her mother was constantly surprised and worried about the vehement driving force of Bonynge's coaching which didn't even allow a pause for a cup of tea. Words flew between them, piano keys were crashed and then all was pleasantly calm again, until the next day. But then came a sudden setback in the preparations for *Lucia*. An Italian opera season was announced for London's Stoll Theatre in early 1957 and *Lucia* was scheduled for presentation with Virginia Zeani in the title role. There were behind-the-scenes moves in an attempt to persuade the Italians to delete it from their season, but to no avail. After a gap of more than thirty years since the opera was last performed in London, it was unthinkable for Covent Garden to mount a costly rival production at the same time as the Stoll Theatre, and the plans were shelved; some hoped they would be dropped altogether.

And so professional life went on. During the Mozart bicentenary year of 1956 Sutherland was engaged to sing at the small but prestigious country opera house of Glyndebourne, the

Countess in *The Marriage of Figaro* in a production by Carl Ebert conducted by Vittorio Gui. There were fears that the small auditorium, seating 600, and her big voice might conflict, but she was a great success. The head of the Glyndebourne music staff, Janni Strasser, had a soft spot for Australians, 'They have wonderful voices', he stated, 'they work industriously, are very humble and easy to teach'. The reasons for this he thought were a combination of climate, good food, a good way of living and the right temperament to make opera singers.

The Countess in *The Marriage of Figaro*, Glyndebourne 1956

77

Life for a Covent Garden soprano in the mid 1950s was hardly one of glamour. The prestige of being a staff singer did lead to many engagements that otherwise would not have been offered, but they required an immense amount of preparation and travel in addition to rehearsing and learning the Covent Garden repertoire which came first. Radio gave Sutherland a wider spectrum of activity including the performance in May 1954 of a special composition by the new Master of the Queen's Musick, Sir Arthur Bliss, to welcome the Queen back from the long tour of her dominions. *Song of Welcome* was set to the words of poet Cecil Day Lewis and was scored for soprano and baritone soloists with chorus and orchestra. Her experience was consolidated by such disparate appearances as Handel's *Messiah* in Liverpool, a recital at Brierly Hill in Surrey, singing at the BBC summer Promenade Concerts, a performance of Dvořák's *Te Deum* and the title role of *Euryanthe* in Weber's opera for a BBC Third Programme broadcast. That contrasted with the title role in *Aida* with the Devon Amateur Opera Company in the Savoy Cinema, Exeter, conducted by Sir Malcolm Sargent, then at the peak of his popularity. Sutherland also gave another Wigmore Hall recital and this time her accompanist was Richard Bonynge who, the *Daily Telegraph* thought, 'accompanied with care and intelligence' in a programme of songs ranging from Arne and Mozart to Schubert and Rossini.

Many of her broadcasts were out of London, particularly in Scotland and the north, and they gave the opportunity to perform on radio the type of repertory she could not get on stage such as Alessandro Scarlatti's most celebrated opera *Il Mitridate Eupatore* in which she sang the leading role of Laodice. One of Covent Garden's regular conductors, John Pritchard, then chose Sutherland to sing in another broadcast opera that was exactly the sort of work she wanted to perform. Pritchard had taken over conducting from Vittorio Gui for the Callas *Norma* when Sutherland had sung Clotilda, but even before that, he had picked out the unique qualities of her voice:

I was conducting the Royal Liverpool Philharmonic Orchestra and we decided to put on a very rarely heard work of Donizetti known as *Emilia di Liverpool*. It's a surprising opera, I don't think it's ever been given thoroughly in the theatre even in Donizetti's day. We cast Joan Sutherland for this broadcast in the part of Emilia. And the piece from which we did an excerpt lasting for about an hour finished with a great coloratura scene for soprano. When we heard Sutherland do this, everybody said, 'My goodness! This is a voice that is going to take over in the Bellini and Donizetti operas with a vengeance.'

Another important engagement away from Covent Garden was a single performance for the Handel Society of *Alcina* at the St Pancras Assembly Rooms in March 1957. It drew attention to the neglect of the composer's dramatic works and helped to restore Handel's standing, at the same time establishing for Sutherland a reputation as a fine interpreter of his music. The year 1957 was another of new roles but with the mixture very much as before. It had begun with her singing for the first time Eva in *The Master-singers* with Kubelik conducting. And then after *Alcina* came Gilda in Verdi's *Rigoletto*, conducted by Edward Downes; a brilliant Mme Herz, one of the warring prima donnas in Mozart's *Der Schauspieldirektor* (The Impresario) at Glyndebourne; and in December she sang Desdemona to Ramón Vinay's title role in Verdi's *Otello* for the first time, with Downes conducting. She continued to receive good press notices. The *Daily Mail* said of her Desdemona, 'Musically and dramatically the point was made so poignant that we all sorrowed with the cruelly wronged and fatally slandered wife'. The *Daily Express* commented, 'Miss Sutherland carried her fast growing reputation up another notch'. Her acting was described as 'powerful' with a 'touching eloquence'.

By the dawn of 1958 nothing had been decided about *Lucia*. The Italian Opera season at the Stoll Theatre had come and gone and their production of the work, which had postponed Covent Garden's, left a great impression on London's opera-goers. Bonynge tried to get a decision about the plans for his wife but was told that none would be made until at least April. And so she and Bonynge had to postpone their *Lucia* preparations again while they worked together on a new production of Poulenc's *The Carmelites*. Ever one to search out the background to a work, Sutherland read not only Georges Bernanos's text, but also as much about the Carmelite order as she could lay her hands on — in the same way that she had gone to Shakespeare's play for her recent *Otello*. The work, telling the story of the martyrdom of Carmelite nuns during the French Revolution, was being seen at Covent Garden just a year after its premiere at La Scala and Sutherland sang the part of the new prioress, Mme Lidoine, with

Top left: *Alcina*, at St Pancras Town Hall, London 1957
Top right: Eva in *The Mastersingers of Nuremburg*, Covent Garden 1957
Bottom left: Gilda in *Rigoletto*, Covent Garden 1957

Bottom right: Mme Lidoine in *The Carmelites*, Covent Garden 1958

Francis Poulenc himself assisting in the musical preparation.

The Covent Garden Board made a decision about *Lucia* in May 1958, agreeing that the production could go ahead if a suitable tenor were found and if a first-rate Italian conductor were available. Finally, one of the world's top opera conductors, Tullio Serafin, was engaged; he was not only thoroughly familiar with the bel canto repertoire, but had first conducted at Covent Garden fifty years before, and in recent years had been behind many of Maria Callas's successes. The Board had wanted an English version of the opera, but Serafin, although delighted to accept the engagement, insisted that it must be in Italian for him to take part. The Board finally let him have his way, and the production was scheduled for the next season, in February 1959.

At this point, with a regular following at Covent Garden, but no records to her credit and relatively small audiences for the BBC's Third Programme, Sutherland was in a secure, but unremarkable position. Her career should have gone forward quicker, had it not been for the delays over *Lucia*. She was now receiving good critical attention, but needed a big role to get wider acclaim. Typical of the notices she was receiving is *The Times* critique of her revival of Gilda in *Rigoletto* in April 1958.

Miss Sutherland was clearly the star of the performance, aware of the expressive possibilities of Gilda's music and technically in admirable command of her glorious voice. Her performance in '*Caro Nome*' at a slow tempo, translucent with exquisite shakes and portamenti and glowing, perfectly placed high notes, was memorable by any standard — and standards in this aria are of the highest. Do we mean that Miss Sutherland could become a Melba or Galli-Curci? Yes.

While waiting for *Lucia*, Sutherland was invited to perform abroad in opera for the first time as a leading singer, although she had already in 1958 left Britain briefly for a performance of Verdi's *Requiem* in The Netherlands. In 1957 the director of an International Festival in Vancouver, Canada heard her sing at Glyndebourne and engaged her for the role of Donna Anna in Mozart's *Don Giovanni* during July 1958. Sutherland found herself welcomed as a celebrity and although Vancouver was hardly one of the world's recognized music centres, she did have a noted producer to stage the production, Günther Rennert. He was born in Germany in 1911 and had emerged as the finest opera producer in West Germany, taking over as Intendant of the Hamburg Opera from 1946 to 1956 and moulding that company into the

Donna Anna in *Don Giovanni*, Vancouver 1958, with Léopold Simoneau

nation's leading ensemble. He guested at Glyndebourne as well as Covent Garden and had a reputation for being able to display an intense humanity in his productions as well as handling stage movement with a sympathetic fluency and efficiency. Sutherland had been directed by him in the roles of Amelia in *A Masked Ball* in December 1952 and three of the four heroines in *The Tales of Hoffmann* during late 1954 and 1955.

She arrived in Vancouver a redhead, having abandoned her blonde image, and from this time her titian hair would be one of her distinguishing features. That, combined with a new trimness and some successful dental work adding a new smile to the repertoire, revealed a personality with a growing air of confidence. The Canadian press described her as 'looking sweet, fresh and unassuming — as untemperamental as they come'. Her figure was noted as 'statuesque — 5 ft 9 inches — though not Wagnerian'. For the first time, Sutherland had a production built around her, not as a company member, but as a guest singer. Her colleagues were of international standard including an outstanding baritone from New York's Metropolitan Opera, George London, who was born in Canada, later making his debut in Vienna in 1949. He had sung at the Met since 1951 with particular success in his roles of Scarpia in *Tosca*, *Boris Godounov* and *Don Giovanni*. Influenced by London's intense acting and Rennert's confident direction, Sutherland responded well and was able to build a performance that, had it been in London, or Paris, or New York might have set her on the road to an international career there and then.

George London was so impressed with Sutherland's voice that he made arrangements for her to stop off in New York on the return trip to London and audition for the Met. Bonynge was not with her in North America and against his telephoned advice she decided to sing '*Caro Nome*' from *Rigoletto* in English. The Met had a whole bevy of sopranos who could, and usually did, sing *Rigoletto* in Italian. The management wasn't very interested in the English version and made no offer of engagement.

Back at Covent Garden a special entertainment to be attended by the Queen was being assembled to mark the centenary of the third theatre to be situated on the site which had opened in 1858. The gala was to be headed by Maria Callas, and Sutherland was listed to sing with John Lanigan an aria and duet from Balfe's *The Bohemian Girl*. Callas listened to Sutherland rehearse, and although she had forgotten their *Norma* association on the same stage six years before, she was impressed with what she heard. Around this time two people were to wield a strong influence on Sutherland's publicity — not an easy thing to get for an opera singer who is not yet a prima donna. Callas herself, at the peak of her career, with a vast range of repertoire and a temper to match the brilliance of her performances, was constantly surrounded by press attention. She would soon make a contribution to Sutherland's fame. The other was a feature writer on the *Daily Express*, Noël Goodwin. In his paper on 30 November, soon after the Covent Garden gala and Sutherland's single performance at the Leeds Musical Festival in Handel's *Samson*, he wrote,

I predict that if Maria Callas, now thirty-four, goes on performing at the present rate, she will have left no professional singing voice by the time she is forty. Joan Sutherland...within five years will be acclaimed as famous an international star as Maria Callas is now, but she will no longer be a member of the Covent Garden Company.

An Israelite Woman in *Samson*, Covent Garden 1958

By the winter of 1958, the long-awaited production of *Lucia di Lammermoor* was finally within sight. Sutherland's health was continuing to be a problem and after a series of x-rays indicated that her ear abscesses could lead to further complications, Ivor Griffiths insisted that she undergo a sinus operation because that seemed to be the root cause of her troubles. Sutherland agreed, but only after she had done the six performances of *Lucia* scheduled for February 1959. At least, if there were complications, she would first have had her chance to reach the heights in the production she most dearly wanted.

84

Chapter Five

It was like a football crowd. My knees were knocking and tears pouring down my face. I couldn't believe it was happening to me.

As part of the thorough preparation for the role of *Lucia*, Sutherland and Bonynge were sent to Venice for two weeks of study with Tullio Serafin, who would be conducting the performance. He was held in considerable reverence in the world of opera and particularly by the Bonynges because of his long association with bel canto. He was already a very senior figure, but active at the age of eighty-one. He had first played the violin in the orchestra of La Scala well before the turn of the century and made his conducting debut in Ferrara in 1900 at the age of twenty-two. Covent Garden first welcomed Serafin in 1907 and his most influential years were as musical director of New York's Metropolitan Opera between 1924 and 1934 and in Rome, where he was the chief conductor and artistic director of the Opera for nine years from 1934. He became the champion of many young artists including Rosa Ponselle and Maria Callas in their early performing years.

After the first session with him, Serafin commented to Sutherland, 'Your husband has taught you very well. I just think you should continue as you are. I am very happy with what he has done.' That was an encouraging omen for the first night and it endorsed David Webster's plan to have Sutherland completely ready for her big role. He was still facing some opposition from those around him but he had always believed in her and was prepared to back his judgement in spite of the risks. 'That is something I never felt', he said, 'I never felt there were any risks, and so we took enormous pains to have her properly prepared for the performance.'

Considerable style was added to the production by appointing Franco Zeffirelli, just about to turn thirty-six, as producer and designer, the most brilliant and busy of the new school of production talent. His interests ranged over a wide area of opera, theatre, cinema and design. Musically, the production was secure with Serafin's confidence in the work Sutherland and Bonynge were doing together, but dramatically the challenge was a huge one for Zeffirelli. Sutherland's stagecraft had improved over the years, helped by her many sessions with Norman Ayrton and, more recently, the experience of working with Carl Ebert at Glyndebourne and Günther Rennert in Vancouver. But *Lucia* was different. Zeffirelli had ambitious plans for his production but the initial encounters with Sutherland were not encouraging. 'He shocked me beyond bounds', she recalls. 'He said, "You can have a much better shape than you've got" and proceeded to coax me to shed a voluminous jacket covering a floppy sweater which I was wearing for warmth.' With the persuasive Italian manner he used a tactile approach to indicate what movements and stance he wanted. Sutherland, with an ingrained Presbyterian propriety shied away from his touch in embarrassment until he had to explain to her, 'Joan, I am sorry. I am Italian, I cannot speak without putting my hand on your shoulder or your arm. I must communicate with my hands. My language is not that good in any case. Let me embrace you', and Sutherland blushed like a small girl. But gradually she overcame her awkwardness to his approach and began responding to his direction. Zeffirelli's method was to involve his subjects in the process of creating a role and much of his direction was the result of a mutual spontaneity. He would plot a particular sequence, giving an over-all idea of how it should go and leave her to see what she made of it. He then took what he considered were useful elements and refined them. Once a sequence of movements had been developed Sutherland found it relatively easy to sing at the same time because she had always done this quite naturally around the house.

Bonynge, who was seeing the culmination of seven years of exacting work, was happy with the way things were working out. He was attuned to Zeffirelli's speed of operation and he was impressed with the way the producer tried to interpret the work from the viewpoint of the composer. Like Bonynge with music, Zeffirelli studied the period he wanted to re-create and thought of himself as an interpreter, not attempting to impose too much of his own personality on the work being staged. As with most Italians, his was an emotional response and although Sutherland and Zeffirelli were poles apart in their reactions to most things, they had a common work bond which was committed to progressive achievement without the need for outbursts of temperament. She was eventually won over by the Italian's completely natural and friendly attitude and the way in which he inspired confidence and affection in those who worked with him.

Zeffirelli's approach to both production and design was essentially realistic and his attention to detail phenomenal. For this new production he seemed to be working around the clock supervising all the minutiae of production. First there was his responsibility of realizing within a conventional framework the plot, based on Sir Walter Scott's story set in the Scottish Highlands in 1699, but which, through its translation into the world of Italian romantic opera had become shorn of much of its literary impact. The novels of Walter Scott had provided a fertile field for opera libretti with almost every one of his works adapted for the musical stage, including Bellini's *I Puritani* derived from *Old Mortality* of 1816, Boieldieu's *La Dame Blanche* from the 1815 novel *Guy Mannering*, Bizet's version of *The Fair Maid of Perth* (1828) and Donizetti's use via Cammarano of the 1819 story *The Bride of Lammermoor*. This makes Scott, with fifteen novels adapted, the leading British source for opera libretti after Shakespeare, and a writer whose subjects attracted the attention of librettists — particularly in nineteenth-century Italy and Germany, when stories of English royalty and Scottish rivalries were considered intriguingly romantic. *Lucia di Lammermoor* was first performed at Teatro San Carlo, Naples, on 26 September 1835 with Fanny Persiani in the title role. The work had first appeared in England three years later and at Covent Garden in 1847. From the 1860s its popularity increased so much in London that it was performed for twenty-three successive seasons headed by Patti, Albani, Sembrich and many other famous singers including Melba with her inauspicious debut in 1888. Tetrazzini made a huge impact singing *Lucia* in London in 1907. Then, apart from Toti dal Monte's single performance in 1925, it disappeared from the British repertory for another fifty years, submerged in the general public indifference to bel canto works.

By reputation, the celebrated Mad Scene was one of the great moments in opera but Donizetti wrote some splendidly melodic music to be sung while Lucia, who has killed the husband she was tricked into marrying, goes through an imaginary wedding ceremony with the man she really loved. It cannot be a raging, stormy madness because the music dictates otherwise. But the long scene, played as a series of increasingly enveloping neuroses, is enough to tax the talents of a good dramatic actress, without having to be concerned about singing. This was a problem facing producer and leading soprano and ultimately it was solved as a combined improvisation. Sutherland was able to react to the passages in the score, and in particular the haunting solo flute, as if they were noises in her head. Zeffirelli moved her this way and that across the stage in response to the vocal changes in the aria. Together they devised an inner madness for Lucia, unlike anything attempted before, but an interpretation close to the spirit of the score. Bonynge made his contribution by adding many coloratura embellishments in the style of early nineteenth-century Italian opera.

While Sutherland, Bonynge and Serafin concentrated on the musical side of the production, Zeffirelli, in his desire for accuracy, turned his attention to costumes. It was a fine coincidence that he had a connection with Scotland through serving on liaison with the Scots Guards in Italy as a partisan in the late years of the war. He developed a great interest in Scotland, which had also been kindled earlier when he had a Scots nanny as a child. In a manner approved by Bonynge, whose passion for collecting antique porcelain, pictures, books and theatrical memorabilia had already become an obsession, Zeffirelli also spent hours in antique bookshops seeking out information on Scotland to add to his own collection of books and prints on history, costume and design. He went personally to the Scotch House in Knightsbridge to select the Hunting Fraser tartan for the Bucklaws of the opera and the authentic Red Innes tartan for the Ashtons. He was committed to creating a striking image for Sutherland and he designed her costumes with a slim waist and flaring skirts to

Lucia di Lammermoor, Covent Garden 1959

88

enhance her figure. The colours of rich greens, browns and blues, complemented her striking red hair to which he added ringlets to show off the facial contours. A final dramatic touch was heavy eye make-up with long lashes. The combined effect was to present Sutherland as she had never been seen before.

For the Mad Scene Zeffirelli chose a simple white nightgown stained down the front and on the hem with the blood of Lucia's murdered husband. It was a theatrical gesture not appreciated by everyone. Serafin thought it vulgar and there was a heated exchange of Italian dialogue between the two of them that surprised everybody after the generally placid progress of getting the work ready for performance. Serafin, an old man and a traditionalist, was not easy to placate, but Zeffirelli had his way in this disagreement bridging a huge generation gap, and the blood-stained dress was retained to have its striking effect in Act III, scene 1.

In the routine turnover from opera season to ballet and back again, new productions at Covent Garden came frequently and were usually regarded in matter-of-fact terms. Occasionally, if an outstanding star was rehearsing — a Callas or a Fonteyn — several of the staff around the Opera House would drop in to watch for a while. By the morning of the final dress rehearsal of *Lucia* word was getting around that all the activity of the past few weeks was culminating in something out of the ordinary. On the day of the dress rehearsal Maria Callas was in London for recording sessions and she rang Webster, asking him if she could attend. He, of course, was delighted and pointed out that she would need to rise earlier than she was accustomed because it was to be a morning rehearsal. There had been talk that she expected to get the *Lucia* role at Covent Garden although, as it had been planned for Sutherland all along, and much delayed, it is unlikely that Callas was given any such undertaking by Webster, even if she was available after a disagreement with the Met. The press caught wind of the possibility of an interesting event and Sutherland was quoted in the *Daily Express* as saying that she didn't want an overnight success, 'I'd rather win it gradually if I can', she said, 'It sticks longer that way.' The three-year-old Adam watched his mother's rehearsal with Ruthli and gained immense pleasure at her knife-wielding powers in the Mad Scene, but was otherwise unimpressed. Also in the audience for the rehearsal was another distinguished soprano, Elisabeth Schwarzkopf, with her husband, Walter Legge, the impresario and record producer. Callas arrived wearing a mink coat with a black leather hat and displaying a beautiful four-strand pearl necklace. 'I have come here to see my friends', she remarked, 'I do have friends you know!' Bill Beresford, the Opera's public relations officer, sensed there was valuable press coverage to be had with two world famous singers in the house to hear a potential new star. He rang the newspapers and soon there were photographers everywhere.

The rehearsal began and, much to everyone's surprise, the orchestra applauded Sutherland after her first big aria, 'Regnava nel silenzio', a gesture that nobody could remember happening before at the Royal Opera House. At the end of the first act Beresford asked Callas if she would mind being photographed; she politely but firmly declined. After the second act he asked again because by this time the photographers were getting restless with the prospect of no pictures after their efforts of coming to Covent Garden. This time Callas agreed and she and Schwarzkopf were photographed together in the Crush Bar, but that was not particularly interesting and certainly not newsworthy for the press who needed an angle for a story.

The third act with its Mad Scene embellished by Sutherland's staccato, flitting movements and her thrilling singing was greeted by the chorus and orchestra with salvos of bravos and it was obvious that Callas was impressed. During the final scene, which didn't involve Sutherland, a hurried discussion took place between Beresford, Webster and Walter Legge about how they could capitalize on Callas's presence. They thought it a good idea to ask her if she would be photographed with Sutherland in her dressing-room.

It was a flushed and excited Lucia wearing her dressing-gown, her make-up running, who opened her door to the minked diva and a horde of press photographers who pushed into the small room filling it to capacity. Sutherland was not overcome by the surprise, she was so excited by the way the rehearsal had gone and was bubbling over with high spirits. The press got the photographs they wanted including one of the two singers together, an elegant and composed Callas on the left, the very model of a prima donna, being cheekily admonished by a dishevelled Sutherland on the right, waving a finger at the star. She was, in fact,

Maria Callas visits Sutherland's dressing-room

suggesting at that moment the photographers should concentrate on her own good side rather than the diva's. 'You were wonderful, just wonderful', said Callas. 'It was I, you remember, who persuaded and encouraged you to sing roles like *Lucia*', she added. Schwarzkopf, with tears in her eyes, greeted Sutherland. 'Listening to you sing today was one of the most moving moments of my life', she told her. That evening the three London newspapers featured the story with photographs and there could have been few who did not know that Sutherland was going to be singing *Lucia*. But that was only setting-up the event; the real test would be in the hands of the audience and the critics the following night.

The 17th of February 1959 was chilly — a typical London winter's day when everyone is tired of the damp greyness and yearns for signs of brighter times ahead. It held the prospect of being the most important day in Sutherland's life, although she had another cold — which now was almost a routine matter in weather like that. She awoke early, suffering from a fit of nerves, anticipating the night ahead. She was reassured by Bonynge that everything would go according to plan because all the elements of the production had been so thoroughly worked out and the rehearsal had gone so well. One tense moment, however, was the substitution at the last minute of Joao Gibin, the tenor who was to play the important role of Edgardo, because of a throat infection. Her fellow Australian, Kenneth Neate, filled in.

In Sutherland's flower-filled dressing-room that evening was a huge stack of good wishes from her mother and aunt and hundreds of others. Norman Ayrton dropped in to wish her well, Bonynge tried to be as calm as possible, keeping in the background while his wife went through the long make-up and hairstyle preparations supervised personally by Zeffirelli who then checked every detail of the dresses as the wardrobe mistress, Gertie Stelzel, expertly fitted them. Outside in the red, cream and gold auditorium there was the buzz of anticipation as the audience settled down and the orchestra began tuning with musical abstractions that soon would be formalized as the doom-ridden prelude and opening chorus of *Lucia di Lammermoor* under the baton of Tullio Serafin. He was one of the last people before the performance to come to the dressing-room to wish Sutherland well on his way to the orchestra pit. For the audience it was another night at the opera, but for everyone who had participated in getting the production to this point on this stage, there was an added air of expectancy that made this occasion more than just another first night.

The curtains parted on Act I, scene 1, to show Zeffirelli's splendidly realistic grounds of Ravenswood Castle in the mountainous Lammermoor district. It is an all-male scene where the feud between the Ashtons and the master of Ravenswood is established. The captain of the guard tells Lord Henry Ashton (Enrico) that he believes his sister, Lucia, has secretly been meeting Edgardo, the rightful owner of the estates. Enrico vows to stop any union between the two lovers, and plans to marry her instead to Lord Arthur Bucklaw (Arturo). This scene, musically well fashioned, was not appreciated by the audience, to whom the Italian text was too dense and the opera itself a novelty.

Sutherland's first appearance was in the second scene, seated by a ruined fountain at night in the park of Ravenswood with the lighting pitched to a low level, but highlighting her red hair against the tartan dress. She was accompanied by her maid Alisa, played by a friend and fellow competitor from the far-off days of Mobil Quest in Melbourne, Margreta Elkins, who watched as she sang her first big aria, '*Regnava nel silenzio*'. As she waits for Edgardo to arrive she sings about a young woman who was murdered many years ago by one of the Ravenswood family. Lucia believes she has seen her ghost. Sutherland was in good

93

voice, in spite of the cold, displaying no obvious nervousness and she finished the aria flawlessly and moved swiftly into the cavatina, '*Quando, rapito in estasi*'. Edgardo arrives and tells his Lucia that he must leave for France but swears undying love. By the end of this scene sung by three Australians, it was as if the whole opera had ended. The auditorium erupted in continuous applause and there was a succession of curtain calls that was so unusual at Covent Garden at the end of a first act that nobody managed to keep score of exactly how many.

The first scene of the second act began so late that it was obvious this was going to be a long evening. In Lord Ashton's apartments in Ravenswood castle, the plot is hatched to convince Lucia by a forged letter that she has been deceived by Edgardo and should reject him in favour of Arturo, the laird of Bucklaw. She falls for the deception, dubbing the luckless Edgardo a vile seducer. The richness of the sets and costumes, together with the precision of the movements and the fluency of the orchestral playing, impressed the audience who were beginning to wonder why this opera had been banished for so long from Covent Garden's stage. The second scene of the act is set in the Great Hall of Ravenswood castle with the marriage deeds ready for signing. The guests arrive for the wedding and, wearing their authentic dress tartans, make a spectacular sight on stage. Lucia, looking pale and worried, signs the contract with the words 'I go now to the sacrifice', at which point Edgardo enters and cues the famous sextet '*Chi mi frena in tal momento*', which once again brought the house down in a storm of applause and cheering for a performance that was not only exciting in itself, but was heralding a return to a style of singing and a repertoire that had been largely absent from England for fifty years. In the bars and foyers they were talking about the electric atmosphere of the evening and the newspaper critics were beginning to sharpen their thoughts for tomorrow's editions. But the Mad Scene was yet to come and that, on the basis of what had gone before, could prove to be extraordinary.

The first scene of Act III continues the celebrations in Ravenswood Castle's Great Hall but they are interrupted with the news that the bride has murdered her new husband. Lucia herself then appears and goes through an imaginary wedding ceremony with Edgardo in opera's most celebrated Mad Scene. Sutherland's

Lucia di Lammermoor

94

appearance in her bloodstained shift and her subsequent darting and flitting across the stage as she sang the long scene, generated an atmosphere of intense excitement within the auditorium. There was something extraordinary happening on stage, a performance unlike anything that had been seen within the memory of most of the audience. The act ended with its '*Spargi d'amaro pianto*' in what David Webster described as 'a riot', and the opera's final scene in which Edgardo learns of Lucia's death and in turn kills himself, was much delayed and an anti-climax to most people without Sutherland on stage. Somehow they managed to get through, but it was obvious that everyone was just waiting to greet Sutherland and give her one of the biggest ovations for many seasons at Covent Garden.

As she took her solo curtain calls at the end of the long evening she seemed a vastly different person from the character she had played only a few minutes before. Now she was self-conscious, a little unsure how to receive such an overwhelming ovation, which she later described as more like coming from a football crowd than an opera audience. Gradually Sutherland began to blow kisses to the cheering throng and they responded more energetically than ever. At last, in the relative calm of her dressing-room she sipped champagne with those who had made her success possible. Zeffirelli was ebullient, like a child; Webster had a glow of pride, knowing that his confidence had been justified — 'it was his faith that made tonight possible', Sutherland acknowledged — and a smiling Bonynge knew that an international career for his wife might now be realized.

Mrs Sutherland
greets her daughter
after the premiere of *Lucia*

The Bonynges en route to Australia 1965
Noël Coward's house party, Jamaica 1965

With host Noël Coward, Jamaica 1965
Richard Bonynge browses in Marseilles

The press notices were more like a hymn of praise with 'triumph' the most overworked word of the week. *The Times* commented, 'Miss Sutherland appeared to be completely inside the conception of the poor over-strained girl, which was in consequence a dramatic as well as a vocal triumph for her'. Andrew Porter in the *Financial Times* wrote,

Anyone who has heard Joan Sutherland sing could have deduced that she would vocalise Lucia's music with high accomplishment. The surprise of the evening was the new dramatic power she brought to her impersonation. The traces of self-consciousness, of awkwardness on the stage had disappeared, and at the same time she sang more freely, more powerfully, more intensely — also more bewitchingly — than ever before.

Peter Heyworth in the *Observer* noted, however,

She had clearly been rehearsed, but her movements often gave the impression of a carefully learnt lesson, lacking freedom and eloquence. A singer, of course, acts in the first place with her voice, but here too Miss Sutherland has yet to acquire something of the alchemy whereby Callas infuses the most ordinary phrase with pregnant meaning and emotion.

Desmond Shawe-Taylor in the *Sunday Times* revealed,

It got round that Miss Sutherland was suffering from a cold, and that she is soon to have a sinus operation. For those reasons, presumably, not to mention the natural effect of nerves, her highly accomplished singing was not flawless. Her arpeggios were marvellously rapid and distinct, her scales a little less so; she trilled at full volume on the high B flat, but tended to reduce the tone when trilling on the lower notes.

As a result of the reception for the first night of *Lucia* the BBC took the unprecedented step of changing its advertised schedule to broadcast the work in full later in the week. The general impression among those regular Covent Garden opera-goers who had watched Sutherland's progress over the years, was that her evolution from gaucheness to radiant assurance put her in the top class of British performers. The display of acting, stiffened perhaps from carrying out every move precisely as rehearsed, was nevertheless impressive. That, together with her genuine humility and wonderment at the reception she received, warmed their hearts; such modesty in the face of triumph admirably fitted into the pattern of the national psyche. When they read the leading critics using such phrases as 'intensely musical and accurate' (Phillip

La Traviata, Melbourne 1979

Hope-Wallace), 'Miss Sutherland is now in the company of the most famous Donizetti singers from Pasta to Callas' (Andrew Porter), and 'that previously unknown creature — Joan Sutherland, the tragic actress' (Desmond Shawe-Taylor), the musical public took notice and knew there was a new star.

Attention also came from outside Britain and reports of the *Lucia* success resulted in offers for Sutherland to sing in several leading opera houses in Italy, the United States, Germany, and Australia. In Britain, inexplicably, the record companies showed no immediate interest in engaging her services. Now Bonynge had the pleasing added responsibility of mapping out Sutherland's career to its best advantage when her current Covent Garden contract came to an end. The £60 a week she was getting was small enough for buying a house, raising a son and paying a nanny. There were now larger rewards in prospect to compensate for the many years of modest income. 'It was a funny sort of overnight success', mused Sutherland realistically. 'I'd been singing there for seven years and the voice hadn't changed overnight.'

Few people noted that Sutherland had laboured under the strain of a heavy cold during the first night of *Lucia*, but she knew through every moment of the exquisite experience of audience adulation that there was lurking in the background the personal medical challenge she had to face after six performances — a real-life event as dramatic as any fictional role she had sung.

Chapter Six

I fail to see how any singer can exist on a purely social, glamorous life, thinking of nothing but lying in bed with her feet up and waiting for the nail varnish to dry — without doing ordinary, everyday things as well. I think that singers mature all their lives and living is part of maturing vocally.

The knowledge that Sutherland would be having an operation prompted considerable response from her public. Some protested that such an act might endanger the future career of one whose voice had burst upon the musical world as the herald of a new Golden Age of singing; no surgeon should have the power to threaten this. Instead, a host of remedies was suggested to obviate the need for tampering with their new star. Letters came from faith healers, religious groups, herbalists, acupuncturists and cranks, all offering suggestions and services. But the decision had to be Ivor Griffiths's alone. He looked after many of the singers at Covent Garden, continuing a tradition started by his teacher and predecessor, Sir Milsom Rees, who had died in 1952 at the age of eighty-six and who during his career had been laryngologist to King George V and Queen Mary. Melba was also one of his charges and he thought she was the greatest of all singers and considered her larynx and vocal cords to be 'the most perfect I have ever seen'. Griffiths in his own distinguished career tended to the oto-rhino-laryngological needs of many notables including the removal of Princess Alexandra's tonsils, aiding Shirley Bassey's throat and treating the ailing press baron, Lord Beaverbrook. With Sutherland, he was reminded of another great British singer, Kathleen Ferrier, who had been faced with the dilemma of chosing between an operation for cancer to prolong her life for a year or two, while depriving her of a performing voice, or keeping

99

her voice intact so that she could sing until a premature death. Ferrier had chosen the latter.

Griffiths patiently explained to Sutherland and Bonynge that she was suffering from a chronic case of hypertrophic sinusitis, which had led to chronic catarrah, infection in both ears, severe chest congestion and symptoms of arthritis. By rights she should be virtually voiceless. After the euphoria of *Lucia* and the flood of offers in its wake, they could only wonder now if there was any future at all — and leave the decision to Griffiths. For him it was something of a dilemma because she was singing so magnificently in spite of the infections. It might mean that an operation would alter the characteristics of every resonance chamber, and completely change the unique Sutherland sound. It was not an enviable decision to be making: to face the possibility of having a notable medical reputation tarnished by making a move that, if the wrong one, would undoubtedly lead to adverse publicity. But something had to be done sooner than later if Sutherland's career was not eventually to be seriously affected by her ailments. She knew the operation must go ahead, David Webster agreed with her, and Covent Garden issued a statement saying that Sutherland would be entering hospital for treatment.

The odds were on her side. She had one of the most experienced surgeons available, a strong physical constitution, and one of the leading hospitals in the world to give her the best care: an establishment known simply as the London Clinic. 'The Clinic', as it had become styled to many celebrities and those with enough wealth to pay for medical exclusivity, is situated unobtrusively at 20 Devonshire Place in London's West End. In its forty years it has cared for many famous people, including royalty, show-business personalities, politicians, and the merely rich. The Clinic built up its reputation of being perhaps the world's most exclusive hospital with a house staff second-to-none and a register of brilliant consulting surgeons. The patients' register has included the Duke and Duchess of Windsor, Princess Margarethe of Sweden, Prince Feisal of Saudi Arabia, Ian Fleming, Yehudi Menuhin, King Hussein of Jordan, Charles Chaplin, Sir Anthony Eden, Ernest Hemingway and Elizabeth Taylor. Most of the clientele go there for the discreet anonymity it affords, but others, like Miss Taylor and her fight for life within its walls, caused a continuing public drama in which, for a while, the Clinic became one of the best-known landmarks of London. Sutherland was admitted on Monday 2 March 1959.

Sinusitis is often caused by acute inflammation of the sinuses or is due to their faulty drainage and aeration because of an obstruction in the nose. In its mild state, it can give high temperatures and headaches with pain over the forehead and a tenderness around the cheeks. Quite often, sufferers get used to the condition and learn to accept it, avoiding treatment. But if it continues and worsens, it can lead to discharge and intense neuralgic pain, which, however, is often intermittent and usually happens early in the day. Temporary relief can be obtained by irrigation of the sinuses — flushing them out with a normal saline solution, which is an uncomfortable, but effective short-term answer. In Sutherland's case, the chronic condition that she suffered but had managed to live with since childhood, was also spreading to other areas of her body — the ears, lungs and legs. It was imperative that something more than periodic irrigation be undertaken.

Griffiths's diagnosis that she had running hypertrophic epithelium meant that an over-active mucous membrane was blocking the sinuses associated with the nose, leading to increasing pain in those areas, a constant impression of being clogged and a general feeling of being run-down. The standard procedure for this condition was named after the surgeons who first performed it — a Caldwell-Luc operation. It is, in fact, a treatment and not necessarily a cure. These days, the use of improved drugs and equipment often avoids such surgical intervention, and the operation is less frequent. In 1959 it was the only answer.

The sinuses are some of the most difficult areas to reach in the human body and being in the head close to so many vital organs of sight, smell and hearing require delicacy on the part of the surgeon to avoid submitting the patient to severe post-operative pain. Being Sutherland, certain extra precautions needed to be carried out during the routine two and a half hour operation. Particular care had to be taken not to damage the vocal cords as a small diameter red rubber tube, a Magill tube, was gently fed down her throat to carry the anaesthetic into the trachaea and then to her lungs.

A week after the operation Sutherland was well enough to leave the Clinic and go with Bonynge and Adam on a holiday to the South of France. Griffiths warned her against singing for three

101

weeks. But as soon as the time was up, she tried a few tentative notes and immediately felt a strange lack of resonance. After practising for some time, the condition remained much the same and they returned to London and consulted Griffiths. He pointed out that as far as he was concerned her nose, sinuses and throat were in perfect condition for the first time. There was no reason why she shouldn't be singing better than ever, all it needed — he hoped — was some concentrated practice. Bonynge was eager to get back to their regular routine of rehearsing and learning, and very soon Sutherland felt her voice getting back to its former state as she grew used to her clear-headed condition.

After two recording sessions — in Geneva for Beethoven's Ninth Symphony and Paris for an operatic recital record — it was back to opera. Covent Garden staged Handel's *Samson* and Sutherland once again sang the small role of An Israelite Woman and thrilled the house with her single aria 'Let the Bright Seraphim'. She was welcomed back to the Covent Garden stage with rapturous applause from a capacity audience. The critics gave her a warm welcome as well, 'Miss Sutherland crowns the evening', wrote Andrew Porter in the *Financial Times*. Her next role was also in Handel, for Sadler's Wells Opera — *Rodelinda*. It was the title part in what Clive Barnes in the *Daily Express* called, 'pure conceit in fancy dress with a plot as thick as porridge where nothing is said twice if it can be said four times'. The male lead opposite Sutherland was originally written for a contralto and Margreta Elkins played it, creating a good deal of Australian hilarity and banter between them at rehearsals. Silly as the plot may have been, and however unconvincing the casting, the result was once again a success with the public — although only a relatively few people were able to see the performance in the small theatre.

Even though Sutherland was exceeding her wildest expectations, had conquered Covent Garden, and was now hailed as a star, it had taken seven long years. Now it was imperative to plan a similar, but much speedier onslaught of Paris, Milan, Vienna and New York — the bastions of opera whose audiences were notorious for being some of the hardest to please in the world, but whose approval was mandatory for claiming a truly international career.

Vienna came first with an invitation to sing Donna Anna in *Don Giovanni*, virtually on Mozart's home ground. After the metic-

Left: Donna Anna in *Don Giovanni*, Vienna 1959
Right: *Rodelinda* at Sadler's Wells, London 1959

103

ulous preparation for *Lucia*, her debut at the huge State Opera had a rather perfunctory air about it. There was no full orchestral rehearsal with Heinrich Hollreiser and only a brief work-out of ensembles with her fellow singers. Fortunately Günther Rennert's thorough preparation of the role with her in Vancouver the previous year had conditioned her for the part which he was again producing. The Viennese audiences greeted the production warmly and the morning after the performance Sutherland signed a guest contract for further appearances at the Staatsoper. The Viennese press said she was the greatest Donna Anna since Lilli Lehmann.

Her next major performance at Covent Garden was one of the most celebrated roles in all opera — Violetta Valéry in Verdi's *La Traviata*. It seemed a foregone conclusion in January 1960 that it would be a success. But this time the many component parts of the production, instead of combining to form an impressive harmony, were working against each other in conflict. Covent Garden did not even name a producer and that, combined with unsympathetic designs by Sophie Fedorovitch, and Nello Santi's sometimes erratic tempi, added to a feeling of foreboding. Sutherland called for help from her friend Norman Ayrton, and together they strove to inject a coherence into the famous part. But now, to add to the already existing problems, she developed laryngitis and wondered about reaching the opening performance — particularly as she had left herself insufficient time to master the role. The fact was that less than a year after *Lucia*, Sutherland realized she had a potential disaster on her hands, being in poor voice, indifferent memory and in a lacklustre, directionless production. A small notice in the official Covent Garden programme credited 'Miss Sutherland's costume designs by Franco Zeffirelli', but that was little enough encouragement to overcome the battle she was facing on the stage.

The last exponent of the part at Covent Garden had been Maria Callas whose vocal accuracy may have been off-centre, but whose characterization of the role set a standard for a whole generation of London opera-goers. The evening would be a test not only for Sutherland, but also for the impartiality and fair play of an audience, most of whom already had their responses tuned to a high expectation. At the same time, the future of British opera in the international sphere was riding on Sutherland's reputation — for it was she who personified the new and exciting spirit permeating the Royal Opera House and being noticed abroad. But she had developed such a severe throat infection that there was no middle voice at all — only a head voice.

Sutherland was understandably nervous as well as hoarse when she began the first act. Adding to the tension there were a few early catcalls from the gallery as she cracked on many middle voice attacks, although the top notes were quite free and brilliant. The house doctor gave an injection to calm her after the first act. A noisy reprimand for the all-too-audible prompter in the second act and Santi's variable but generally slow tempi added to the difficulties. By the end of the evening her performance had improved, but most of the critics were not impressed. *The Times* noted,

When once Miss Sutherland had gathered spirit after her first nervousness she sang Violetta's music with the purity and pathos that are prominent among her accomplishments. Much of her acting was characterless (in this of all roles, a producer's aid is essential, but Covent Garden had not the courage to name a producer for the revival), and she was ineffectively made up as an ageing invalid, not a bright light of society — Violetta's illness should come as a surprise to her circle of acquaintances.

The Times concluded, 'The role is Miss Sutherland's for the taking; she is already a gratifying exponent, but not yet the great interpreter of it in word and tone and gesture that she will yet be'. 'Not an Evening of Fine Singing', was the headline in the *Guardian* and references were made to Santi's heavy conducting. The *Sunday Times* made mention of 'lugubrious tempi' and thought that Sutherland had been thrown very much on her own resources. The popular press also covered the first night of *La Traviata* extensively because anything Sutherland did was now news. The *News of the World* headed what was for them a long review with, 'Miss Sutherland Out of Place'.

Next day the throat infection became worse; it had developed into an attack of tracheitis. She sat at home and glumly read some of the reviews. Andrew Porter in the *Financial Times* wrote,

It was an unhappy performance, for nothing seemed to go right. Dramatic and musical shortcomings formed a vicious circle. There is no great point in going into details of the evening since it was obvious that a mixture of nerves and a lack of confidence in the dramatic conception had affected Miss Sutherland's voice so as to mute it and reduce its expressive powers to an unvaried, tear-laden gentleness. There was no energy in the singing. The rhythm of the

Top left: Desdemona in *Otello*, Vienna 1959
Top right: Violetta in *La Traviata*, Covent Garden 1960
Below: *La Traviata*

106

phrases slumped, the beautiful and delicate effects which should have enhanced the performance lost any dramatic meaning.

In fact, Sutherland should not have sung at all in her condition because of the danger of permanent damage to the voice. The next scheduled performances of *La Traviata* were cancelled and instead Covent Garden put on *Cavalleria Rusticana* and *I Pagliacci*, while issuing a press statement explaining the position. It read, 'Miss Joan Sutherland is suffering from slight laryngitis. In the opinion of her throat specialist she should be able to sing in the other advertised performances of *La Traviata* if she is not required to perform tonight, whereas if she were to sing this evening, she would be unable to appear for the remaining performances.' In the few days off she went back to Ayrton for more acting and movement coaching and then returned to the production in much better voice and spirit. It was a new Violetta that audiences saw on her return. The accompaniment from Santi was also a little tighter, with better balance and instrumental ensemble, but still lacking the supportive drive needed by the drama.

Andrew Porter was, however, the only major critic to re-visit the production and write about it. 'I was wrong', he said about Sutherland's dependence on a strong producer and conductor.

Laryngitis compelled her to retire from the next performances. I went again to the last one she gave — and heard, and saw, a new Violetta. And in so far as this entirely successful performance was achieved without those Svengalis, Serafin and Zeffirelli, being at hand, it can be reckoned an even more brilliant achievement than her *Lucia di Lammermoor*. Last year there was only one soprano equipped to sing every part of this most taxing role: now there are two...

Once again it was a Callas-Sutherland comparison, 'Miss Sutherland has transformed what was nearly a failure into a triumph, acclaimed by an excited audience'.

It became obvious that closer attention must be given in future to each production to avoid lapses in any aspect that might lead to an indifferent result — or even worse. Bonynge had to be firmer than before, vetting the musical and artistic elements of his wife's productions and also overseeing a whole host of other aspects — such as fees, locations, travel, conductors, producers and designers. He was good at it, but the apparent confidence with which he made decisions, and his single-minded purpose were sometimes interpreted as arrogance. The British particularly were accustomed to a leisurely, more 'clubby', approach. In opera

107

circles they were not used to having a home-grown international prima donna, and were not quite sure how to handle the situation. Bonynge was not prepared to waste time, and his decisions gained him the reputation of being a hard taskmaster, not only with his own wife — that was his own business — but also in dealings with opera and concert administrators. His attitudes were understood, however, by most of their singing colleagues because they realized how easy it would be for Sutherland's career to take a wrong turning if it were left in too many hands. You cannot be a prima donna by committee.

The leading American baritone, Robert Merrill, with whom she would soon sing in New York, observed the Sutherland-Bonynge relationship and noted, 'I think he has helped her a tremendous amount and the unusual part is that she listens to him. You see, she realizes, which is rare in a man and wife combination, that Ricky really does know his business.' The Sydney-born writer Russell Braddon, who was to publish an early biography of Sutherland, was a close friend of the Bonynges. He saw that Bonynge was getting the reputation for being a 'Svengali' and thought it unwarranted:

This is not true except in one respect and that is Sutherland quite rightly, since she's taken a maestro upon her who is also her husband, does only what he says. And Bonynge as a brilliant musician has extremely strong views about what his wife should do, and she doesn't question them. He has proved himself right. The grave risk is that one day he will drop a clanger and he'll be wrong and then she will have done what he says and she'll be wrong too.

Braddon saw Sutherland being happy — even anxious — to let her career be orchestrated entirely by Bonynge. 'There is undoubtedly a lack of initiative on her part in choosing roles. He chooses the kind of music and says "You will like this". And she does. But then you realize the endless business of their professional life. So all singers need someone like Richard Bonynge behind them.' Bonynge's aunt, Anne Roughley — known to them affectionately and constantly as 'Weenie' — was to become their secretary for several years. 'It is not one completely dominating another', she observed, 'because if she really didn't like it, they then would talk it out and work it out between them. What amuses one, amuses the other very much, and so I think they knock quite a lot of fun out of life, one way or another, particularly when their son's around.'

The picture of the relationship as seen by those close to them indicated a dominance by Bonynge, some saw it as a unilateral ruthlessness that knew exactly where it was going. But that discounted the strong individual personality behind the compliant image of Sutherland. And it was the star herself most people noticed. The English conductor, John Pritchard, with whom she worked frequently at Covent Garden and on recordings, put it this way,

I could say she's a down-to-earth person. But she is not, in fact, because one has to distinguish between the public image of a prima donna — and sometimes it surprises me when I think of the difference between the public image and the actual person. Joan is different in that she scorns the more airy-fairy aspects of prima donnaism. She is a person who reacts very quickly, for example, to illness or sickness or pain in one of her colleagues. She is tender and sincere about this — and this is a great quality.

Bonynge, of course, was not yet in the public limelight. His change of career and the behind-the-scenes success of their partnership would not be fully appreciated until later, but his ideas and ideals were now being realized through Sutherland in a way even he couldn't have imagined ten years before. His background was, in fact, similar to Sutherland's. He was also from Sydney, although born closer to the surf of Bondi Beach rather than beside the placid waters of the harbour. The Bonynge family was not particularly musical, but the father played the piano quite well, although he'd never had formal teaching. Richard himself started piano at the age of four and could already pick out thirds and sixths on the keyboard at the age of seven. There was a cousin who sang opera in Melbourne, but that was the only contact with musical theatre except for Gilbert and Sullivan which was performed frequently in Sydney. He began to study at the Sydney Conservatorium with Lindley Evans, who instilled in him a love of Chopin and, by the age of thirteen, an awareness and growing appreciation of the music of a wide range of composers. Bonynge had already bought and memorized the complete score of *I Puritani*, and proved himself to be good at languages. One day at the Sydney Conservatorium, when the regular accompanist for the opera class became ill, the director, Eugene Goossens, suggested that Bonynge take over for the rehearsal of the second act of *The Marriage of Figaro*. The session was such a success that he was soon made the regular accompanist for the class. The director

109

of the class would swear at him when he played sharps instead of naturals and this grounding in piano technique and experience was invaluable. He pursued his teacher's diploma, passed the examinations, and won the scholarship to London. Bonynge had been performing in public since the age of fourteen when he played the Grieg Piano Concerto under the direction of Bernard Heinze, followed by the Liszt E Flat Concerto with Goossens conducting, and some of the Mozart and Beethoven repertoire.

There was hope of losing the unpleasant taste left by the *Traviata* incident with the prospect of working once again with Franco Zeffirelli. While they were in Rome preparing for *Traviata*, making recordings and snatching a short holiday, he had suggested to them that a large, flamboyant performance of Handel's *Alcina* would be ideal for La Fenice opera house in Venice — a production on the stage to match the baroque splendour of the early eighteenth-century opera house's richly decorated interior. Sutherland's Handel reputation in England was already firmly established with *Samson* and *Rodelinda*, and in *Alcina*, which she had also previously sung, she would undoubtedly be impressive. The problem, as Bonynge saw it, was that Handel was virtually unknown in Italy and those few music lovers who were aware of him were likely to favour instead the baroque repertory of their own national composers. Why should they care about an Australian singing what to them was English music? But Zeffirelli wanted to do it — and his reputation together with Sutherland's was enough to persuade the management of La Fenice to go along with his wishes.

An amusing diversion occurred at this time when Sutherland and her singing friend Margreta Elkins, who was staying with the Bonynges in Rome, were followed on several days by two Italian men as they made their way across the Piazza di Spagna on the way to recording sessions at the Accademia di Santa Cecilia. The two handsome and tall Australian women, one with red hair and the other blonde, attracted considerable attention from the local males. Eventually they were approached by their two regular followers and asked if they would like to appear in a film. The men were assistants of Federico Fellini who was casting for his movie *La Dolce Vita* and they thought Sutherland and Elkins would be ideal for the parts of ladies of the Roman streets in the production.

110

However, Zeffirelli advised them against taking part in such a film, fearing that their reputations in the world of opera might be affected.

Although only in his mid-thirties, Zeffirelli was already a name to be reckoned with on the European cultural scene. He had begun his career in Florence as a radio actor, and in his leisure moments he was producing amateur theatricals and designing them as well. He went to Rome in 1947 where he appeared in a stage version of Dostoievky's *Crime and Punishment*. His first major assignment as a designer came soon after when he worked on Visconti's production of *A Streetcar Named Desire* and his first major success was when he designed the strikingly beautiful sets and costumes for Visconti's production of Shakespeare's *Troilus and Cressida* in the Boboli Gardens in Florence. Zeffirelli then turned to cinema and began a film career as an assistant director on several Italian features including *Senso* with Alida Valli and Farley Granger, and *Bellissima* with Anna Magnani. His first association with opera was in 1948, but it was the 1952-53 season at La Scala that brought him into prominence. His sets for *L'Italiana in Algeri* by Rossini were an accomplished essay in romantic opera of the grand manner. His love of the early nine-teenth century was reflected in the meticulous attention to detail he put into his productions — and it was no coincidence that his finest designs were for Rossini, Donizetti and Verdi. Rossini's *La Cenerentola* was the first production that Zeffirelli both directed and designed; that was at La Scala in 1954. By the time he first worked with Sutherland in 1959 he had behind him the experi-ence of five years at the peak of operatic standards — as well as a growing cinema and theatre reputation. In fact, 1959 had been a particularly significant year for him as he rushed between the leading opera houses of Europe, working at a pace that, while admirable in its achievements, was exhausting for all those who tried to keep up with the mercurial Italian. The year had begun with *Don Pasquale* (production, sets and costumes) at Milan's Piccola Scala. In Genoa he then designed and produced both *Il Barbiere di Siviglia* and *Il Trovatore*. There followed *La Figlia del Reggimento* in Palermo, two more operas for Siena and then Sutherland's *Lucia* at Covent Garden. And that was only the start.

In between his hours at the opera houses, he would be scouring the antique markets of Europe, particularly London's Portobello

Road, to add to a collection of paintings and nineteenth-century prints housed in his apartment near the Piazza di Spagna in Rome. Zeffirelli worked at a pace that was completely in tune with Bonynge's approach and the two of them shared a love and a rivalry for collecting that, in its fervour, was almost an addiction.

Zeffirelli wanted to produce *Alcina* with the correct emphasis on the baroque era — when it was composed. It was a new style for him to explore, a fascinating challenge, after so long in the early nineteenth century. Now he would go back to the early eighteenth century and Bonynge was confident that Zeffirelli's researches and approach would have much more validity than the recent version of the same composer's *Rodelinda* which he thought had been overpraised in London. Desmond Shawe-Taylor's had been typical of the generous comment lavished on Sutherland's performance. His review in the *Sunday Times* stated, 'She swept grandly around the stage, coruscated with brilliance and improvised with gusto, even throwing an occasional flourish into her recitatives; her quieter pieces were delivered with much art and sensitivity of phrase'.

As with *Rodelinda*, performed at London's Sadler's Wells Theatre, Sutherland would be singing away from the main focus of operatic activity. Venice's Teatro Fenice had a proud tradition, with several notable premieres credited to it, but had drifted into a backwater of provincial production and short seasons. In the normal run of events, success there would go unnoticed, but Sutherland's presence in a Zeffirelli production was enough to attract the leading Italian music critics to the opening night as well as some from London.

Franco Zeffirelli supervises *Alcina*, Venice 1960

Lucrezia Borgia, Sydney 1976
The Merry Widow, Sydney 1978

One of the dozens of portraits painted in the past twenty years

Although the work itself was something of a mystery to Italians, who were unfamiliar with Handel's operas, *Alcina* was one of the most popular musical stagings of eighteenth-century London, composed for Covent Garden in 1735 and abounding in transformation scenes and ballets. But in deciding to produce the piece against a permanent set, Zeffirelli lost one of the principal ingredients. There was plenty of ballet, but no transformations, making it difficult to accept the change of scenes which range from a barren seashore to the glittering court of Alcina. The music alone is not enough to suggest these transitions and consequently the production tended to emphasize the inherently static nature of eighteenth-century opera. Zeffirelli concentrated on the idea of an entertainment — almost a masque — in a sumptuous ducal court with action set on and around a rock on a revolve in centre-stage. The chorus and dancers played the parts of guests for this entertainment.

Zeffirelli supervised the entire production with his attention to every facet of it. Sutherland was not called upon to act very extensively: in fact, the range of movements was small. Instead, he concentrated on making her the most glamorous element in a brilliant production. The detail given to costume, make-up and hairstyle, was to present Sutherland to the Venice audience with an aura of theatrical radiance that had not been attempted with her before. The whole concept was designed to bring into the drizzly Venetian February a warmth of personality, a brilliance of voice and an inventiveness of production to make local residents forget about the dank, subsiding city outside, to ignore the winter flooding of the Piazza San Marco, and to re-live some of the glories of

Sightseeing in Venice

the city's past and the particular traditions of their own opera house.

Venice opera-goers are not easy to impress, but Sutherland's singing and Zeffirelli's production quickly won them over. In the intervals there was a buzz of enthusiastic comment. Noël Goodwin of the London *Daily Express* was in the audience. He had been one of the first critics to write about Sutherland's potential, and had followed her career with interest ever since. He listened to the audience talking about the Australian soprano in the foyers and bars. '*È stupenda*', they kept saying, 'she is stupendous'. During the last scene, the phrase kept running through his head and he knew it would make a perfect headline for his story.

Zeffirelli thought up a novel scheme to end *Alcina*. It was the device of adding a request item from the Duke, which just happened to be Sutherland singing the music of 'Let the Bright Seraphim' from *Samson* with the words adapted from Alcina's final aria. It achieved his intention of ending the evening on a high note — and without any apparent incongruity. The audience was completely won over and, while Sutherland was taking curtain call after curtain call, Goodwin cabled back his report to London. It was headed 'La Stupenda', a name that would be indelibly associated with her from this time.

After the performance they all walked to the nearby restaurant which has long been a favourite with so many of La Fenice's performers, La Colomba. On the walls of the dining-rooms are framed menu covers designed by some of the greatest artists of the twentieth century, and on the tables, the finest Venetian cuisine. Sutherland was still a little dizzy from the showers of pink carnations that had decorated the boxes of the theatre, but which had been thrown at her and around her at the end of the performance. 'I never thought we would bring it off', she exclaimed to a smiling Zeffirelli, who was now becoming to her what Visconti had been to Maria Callas. Both he and Bonynge knew how they had brought it off by a combination of patient preparation and long hours of rehearsals, which had seen them working from ten in the morning to well after midnight for many days before this first night.

The Italian press reported the premiere extensively. *Corriere della Sera* described Sutherland as having 'a soprano voice that is most impressive both in technique and expressiveness, and a fault-

Opposite: *Alcina*, Venice 1960

less artist, perhaps even comparable, in the rare completeness of her means, to our Callas'. *Il Gazzettino* stated, '...in the voice — impressive, in its staying-power — precision and fullness, in the singing — all interior, and greatly expressive. Of this Australian soprano, we recognize an artist of great value.'

'Joan Sutherland revealed the secret of Handelian opera', wrote *Il Tempo*. 'In passagework of immeasurable purity, and in the sustained quality of her singing, she laid bare the intricate workings of a soul.' *L' Avvenire d' Italia*, 'The voice of Joan Sutherland belongs without question to that small and distinguished band of singers who, through natural quality and a good technique, succeed in obtaining precious results in the execution of the most difficult scores... We hope to hear this exceptional singer again soon, in a repertory opera.' *Venezia Notte* noted, in those convoluted sentences so beloved of Italian journalism,

Endorsed with a stupefying technique, Joan Sutherland knows how to overcome with ease the most formidable virtuoso passages, more instrumental than vocal in style, of Handel's writing; and at the same time to give a dignity, both in her acting and her expression, to the figure of Alcina — with a musicality that was pure and at the same time rich in subtle shadings. Here is certainly one of the greatest singers of our time.

Sutherland was now on an international roundabout that she couldn't step off — even if she wanted to. Next it was on to Palermo, Genoa, Barcelona and a return to Vienna, with cheers all the way. Paris was the next major challenge with the knowledge that the Opéra's audience was extremely partisan and didn't easily take Anglo-Saxon newcomers to its heart. The building itself, Garnier's grand creation so dramatically placed at the head of the Rue de l' Opéra, is enough by its facade alone, to strike apprehension in the hearts of performers. Above the entrance colonnade stand the busts and the names of composers who have created so many of the great entertainments witnessed within — Mozart, Meyerbeer, Offenbach, Halévy, Rossini, Bellini...the names go on and on. Inside the building, beyond the marble grand staircase and the sumptuous corridors, the auditorium stands imposing, but compact, dominated by a huge chandelier which gives a yellow sparkle to cherubs and angels and statuary. In contrast to the public areas, backstage at the Paris Opéra is so unprepossessing as to belong to another building. Where an eternity of care and polish is lavished on the foyers and auditorium,

I Puritani, Palermo 1960

the endless dingy corridors, flights of stairs, dressing-rooms and rehearsal-rooms, appear to have no part of an architectural plan. Garnier obviously gave little thought to the legions of artists who would spend many long hours in these cheerless surroundings behind his brilliant facades.

An exception to the backstage drabness is a dressing-room that looks as if it has come out of another time. And indeed it did. It is spacious, draped in pastel silks, with a marble fireplace, chandelier and authentic Louis XV furniture. It is the room used by a former star of the Paris Opéra, Fanny Heldy. In the past all the great singers of the Opéra were given their own suites which remained almost as personal property. Their names appeared on a brass plate on the door and they were invited to decorate the rooms to their own specifications. Heldy was born in Belgium and, like Melba, made her operatic debut at Brussels' Royal Opera House — La Monnaie. She had considerable success in Paris — so much so, that when she married and gave up her singing career, the management decided that her dressing-room should remain just as she had left it. For many years she retained

117

the right to say which other singers could use it. Callas had not been extended the privilege, Tebaldi had, and now Sutherland was also granted the use of the room. That, at least, put her a little more at ease for the production of *Lucia* that would introduce her to Paris audiences.

There was considerable press comment about this new star of opera. References were made to her Australian character and how it embodied several of the national caricatures — such as an inborn sporting ability and love of the great outdoors. There were many attributes that were patently not part of the Sutherland persona — and if they ever were, she would have abandoned them years before in favour of concentrating on her career. Her straightforward nature and apparent lack of temperament also attracted press attention. She typified an Anglo-Saxon 'calme' — some thought a coolness — and although that might be a highly desirable attribute in Britain and the Empire, it is not usually a plus for performers in France. Sutherland had now begun a long and lively association with the press in many parts of the world, that would result in a library of scrapbooks crammed with cuttings. Curiously, she was constantly referred to in France by her country of origin as if being Australian added a certain glamour — or perhaps exoticism. The main part of the Opéra's season was in the winter months. Now with spring in the air, the usually chauvinistic Parisians seemed to be demonstrating a little of what Sutherland knew to be a typically genuine Australian attitude — that of fair play, or 'give 'er a go!'

Springtime in Paris 1960 had all the elements of nationalistic cliché, as well. One could take the lyrics of half a dozen American popular songs penned on the subject of the French capital, and apply them accurately to the scene. The chestnuts *were* in blossom; Paris's heart, despite the war in Algeria and internal political strife, *was* young and gay; the noisy taxicabs, the sidewalk cafés, the reek of Gauloises, the aroma of garlic and the sound of accordions *were* all in abundant evidence. British school parties and German honeymooners were everywhere, and the Americans, with plenty of hard-currency dollars, were back in force once again; the ubiquitous columnist Elsa Maxwell was among them, eager to report the opening-night proceedings at the Opéra, where the atmosphere was rather chilly for rehearsals in spite of the warm spring weather outside Garnier's walls.

Zeffirelli had arrived to supervise what was, in fact, his Palermo production of *Lucia*. He had to work harder than usual on the French principals and chorus, to drill them into a routine that he knew, from experience, was a successful formula. For him, too, it was important to have a Paris success.

The opening night coincided with an orchestral concert by Herbert von Karajan and the Berlin Philharmonic Orchestra. The opera began at 8.15 and the concert at 9 o'clock. Von Karajan was keen to hear Sutherland sing, having read and heard so much about her, and he planned to attend the first thirty minutes of the opera, with a car waiting outside to whisk him across town to his orchestra. The carefully contrived logistics failed him, however, when the car was caught up in a typical Paris traffic jam and his concert was late in starting all because of — and unknown to — Sutherland.

In spite of Zeffirelli's presence, the Paris *Lucia* was different. The lighting on the large stage was indifferent and the production, which had looked fine in Palermo, seemed faded and old-fashioned here. This was not helped by a leaden chorus, singing in French while the principals performed in the original Italian. In the audience, to hear Sutherland, was the former French and singing teacher at St Catherine's School in Sydney, Miss Amy Chicken. She had managed to get a seat in the top gallery to see her former pupil. At first, the audience response was cool and reserved — unlike any previous reaction Sutherland had received to the role. The pause during the Mad Scene had always — until now — been punctuated by applause. Artistically perhaps it was not so admirable, but it did give a breathing space before the demanding cabaletta. When the point was reached in Paris, the few audience reactions were quickly hushed, and Sutherland had to continue without her accustomed rest. The reception at the end of the night was all the more remarkable because of the restraint during the opera. She was called back thirteen times during an ovation that was exceptional, even by the standards of the house. Afterwards, Miss Chicken managed to find her way through the backstage maze to Sutherland's dressing-room and was told, 'I seem to have done better out of your singing classes than out of your French lessons. My French is woeful.'

After the performance a small group went to a little Left Bank restaurant called Pavet to celebrate over supper. Elsa Maxwell

Top left: Fanny Heldy's dressing-room at the Paris Opéra
Top right and bottom: *Lucia* in Paris 1960

was there and she told her readers afterwards that she had found the prima donna was 'very simple, nothing pretentious or conceited about her'. Miss Maxwell thought it admirable that Sutherland had some good words to say about other singers. She thought it nice, 'to hear one artist being kind to another. Joan has not learned yet about jealousies, meanness, stage tricks and so forth. I hope to heaven she never does.'

Next day, the more substantial comments in the French press were favourable. *Le Figaro* noted with gracious verbal arabesques

...not the texture of her voice — which is very beautiful, but not incomparable — nor even in her ease in the upper register, so much as the musical quality of her expression. These arpeggios, these fioriture, all this luxury of vocal acrobatics, like creepers climbing around a statue forsaken in a park — she gives them dramatic significance and human importance, she clothes them with feeling.

Zeffirelli's sets and costumes received a cool reception from *Le Figaro*'s critic. *France-Soir* described it as, 'one of the finest productions that has been seen for a long time. At the same time it showed us an admirable singer, the equal of Maria Callas and Renata Tebaldi, one of the century's great voices.' *Le Monde* said, 'She now joins the very restricted ranks of those singers who can triumph in such works'. With a certain amount of pride *The Times* of London gave an extensive coverage of the French newspapers' critical reaction to Sutherland. It ignored American *Variety* with the headline, 'Joan Sutherland's Mad Lucy Clicks as Paris Borrows Sicily's Scenery'. *Variety*'s Paris reporter went on to say,

I know you asked for a review of the show. You don't really want it, do you? This is a pretty silly opera by Donizetti, but a lot of people like the arias, so what's the point of panning it at this stage of the game? Or praising it, for that matter? The Sutherland girl is great, no doubt about it, and she handles the second act finale warbling magnificently; this is the hunk, you will remember, which has thrown many a girl in the past.

It has long been a tradition for special dishes to be named after famous divas. Most of these gastronomic gestures are forgotten after the reason for their creation has passed. The only survivors are Melba, whose name is associated with a type of toast as well as a peach dessert, and Tetrazzini, whose name lingers in a way of serving chicken. Sutherland, too, after her success in Paris had a dish created in her honour by the chef at one of France's greatest restaurants, Lasserre, on the Avenue Franklin Roosevelt. On 3 May 1960 the *plat du jour* was '*L'Aile de Bresse Sutherland*'. It cost twelve francs, and forty-seven diners on that day availed themselves of the braised chicken wings in a special sauce. Sutherland and Bonynge were taken to dinner there by Decca's Paris representatives to sample the new creation. Later in the week Madame Heldy attended a performance and met Sutherland in her own dressing-room.

In October of 1960 Sutherland added another role to her repertoire with Amina in Bellini's *La Sonnambula*. It was the first time the opera had been seen at Covent Garden for forty-nine years; the last to sing it there was Luisa Tetrazzini in 1911. The first night was a Royal Gala for the state visit of the King and Queen of Nepal. Clive Barnes's review, going one better than Noël Goodwin, was headed 'La Stupendissima'.

Sutherland's favourite conductor, Tullio Serafin, had said she would become a great singer if she didn't accept too much work at once. But now, as if to contradict him, her schedule was crowded. There were more *Traviatas* in London, the preparation of Glyndebourne's *I Puritani*, and studying the unfamiliar and difficult arias for recording 'The Art of the Prima Donna'. The immediate future included the Edinburgh Festival, an American debut in Dallas with *Alcina* and *Don Giovanni*, back to Covent Garden for more *Lucias*, Rome for major recordings. Then it would be time for the Edinburgh Festival again and another American tour, culminating with her debut at the Metropolitan in late 1961.

Left: Amina in *La Sonnambula*, Covent Garden 1960
Right: Elvira in *I Puritani*, Glyndebourne 1960

The prospect was for eighteen months of intense activity with barely four weeks of leisure in between. Sutherland had reached the point where any possibility of her life being private was fast disappearing. She was now public property wherever she went — the product of an age that expected its stars to jet across the world and be available as easily as television could be summoned at the flick of a switch, and records played at the press of a button. Under these conditions of constantly-changing hotel rooms, long hours in the throat-drying atmosphere of jet planes, press conferences and work sessions, Sutherland's and Bonynge's private life was under considerable strain. Their son Adam, now beginning school in London, could not travel with them, and although he was in the very capable hands of his nanny, Ruthli, it didn't make it any easier to face the increasingly long times when they were separated from him.

They made plans for an escape. 'It was quite obvious that it would be necessary to have some sort of retreat', says Sutherland. 'For a while we toyed with the thought of houses in the country outside of London. It was a romantic idea then to have a place in the English Lake District.' But all these schemes were replaced by thinking about going south and spending some time in the sun. In November 1960 Bonynge announced that he'd leased a fourteen-room villa beside Lake Maggiore in southern Switzerland, just outside Locarno. 'Our doctor has advised my wife', he told the press, 'that the cold, clammy climate over here is not good for her voice. She has been getting far too many colds and sore throats

At home in London 1960

lately.' The location of the villa seemed to be ideal for their future commitments.

It is only twenty minutes drive from the Italian border and two and a half hours from La Scala, Milan, so it is very handy when Joan is singing there. Our four-year-old son will go to school in Switzerland. We are taking the villa on a long lease with the option to buy if we like it there. The main thing of course is to have a place in the sun for my wife.

Sutherland was asked by *Go* magazine at this time to state her favourite holiday spots. She wrote,

Being Australian, I regret very much not having been to the Barrier Reef, and if I could that is where I should like to go for a holiday. Our holidays have to fit in with my engagements, and our son's holidays from school. We always want to go somewhere different every year and we are always saying, 'We'll go to Spain next year'. We never do and invariably we end up in Italy. We love Lake Garda. I hate super-comfortable hotels and smart resorts — except the Imperial in Venice.

Some idea of the travelling pressures on a busy singer can be gauged from Sutherland's notes of her first journey to America. She wrote,

We left London early in the morning of 8 November a few hours after singing *La Sonnambula* at Covent Garden. A day's packing, not knowing what climate to expect — and 7 November was my birthday! A seven-hour flight to New York arriving on election day — sinus problems caused by cabin pressurization — a three-hour wait at Idlewild then a three-hour flight to Dallas. The wait at New York was impossible — all bars closed, not even a drink at the airport. Met by Terry McEwen and Henry Principe of London Records and Ann Colbert. It was 8.30 p.m. on arrival in Dallas. On the go for twenty hours. Welcoming committee — an illuminated scroll, complete with red ribbons and gold seal, making me an honorary citizen of Dallas and then the invitation to a big election-night dinner party. I had to turn this down explaining the twenty hours of strain and fatigue was too much — we just had to go to our hotel and sleep. Next day started a week of rehearsals.

The reward for all this was a standing ovation from the audience of 4,000 and thirty curtain calls for the star of *Alcina*.

Back in London at the end of 1960 Sutherland appeared again in *Lucia di Lammermoor* to an ecstatic audience. She took seventeen solo curtain calls after the Mad Scene and the applause lasted for twenty minutes, all through the interval and until the orchestra returned. That broke the previous Garden record of fifteen calls and applause lasting thirteen and a half minutes held by Dame Margot Fonteyn.

124

Meanwhile, the *New York Post* reported that Sutherland had been engaged by the Metropolitan Opera for the 1960-61 season with an estimated salary jump to £500 a performance — a long, long way from the £10 a week of less than a decade before.

Covent Garden was obviously going to see much less of their star in the future, but they had every reason to be happy with her because in 1960 they made a profit for the first time in seven years. The directors, headed by Lord Drogheda, celebrated the event by raising the admission prices. The gallery went up from 6s to 7s 6d, the grand tier from 28s to 31s 6d. It was explained that the surplus of £46,000 came largely from a Royal Ballet tour of America, but at home the biggest pulling-power came from Maria Callas, Joan Sutherland and Dame Margot Fonteyn, with Sutherland's *La Traviata* being the most popular performance of the year.

At the end of the most eventful year of their lives, Sutherland and Bonynge reflected on how far they had come since leaving Sydney. 'I originally started out in heavy roles in Australia', she remembered. 'I'd a big, rather wild voice, and I was singing Wagner when I was nineteen or twenty. Really, my voice isn't heavy enough for that. When I came abroad, it was then that my husband — he was coaching me then — suggested the old Italian operas, and I came to love them as he does.' Bonynge explained why he thought there was a decline in their presentation.

Singers just did not sing them well enough. They treated the older operas as though they were concert music; they sang with too little drama. The demands of the new operas stopped singers practising roulades, variations, chromatic scales, so that opera-singing became a matter of a louder voice to cope with heavy and involved orchestration.

Sutherland continued,

Too much attention to the later style of opera robbed people of the gift of singing a simple line. They forgot that opera is music as well as drama. My mother was a mezzo-soprano of the older period, and I used all her exercises. Mastery of bel canto style, however, does not narrow the singer's range in any respect. It does not make the voice any smaller, but the maximum power is used only for the climaxes.

Sutherland was realistic and modest about her newly-acquired fame. 'The more famous one becomes, the harder one has to work', she explained. 'I find that to maintain or surpass a standard is much harder than to arrive at it. I am grateful that I have been given so much in life. In return I try to sing well. It's the only way I know how to say "thank you".'

Chapter Seven

When an opera becomes a fight in public between the singer and the conductor, that performance becomes an impossibility. The conductor must be an accompanist.

The Australian press in early 1961 viewed Sutherland's successes on the opposite side of the world with a great deal of pride. The Sydney Opera House was in the course of construction and its unique architectural design captured the imagination of Australians everywhere and focused attention on opera itself — although the structure was to be a performing arts complex, rather than exclusively an opera house. Its completion was still at an unspecified date in the future but, while the Opera House was little more than a very expensive hole in the ground, the *Sydney Morning Herald*, in a splendidly premature leader headed 'The Queen of Bel Canto', wrote,

It is inevitable that Miss Sutherland should be linked with the opening of Sydney's Opera House. She is this city's particular star in the world of music, and an Australian cultural asset of unchallenged worth. But no boundaries confine her now, and if we want her we shall have to compete with the claims of opera-lovers everywhere.

A lot of water would flow under the adjacent Harbour Bridge before the Opera House opened, but Sutherland's name would continue to be linked with its progress over the next twelve years. She had already been away for nine years, and now there were plans for a concert tour in 1962.

Sutherland's Metropolitan Opera debut was scheduled for November 1961 and it would set the seal of international approval on her career — the grand slam of opera. But before that, she made her first appearance in New York at a concert performance in the Town Hall of Bellini's *Beatrice di Tenda* in circumstances that were extremely trying. On the afternoon of the rehearsal, Terry McEwen took a telephone call from London. It told of Mrs Sutherland's death. He informed Bonynge, who was faced either with going ahead with an important concert and informing his wife afterwards about her mother's death, or telling her and then perhaps having to cancel the event altogether. He told Sutherland immediately and she realized that nothing would be gained by disappointing her sell-out audience and flying to London. It was decided the concert should proceed, as her mother would have wished. Singing with her for the first time on this occasion was the American mezzo-soprano, Marilyn Horne, who was also making her New York debut, and she was amazed at Sutherland's ability to give a sustained performance in spite of the shock and the sense of loss she was experiencing. Most of the capacity audience were unaware of the strain that night and the critics were complimentary. Only a handful of those close to Sutherland were aware of how far she was from feeling her best.

In the meantime, the Italian weekly magazine *Le Ore* attempted to generate a story of conflict and rivalry between Sutherland and Callas over her forthcoming Milan debut in *Beatrice di Tenda*, claiming that Miss Callas considered it to be her own property at La Scala. She was quoted as saying that she thought it an affront that 'a newcomer with poor vocal powers' should be given the role before she had the chance to sing it there herself. Callas was said to have contemplated walking out of the season, which she had opened in December 1960 with Donizetti's seldom-performed *Poliuto*. She denied the story and accused the magazine of a stunt, 'I have no reason to be jealous of Joan Sutherland or any other singer', she snapped.

Beatrice di Tenda would prove to be a rather annoying opera for Sutherland at times. The eminent maestro, Vittorio Gui, who had conducted *Norma* when she sang with Callas at Covent Garden in 1952, and also her *I Puritani* at Glyndebourne in May 1960, was the conductor for La Scala's production and he had his own version of Bellini's score. Gui changed certain plot emphasis in an attempt to inject credibility into the out-dated confusion, which is virtually a parody of Italian opera libretti. This was aimed at making the musically brilliant bel canto work more acceptable to modern audiences. The music itself was also the victim of his reshuffle because he planned to delete Beatrice's dramatic cabaletta from the final scene where she goes to her death. He was, in fact, ending the opera as Bellini himself originally intended. The composer had written — against his wishes — the final cabaletta for the work's Venice premiere with Giuditta Pasta in the title role in 1833. After the Paris production of *I Puritani* in 1835, Bellini sketched out the rudiments of a new final scene to *Beatrice*, which is in the Bellini Museum in Catania. Vittorio Gui had 'realized' this for a performance in Palermo two years previously and intended to use his reconstruction again for La Scala. None of this was a surprise because Bonynge had exchanged letters about the edition to be used, but when it came to rehearsals, Gui's interpretation seemed to make a mockery of the version acceptable to Sutherland and Bonynge which saw Beatrice going to death defiant rather than in defeat. They were aware by now that Gui had an intense dislike of showy cabalettas.

The tension was relieved briefly by the presence in Milan of Queen Elizabeth and the Duke of Edinburgh during their royal tour of Italy. They were given an inspection of the famous old opera house and a short performance was arranged for them. It

Royal visit to La Scala 1961

was a rest day during rehearsals and the management of La Scala persuaded the singers, including Sutherland, and the orchestra to present the sextet from *Lucia di Lammermoor*. The existing *Lucia* set was considered to be too old and worn for royalty and the twelve-minute performance was sung against a backdrop from *I Puritani* hastily taken out of the scenery stores. The royal party, sitting in what was once the royal box before Italy became a republic, was not informed and was unaware of the anomaly.

Sutherland's side of the *Beatrice* situation was this:

A little before arriving in Milan, I was informed that the final cabaletta for soprano, the heroic bravura closing of the opera, just before Beatrice goes to the scaffold, was to be cut — the conductor did not like it, and he had provided another ending. I was told also that a duet, not in the original score, was to be inserted in the final scene. Bellini, it is true, sketched a few fragments of melody after the first presentation of the opera, but he had never orchestrated or even harmonized them. For this Milan production the sketches had been scored for the occasion with harmonies that I thought were better suited to the French Impressionists than to Bellini.

Reluctantly, Sutherland told the management that she would prefer not to sing at all than accept Gui's version of the work.

There had been widespread publicity about her debut at La Scala and the thought of having to cancel the advertised appearances was unthinkable to the management. There was an impasse: neither Gui nor Bonynge would budge from his own stand and so, as a compromise, it was suggested Sutherland should appear in *Lucia; Beatrice* could wait for later. This was agreed; the *Beatrice* sets were put into store and the ageing Donizetti properties, that had been unsuitable for the Queen of England, were taken out and dusted off. The designs owed more to the style of the nearby, age-blackened Galleria, than to anything resembling a Scottish castle. There also seemed to be little subtlety in the lighting, which was either full flood, showing up the wrinkled inadequacies of the sets, or as crepuscular as the interior of Milan's great Gothic cathedral, the Duomo. Quite naturally, Sutherland wanted to perform within the spirit of the interpretation she and Zeffirelli had worked out together, but he was not present, and La Scala knew best. During the rehearsals, the Mad Scene was played as she had always done it, by moving around the stage in the swooping and darting actions that seemed to express so admirably the inner madness gnawing away at the heroine. To carry this off effectively needed a couple of alert spotlight operators who could follow the movements and, literally, highlight the drama. But the operators at La Scala were not used to such quick action on the venerable old stage, and Sutherland was asked not to move so speedily, so they could have time to follow her. Added to this, Zeffirelli's master touch of the blood-spattered dress after Lucia has killed her husband was rejected by La Scala's directors as being too vulgar. It was enough, they said, to suggest death by clutching a dagger without seeing the gory results on a white shift. The combination of a fettered heroine and a static chorus within a dull production was a difficult compromise for Sutherland to accept, but preferable to a false version of a Bellini opera in which she and Bonynge did not believe.

At La Scala it is the dress rehearsal which gets critical attention from the press so their reviews can be published after the first night because the performances generally end too late to catch the presses for the following morning. Into the otherwise empty ivory and gold auditorium they came, together with a group of the theatre's leading sopranos who were curious about the newcomer from Australia — they included Giulietta Simionato, Antonietta Stella and Renata Scotto, all of them accomplished singers with international reputations, particularly at the Metropolitan. Sutherland felt uncomfortable because she had problems with her hair, which hadn't been dressed for the rehearsal, and the stand-by red wig from London had been incorrectly prepared by La Scala's wardrobe department. The performance went ahead in an unnerving silence with no apparent reaction from the small groups in the theatre. The only response was from the orchestra who applauded after the Mad Scene.

There were a couple of days between rehearsal and opening night and Bonynge took the opportunity to drive into southern Switzerland to supervise the arrival of van loads of furniture, paintings and household goods at Villa Rocca Bella, as their new lakeside house was named.

On the night of the *Lucia* opening, a capacity audience crowded into the theatre. Top prices were being charged and every seat had been sold several days in advance. There was a continuing Milanese tradition of factional support for favourite singers and the rivalry was clear-cut — between Renata Tebaldi and Maria Callas, with neither side having a clear lead in a continuing contest which swung from one to the other with successive performances. Sutherland's confidence had been boosted by the last-minute arrival of Franco Zeffirelli to wish her well. He was his usual ebullient self, a whirlwind of information and advice, but he couldn't stay to see the performance as he had an appointment in London.

The dressing-room was overflowing with flowers and one of the largest bunches bore a card with an encouraging inscription, 'I'm sorry that I cannot be with you tonight except in spirit, Joan Carissima. But I pray and know that you will have a marvellous success. Onward always to triumph.' It was signed 'Maria Callas'. The performance, according to tradition, began on the stroke of 9 p.m.; the audience reactions ran true to the London and Paris form, and by the end of three-and-a-half hours, Sutherland had notched up La Scala on her tally of triumphs. Within a few weeks she would be back there to sing *Beatrice di Tenda* — in the original version without Vittorio Gui as the conductor.

Left: *Lucia* at La Scala 1961
Right: *Beatrice di Tenda*, La Scala 1961

'La Stupenda' and 'La Divina' at La Scala 1961

During the season, the Italian press continued their attempts to give Sutherland the hackneyed image of a prima donna. They were after a show of temperament — a three-way clash perhaps, along the lines of a Callas-Tebaldi-Sutherland triangle. It never happened, of course, in spite of their strenuous efforts, because Sutherland was regarded in high esteem by both Tebaldi and Callas, whatever they or their claques thought of each other. The sort of incident the press was after was to happen soon, however, in Venice — and it needed no fabrications.

Sutherland was constantly concerned about her duty to the public. 'They pay a great deal of money to hear me sing', she said, 'and I certainly do not want to displease them. However, the public should learn to realize that singers, no matter how beautiful their voices, how great their technical skills, are human beings. Under the best of circumstances it is not always easy to sing at one's best.' She was referring to conductors as being the main causes for less than perfect performances.

My very dear Maestro Tullio Serafin said to me one day when I asked his advice concerning a tempo in *I Puritani* : 'My dear, you are an artist. Sing whatever tempo you feel to be correct, and I will accompany you.' And how he accompanied! He inspired and helped, and never made me do anything I did not feel was perfectly natural. How I have loved singing with him in Bellini's *I Putritani* and *La Sonnambula* — wonderful, unforgettable experiences.

132

Amina in *La Sonnambula*, La Scala 1961

Sonnambula, with another conductor, provided a new and unforgettable experience for Sutherland. The Teatro Fenice, that happy hunting ground of the previous year, had negotiated with Bonynge a special gala performance soon after the final performances in Milan. It was then brought forward a couple of days, and they were both apprehensive about the short preparation time. La Fenice's management wanted Sutherland to head the gala because of her outstanding reception there in *Alcina* the previous year, and they gave the indication that the production would be entirely staged around her interpretation of Amina — a part she knew well. Sutherland was tired and bruised from a fall in her bath on the last night of *Beatrice*. Her head had struck one of the taps just above her eye, causing some swelling and a bad headache. Soon after arriving in Venice, her patience was stretched when, during the first walk-through by the producer, conductor Nello Santi insisted on playing sections of the score on the piano, which were mostly irrelevant to the action she was trying to rehearse. Santi was no stranger; he had conducted the *Traviata* in London which so nearly became a first-night failure, and she had worked with him in Paris on her first recital record in April 1959.

Sutherland asked Santi if he would play over the score for her on the piano in the rehearsal room before the orchestral rehearsal; he refused, saying there was no need. She recalled, 'At the orchestral

133

rehearsal the tempos were different from mine for all the major numbers of the opera. I tried to see if we could compromise a little, but his reply was, "I am the maestro here".' La Fenice's director had stated that because of severely limited rehearsal time the production would be according to her wishes. But Santi was unrelenting, and to make matters worse, there was a disagreement between him and the chorus which precipitated a walk-off. Appeals were made to their sense of occasion and they reluctantly came back to the stage.

Next day, the final rehearsal was faced by Sutherland with a little more equanimity. She had rested overnight and was sure that a spirit of compromise could prevail. While singing her first aria she stopped and once again complained about the tempo. Santi explained that he was in favour of slow tempi for the work, and anyway he was the conductor and therefore in charge. Sutherland now repeatedly requested faster tempi, while Santi, becoming more and more stubborn, refused to listen to any of the requests. It was a situation she had not faced since her altercation with Rafael Kubelik over the *Carmen* dialogue, but then she was a Covent Garden staff soprano, not an international star. Bonynge was not dismayed by this show of spirit from his wife. He was rather delighted to see her firmness in the face of such frustration, but he also realized that tension generated by the argument might tighten her throat and affect her performance. There was one further attempt at rapprochement which failed and for the first time in her life Sutherland walked out of a production. The director of La Fenice, Dr Ammannati, pleaded with them to change their minds. It was, he pointed out, a gala performance with all seats sold and, after all, it was here that Madame had become 'La Stupenda'. He begged for reconsideration. Ever reasonable, they agreed to try once again. But Santi proved to be intractable, the tempi remained and he suggested Sutherland was only there for the money. There was now nothing for the Bonynges to do but leave. They booked a flight to London for the next day, while La Fenice's management threatened to serve a writ for breach of contract, claiming moral and material damages. She said, 'I left preferring to disappoint the public in that way rather than to sing what I believed to be incorrect. Some elements of the press called me "*La Capricciosa*". If being unwilling to sing my roles at all unless I can sing them in what I feel to be

134

the spirit of the composer is being capricious, then I am indeed capricious.'

The gala performance went ahead as scheduled, with the Italian soprano Elvira Ramella singing Sutherland's part, and the management of La Fenice issued an official statement which gave their side of the story:

At the preliminary rehearsals on Tuesday, toward the end of the first act, La Sutherland manifested certain signs of impatience, insisting that the tempo should be less rapid than that followed by the director of the orchestra, Maestro Nello Santi. He did not retreat, saying that artistic exigencies must not be adjusted by a performer. There was a lively exchange of opinions and every-thing ended there. The incident was repeated that night at the general rehearsal. La Sutherland started to sing but her voice became choked in her throat when she realized that Maestro Santi was directing as he had a few hours earlier, according to a tempo too rapid for her, and according to an aesthetic interpretation that was certainly correct, but not congenial to her. Furious, mumbling words in English made incomprehensible perhaps by her Australian inflection, she left the stage, went to her dressing-room, undressed, throwing her costume on a chair, put on her street clothes and went to a neighbouring restaurant to eat.

News of Sutherland's walkout spread quickly and she was beseiged by the press on arrival at London Airport, wanting a story. There was no comment from a grim-looking Sutherland wearing dark glasses. At the Bonynges' Cornwall Gardens apart-ment a flock of reporters knocked on the firmly-bolted front door or attempted to get through on the disconnected telephone. Franco Zeffirelli visited them on their return and agreed to take with him to Venice a medical certificate which stated that Suther-land had blood clots on her antrum as a result of coming into contact with a bathroom tap and that she must rest for two weeks. This was to indicate to the management of Teatro La Fenice that she should not have been singing at all in Venice.

Meanwhile, Sutherland pointed out that the Fenice statement was incorrect. She said that everyone had been co-operative except the conductor. She had asked if the tempi shouldn't be a little faster — not slower — and Santi had snapped back, 'It's my tempi'. 'I told the producer that one of us would have to give way or one would have to go. The maestro has a very unfortunate habit of saying "Si, si. Is all right", and then doing exactly as he pleases.'

Yet another view of the affair was given in a statement from Joan Ingpen, of Ingpen and Williams, Sutherland's agents:

135

The Italians are making Miss Sutherland out to be very fiery, temperamental and inconsiderate. That is not so. Success has neither spoiled her nor gone to her head as it has other stars. She remains the same sweet and simple girl she was before fame overtook her. Miss Sutherland is ill and in fact should not have attempted to play the role. On Saturday evening on finishing her performance in Milan, she slipped in her bath and injured her head and nose. From then on she had severe headaches. It's just not good enough of these people in Venice. They begged for her to stay extra days and now this is how they treat her.

The affair had now become a minor international incident with Italian honour and British fair play at stake. The directorate of La Fenice realized, however, that little would be gained by legal action and that reputations on both sides might be damaged if the suit were protracted, as seemed likely in such a dispute. A truce was declared by Dr Ammannati, and he sent a leather make-up case as a peace offering with the hope that she might sing again in his theatre in the near future. A short time after the incident, Sutherland went to a performance of *Boris Godounov* at Covent Garden to hear Margreta Elkins who was singing Marina in the production. As she entered her box after the first interval she was noticed just before the house lights were to be dimmed and spontaneous applause broke out in the auditorium. Sutherland stiffly acknowleged the tribute which, although common in some continental opera houses, was virtually unheard of in Britain. Boris Christoff, who was waiting to continue the title role, was less than happy with the ten-minute delay. It was a positive comment from the partisan British audience who were firmly on Sutherland's side in the much-publicized dispute. Soon after, the Queen's Birthday Honours for 1961 announced the award of the C.B.E to her — an honour she shared with several others including the African tribal leader, Seretse Khama, and the dance band leader, Victor Silvester.

There was growing interest in Australia about her forthcoming concert tour. The general manager of the Australian Broadcasting Commission, Sir Charles Moses, whose organization was sponsoring the visit, said he was 'highly excited by the return of Joan Sutherland. We are proud that we are able to bring this artist to Australia while she is at the peak of her fame and in demand all over the world.' Her visit was to be one of the highlights of the Commission's extensive concert and recital season for 1962, and many people were buying season tickets to guarantee a seat for

Sutherland. Already she was receiving invitations from people who wanted to entertain her when she arrived the following June for the nine-week tour. In the meantime, interest was kept alive by press comment and statements from Sutherland — such as the rather pious piece she contributed to the magazine *Our Women* for its October-December issue of 1961. Its sentiments echoed the type of message Dame Nellie Melba had sent back from the hub of Europe fifty years previously.

During the years I have been singing in the countries of Europe and in America it is natural that I should meet many people in high positions, performers and students of all the arts, and perhaps the most important branch of humanity — because so much may be obtained from its applause and criticism — the listeners and lookers. In every place I've visited I have met fellow Australians either at the top of their field or on the way. Many times I have heard words to this effect — 'You must come from a wonderful country, just look at the people it sends us!' And, of course, it's true. We have a beautiful country and a climate that so many of us do not appreciate until we leave it. What more can I say? Love what you have right there in Australia, and help yourselves — your children if you have a family — by appreciating and working for a land in which it is possible to raise a nation of people with the vitality, ability and ambition to obtain any position in any part of the world.

Elvira in *I Puritani*, Covent Garden 1961

137

It was a statement destined to keep the colonial spirits high until the arrival of their prima donna on Australian soil after an absence of eleven years.

Sutherland and Bonynge continued to build up a repertory of roles, including several she had not yet been asked to sing. 'None of this will be wasted', commented the American *Hi Fidelity* magazine in November 1961, 'now that she has established herself. Joan Sutherland is in the position to create the demand which she is only too happy to supply. The initiative is very much with her.'

The demands of retaining that initiative meant an increase in the number of staff necessary to keep Sutherland on the road. In England there was a secretary looking after their routine affairs; Bonynge's aunt, Anne Roughley — 'Weenie' — had come from Australia to tour with them and look after the many and varied needs while they were away from either of their homes — in England or Switzerland. Meanwhile at Villa Rocca Bella or in London, Ruthli was looking after Adam. 'Weenie' had a special insight into how Sutherland worked and lived. 'It is a little difficult to get her to ease up because she wants to be an ordinary human being and doesn't like being coddled. She loves to do things around the house and she will stretch up for something and someone will scream at her, "Don't do that!" She can't remember all the time that she must look after herself.' There was also the question of looking after the voice — a precaution that Sutherland had never been terribly concerned about, unlike many top singers. 'Weenie' added, 'She gets fed up with staying indoors and sometimes wants to go out in the pouring rain. So everybody sits firmly and she doesn't go out. But generally speaking she looks after her voice. 'I've known a couple of tenors who wouldn't go outside without a six-yard muffler around their necks but she doesn't coddle herself and I think it's quite a tough throat really.'

In the European summer of 1961 Sutherland managed to ease off a little in the sunshine of Lake Maggiore. For a few weeks the Bonynges and their friends spent a relaxing holiday at the Swiss villa. A gregarious informality reigned as they swam and fished and talked and ate and put up pictures, arranged furniture, painted walls. There was an attempt to clear a huge backlog of personal mail and discussions about the future, together with some intensive rehearsals for the forthcoming recording of

Rigoletto and *Lucia*. It was a time, away from the pressures of travelling, for recharging, studying and reflection. If the 1950s had been a period of consolidation for Sutherland's career, the 1960s were seeing a full-flowering of what it meant to be a prima donna. In an era of instant communications, satellite television, myriad newspapers and a cacophony of radio, the old-fashioned world of opera still demanded the personal appearance. It was necessary to travel to the leading opera centres to establish a career and be able to demand the top fees. For Sutherland by now, most of the essential places could be ticked off the list as a job well done and they could decide at their leisure whether to return or not.

The Metropolitan debut would come only at the end of a gruelling tour across the United States, starting at San Francisco and ending in New York. Sutherland's health problems were far from over and appearances at the 1961 Edinburgh Festival were marred by the development of abscesses in the ear that caused the cancellation of one of the performances of *Lucia*. Her Madonna had failed to help. In early January 1960 Sutherland had sung *Puritani* at the Liceo Theatre in Barcelona. It was a bad first act; she'd just flown from London and had caught the inevitable cold. In the interval her dresser handed her a small statuette of the Madonna of Monserrat. She suggested that Sutherland kiss it and place some of the flowers in the dressing-room around it. Suddenly the coughing stopped and her bronchitis cleared up. 'Wherever I go the Madonna goes with me', she then said. In Edinburgh for *Lucia*, she admitted that she kissed the statuette before every performance, but hastened to add in that bastion of the Reformed Church, that she was a Presbyterian and had no intention of becoming a Roman Catholic. 'I have faith in the Madonna. Surely it is not a question of sect.' The ever-reliable Ivor Griffiths in London referred Sutherland to an Edinburgh specialist and he put her on a course of antibiotics and ordered immediate rest under the supervision of Anne Roughley who, apart from coping with her secretarial and travel duties, was now getting experience as a nurse again — she had previously been a nursing sister in Australia.

Sutherland was undoubtedly working too hard, and not heeding the advice of Tullio Serafin. She was concerned with her domestic life as well and there was the realization that time was slipping away far too quickly. Even during rare moments of relaxation with Adam, happily sewing curtains or making cushion covers, there was always another challenge just over the horizon that could only be met by work and more work. That meant long and often stormy sessions with Bonynge at the piano. Having finely tuned her career to this pitch, he was aware that any false steps could rob them of the position Sutherland was close to attaining. Press and publicity descriptions such as 'La Stupenda' and 'The Voice of the Century' sounded to them a little too glib, too contrived, to be applied overnight to someone who had spent a lifetime striving for the best. But such accolades were part of the marketing process necessary to stay at the top — and they would remain for as long as she continued to give a succession of first-rate opera, record, concert and recital performances.

The United States tour started rather badly because of Sutherland's enforced rest after Edinburgh and a late start for the planned season in San Francisco. Anna Moffo sang *Lucia* in her place. But then she was ready to take the part herself and received a huge ovation in spite of more problems with tempi — this time with another Italian conductor with whom she'd worked before, Francesco Molinari-Pradelli. Bonynge disapproved of the ponderous pace one evening while he was sitting in the box of Kurt Herbert Adler, the director of the San Francisco Opera. He couldn't restrain himself any longer and hissed '*Porco!*' as the conductor received an ovation. Later during the performance he hissed and booed him for the same reasons. The other occupants of the stage box politely asked Bonynge to refrain from such porcine comments. Molinari-Pradelli was originally engaged to conduct Sutherland's Metropolitan debut but because of their artistic incompatibility Silvio Varviso was signed instead.

Sutherland was surprised at the capacity of Americans to demand autographs. 'I was absolutely amazed at the number of people who came around to my dressing-room. I couldn't believe I had more than two or three fans. There must be a bigger fan proportion in the United States than anywhere else in the world and, although they've cottoned on to it elsewhere, the American fans are more frantic about it.'

There followed a trio of recitals in which Bonynge accompanied his wife and received the plaudits of the large audiences as a performer in his own right. Chicago came next for Zeffirelli's

140

production of *Lucia* at the Lyric Opera. The excitement generated by the performance was becoming normal in America — as everywhere else. Then came a schedule that looked as if it had been drawn up at random: after Chicago, recitals in New York and Washington and back across the continent for more *Lucias* in San Francisco. There they met fellow Australian Dame Judith Anderson, and watched her give extracts from her classical stage repertory including *Medea* and *Lady Macbeth*. Sutherland was contacted by one of the great opera singers of the past, and one of her idols, Amelita Galli-Curci, beginning a firm friendship based on mutual admiration. Next, Los Angeles for several more *Lucias* to capacity houses of 6,000 people at the Shrine Auditorium. *Lucia* travelled to San Diego before they returned to San Francisco for a recital on Sutherland's 35th birthday.

With Amelita Galli-Curci, California 1961

This time they had longer to spend with Galli-Curci, who was living on the West Coast in retirement, and they spent many hours talking with her about opera, and particularly the place of the coloratura in the bel canto repertory. 'She gave me a great deal of good advice', says Sutherland, 'gave it so freely and sincerely that I hope I may always be able to live by it. She told me to set myself a goal and to take no notice what anyone might say so long as I believed I was right; and to head straight for that goal.' Galli-Curci, in her delightful accent, told Sutherland, 'You must, 'ow you zay? — put on ze blinders and keep on looking straight ahead'. Sutherland was impressed by her meeting with the famous soprano, whose brilliant career had been cut short when she developed a goitre and had to have it removed.

Sutherland's voice was weathering the demands put on it, even if at times the combined effects of travel, tiredness and the anti-biotics she needed to continue taking, produced some ragged notes. 'Jet age travel together with impresarios who think we are made of iron require a prima donna to be built as tough as a work horse', she said. 'You miss hours of sleep, you get your days and your nights mixed up, and sometimes the flights leave you deaf in the ears. How can that help a singer? It drives you crazy.' The public presence she had developed, together with Bonynge's support in their many recitals, combined to keep a vital atmosphere going wherever she performed. Bonynge was now getting offers of conducting engagements for the following year in Europe and America and they could sense the time approaching when some of their opera performances would be in partnership — like the recitals which were proving to be successful.

Sutherland remembers the old Metropolitan Opera House in New York with a great deal of affection. In her years of thinking about opera in Sydney, it was always London's Covent Garden she had aspired to because that was the centre of a sense of Empire that lingered in Australia long after it had really ceased. The Met was something else — a place of immense power, a certifier of reputations, of opulent productions and high fees. But to far-away Australia in the late 1940s it was little more than a place where a handful of Australian singers were said to have left their mark — Melba and Marjorie Lawrence among them. Now in late 1961 Sutherland's attitude was different. She knew it to be the centre of operatic influence, through its ability to pour money into productions and through New Yorkers' fervour to ensure that the Met was the greatest and most interesting opera house in the world. Added to this, Rudolf Bing's regime as general manager was in its eleventh year of flamboyance. With him as figurehead, attracting the greatest singers in the world, and his continuing dialogue with the New York press which gave the Met wide publicity, the old house was the liveliest anywhere at the time.

'I remember the old Met with a great deal of affection', says Sutherland.

It was very dark, there were holes in the floor, you tripped on dents in the floorboards and on the stage. There were horrible little steps everywhere and you could easily fall over. The sight-lines in the theatre were horrendous, most people couldn't see the stage very well, but the sound was wonderful — especially for the singers. But there was a fantastic atmosphere and I often thought back to the great people who had sung in it like Caruso and Tetrazzini, Ponselle, Swarthout. It was a theatre of history.

There were already plans for a new Met as part of the Lincoln Center, but they were several years away and, in spite of the old building's obvious shortcomings, New Yorkers were so attached to the crumbling old structure, that there was pressure from historians and conservationists to restore the Met to retain its position of pre-eminence. Others argued that the city needed a new, efficient opera theatre to perpetuate the same aims.

The production of *Lucia* that was to introduce Sutherland to the Met was rather well-worn. It originated in 1942 when Lily Pons sang the role, and many notable singers had performed in front of the increasingly dusty and battered sets over the years. The atmosphere in the theatre as rehearsals began was different from anything Sutherland had experienced before. It was rather like an exclusive club of the type so beloved of New York's business and social élites, ruled over by its famous president, Rudolf Bing, and whose members included some of the city's most distinguished families. Richard Tucker was to sing with her in *Lucia* and this famous tenor of the Met greeted Sutherland with a warmth and a disarming American sincerity. In fact, the whole company accepted her in a similar way, whilst paying show-business deference to her star status. The chorus seemed to be far more agreeable and eager than their colleagues elsewhere and the backstage atmosphere was reminiscent of the days at Covent Garden in the early 1950s.

143

Sutherland had been using her singing voice very extensively over the past few weeks and the rehearsals, although fully worked out, were aimed at saving the voice for the actual performance — so that she attempted none of the highest notes or coloratura displays that were now a legendary part of her interpretation of the role. Nevertheless, at the end of the first rehearsal she was applauded enthusiastically by the chorus. The dress rehearsal a few days later went well enough, although Bonynge found the sets and costumes to be uninspiring and certainly not good enough as a showcase for Sutherland. If the Met debut was the success it should be, he realized they could insist on future productions being new ones, built around Sutherland — and showing off her talents to the best advantage. He could do little about the staging, but he did work extensively with the conductor — the Swiss, Silvio Varviso — on the finer points of Sutherland's interpretation. Varviso was conducting *Lucia* for the first time and was happy to hear Bonynge's comments about the acoustics and the balance between the singers, the chorus and the orchestra — and how it was being received in the auditorium. All too rarely can a conductor know how a performance sounds to the audience.

The opening night on Sunday evening, 26 November 1961, was a benefit performance, which meant that the socialites would be out in force in their bejewelled finery. Their main concern was likely to be who was sitting where and wearing what, rather than being involved very much with the proceedings on stage. *Lucia* had, however, been a regular part of the Met's repertory over the past twenty years, unlike many European centres, and so it wasn't as if this audience was subjecting itself to anything outrageously unfamiliar.

The pre-publicity had been enormous and Sutherland's first appearance on the stage was greeted with a storm of applause — almost like a cued ovation for the celebrity guest on a television show. For a few minutes of agonizing tenseness she had to wait for the acclaim to die down before the performance could continue. 'I hadn't sung a note yet and I knew I had to go on and live up to the expectations of such a reception.' This unnerved her and the aria 'Regnava nel silenzio' was below its usual form — not obviously so to the audience, but an equally-tense Bonynge was well aware that

Opposite: With conductor Silvio Varviso, New York 1961

144

METROPOLITAN
OPERA
FIRST TIME
SOLD OUT
SUNDAY EVENING, NOVEMBER 26 AT 8 P.M.
BENEFIT - THE METROPOLITAN OPERA GUILD
GAETANO DONIZETTI
LUCIA DI LAMMERMOOR
SILVIO VARVISO (DEBUT)
DESIRE DEFRERE
LORENZO TESTI

it could lead to an indifferent performance if she didn't relax and sing naturally. There was an improvement as she moved into the faster and more joyful '*Quando, rapito in estasi*' and this brought a bellow of approval from the audience. Later, the sextet became a *tour de force* with Sutherland and Tucker seeming to coax each other to greater heights and that, too, was greeted with a huge ovation. At about 10.30 there was a tiny pause in the proceedings and then the audience went wild. Sutherland had just finished the first half of the Mad Scene with an exquisitely placed high E flat — confidently right on pitch. It took a full five minutes before order was restored and she was able to start the second part, '*Spargi d'amaro pianto*' — and at the end the house erupted for a full twelve minutes. There was still the final scene to be played where Lucia's death is lamented by the luckless Edgardo. It was unfortunate for Richard Tucker, who was singing the part, because the audience would not let Sutherland go. The auditorium lights were dimmed, but to little effect. There was no way the orchestra could have been heard for the final scene if Varviso had cued them to start playing. And so he stood, smiling and patiently waiting while the orchestra members craned their necks to get a glimpse of Sutherland taking her repeated bows on stage. At the fourth attempt the final scene did start and Donizetti's opera was brought to its quiet, sad conclusion. Then, adding to what had gone before, Sutherland took ten curtain calls — and from the sixth she received a spontaneous standing ovation. Old-timers in the press room could not remember such a reception — not since Callas anyway.

The star's dressing-room was crowded with celebrities after the applause had finally subsided and the audience had gone home. George London, the baritone who had encouraged Sutherland to audition for the Met in 1958, was there congratulating her. Elsa Maxwell arrived breathless and excited and later told her readers in the New York *Journal-American* that she knew Joan 'had it all the time' because she had seen her in Paris two years previously.

On leaving the theatre they were faced with a huge crowd at the stage door making it impossible for them to reach the rented Rolls Royce waiting to take them home. Bonynge, assisted by theatre ushers and police, had to form a 'human wall' to let Sutherland through. On the short but hazardous journey her dress was pulled, her slip torn and her hair ruffled. Bonynge had his jacket frayed

Above: *Lucia* at the Met
Below left: Lucia's Mad Scene
Below right: Sutherland's dressing-room at the Met

147

and shirt ripped. 'It was more like a football game', Sutherland said. 'Even when we were in the car I thought they would crush it.' The crowd rocked the Rolls in an alarming way, but eventually they were able to pull away from the kerb and go home. The reviews were brought to her and she propped herself up in bed to read them until 3.30 a.m. and then fell asleep, happy and exhausted.

One of the most influential music critics in the United States, Harold C. Schonberg, wrote in the *New York Times*,

There have been others of this generation who have had bigger voices; Milanov, Tebaldi or Nilsson can produce more volume. There are others who may have a sweeter quality of tone — de Los Angeles, say, or Price. Callas undoubtedly for temperament. But there is none around who has the combination of technique, vocal security, clarity and finesse that Miss Sutherland can summon.

Henry Long in the *New York Herald-Tribune*, stated,

She can sing like a flute — but the sound is never flutey; she can sing staccatos that can cascade like raindrops; her trills are not the usual uneasy vacillation between two neighbouring tones, but an utterly musical warbling that a pianist could not execute with more security, and she can make a melody arch as if it were supported by marble columns.

After the premiere, a press conference was hastily arranged so that the new star could be interviewed for the many magazines and wire services who wanted to do Sutherland stories and find out who it was behind the previous evening's success. Her speaking voice confused some of the American reporters who thought it was a kind of cultured cockney. Sutherland was in good form and presented a few quotable lines for them. Asked about her favourite operatic roles she was then reported as saying, 'I love all those demented dames of the old operas. Loony? Sure they are. But the music's wonderful and I get a kick out of doing 'em.' Commenting on the crush outside the Met when she had to fight her way to her car, 'I'm going to send a cable to Elvis Presley and tell him now I know how a dinki di celebrity feels'. They also referred to her 'bel canto kick'. These were all fabrications by the press but they certainly did no harm to her reputation.

Sutherland was approached with several offers to endorse products, including one from a large household equipment company called Prima-Donna Products Incorporated. Their suggestion that she be photographed with their brooms and buckets was politely turned down.

The following week the two news magazines, *Newsweek* and *Time*, reviewed *Lucia* for their international readership. *Time* stated,

Standing there beside her are five singers, whose achievement challenges the memory of some of opera's most hallowed names. The other five: Maria Callas, Renata Tebaldi, Eileen Farrell, Birgit Nilsson, Leontyne Price. No two of the group come to the public equipped with the same technique or bearing the same musical gifts. The Sutherland fans fortunate enough to crowd into the Met last week heard and witnessed the best modern demonstration of bel canto singing — which has come to mean the florid, highly ornamental vocal style that almost became extinct a century ago.

Newsweek reported,

Miss Sutherland does not generate on stage the hypnotic theatrical illusion of the blazing electricity of Callas. Nor does she invest the words she sings with deep dramatic meaning. But such comparisons are not really to the point. The remarkable thing is that both a Callas and a Sutherland have been heard in one decade of opera.

Another Australian was praised for a role at the Metropolitan at the same time. Cyril Ritchard, better known for his stage and musical comedy performances, was described by the New York *Daily News* as 'one of the smoothest comedians in our theatre', for his acting in Offenbach's *La Périchole*.

Every age, almost every season, in dozens of opera houses around the world, produces a new crop of potential stars. Very few of the newcomers ever become prima donnas or leading tenors because there is only room for a handful of big names at one time. The star system is an essential part of opera's continuing existence but at the same time it becomes a headache for managers and administrators. The most acclaimed singers are bid for at the highest market rate. Sutherland, after the Met, was one of this élite group who demanded and got the top fees. As Bonynge says, 'Opera is the sort of art that breeds stars because the public expects it'. Sutherland agreed with him — but she was still apprehensive of fame in spite of a growing confidence. At the time of the Met's *Lucia*, Bonynge admitted she had been a most reluctant prima donna.

In the beginning she was extremely inhibited. But it was just a development and those sort of things pass when you've had a great deal of experience. She has now sung in all the leading opera houses of the world and she's lost her inhibitions. In fact, she's matured emotionally, matured personally, and if I've helped her realize what she's capable of, it is because there are so many things in

149

music that she just didn't think about before. Now she realizes and loves the bel canto period of music so much that she feels it emotionally — it becomes a part of her.

In spite of continuing successes there were many times when the pressures of travel, rehearsal, performance and then moving on, together with the frustrations of not spending nearly enough time with Adam, made Sutherland reflect on the life of a celebrity. There was often disenchantment with the necessary paraphenalia and periphery of success — the hangers-on, the social commitments, the need to present a public face much of the time. Anne Roughley thought she carried on because of an absolute commitment to singing and that was the price she had to pay. 'I asked her once if she could ever give up and she thought very hard for about fifteen seconds and then replied simply, "No, I couldn't".' Sutherland had reached this stage with few outward signs of personal ambition. She never imagined she would achieve this degree of success, and so it was not of immense concern to her. After the New York *Lucia* she said, 'It was all a marvellous dream, something that I thought would be very nice — but I never really thought it would happen'.

A week after the opening of *Lucia*, Sutherland, in a burst of extra energy, sang Amina in a concert performance of *La Sonnambula* at Carnegie Hall to another huge New York ovation and appeared on the Ed Sullivan television show coast-to-coast. Christmas 1961 saw the Bonynges in Naples and Adam still in New York. Feeling rather homesick, the highlight of their Christmas Day was a long trans-Atlantic telephone conversation with their son.

By early 1962 the Bonynges' domestic demands in London had become too pressing for life in their small Kensington apartment and they bought a house in the same street, Cornwall Gardens — a large mid-Victorian property overlooking the leafy gardens and containing fifteen rooms and five bathrooms. The London *Evening Standard* reported a purchase price in excess of £20,000.

Sutherland was looking forward to her return to Australia after more than a decade and, in the intervening months there were concerts, operas and travelling as before. A significant development of their public professional partnership was Bonynge's conducting debut in early 1962 for a concert in the Teatro Eliseo, Rome. There were four rehearsals with the Santa Cecilia

At home in London 1962

orchestra for the full concert programme which included arias by Sutherland. 'I wondered what I was letting myself in for', Bonynge remembers. 'I was surprised it wasn't a disaster, although whatever the concert was like, I did know the music.' Sutherland sang arias by Bellini, Handel and Thomas, and Bonynge conducted Handel's *Water Music*, the overture to *La Belle Hélène* by Offenbach and ballet music from *Alcina*. The Roman press was not very complimentary about his technique; *Il Messaggero* commented that he 'is nothing more than a café conductor who beats time with the strange gestures of a ballet dancer'. *Paese Sera* thought that too much time was taken up with the orchestral pieces and not enough with Sutherland's singing. It was, however, a triumphant evening with a huge ovation for Sutherland's debut in the Italian capital. At the end of the concert the musicians packed up and went home while the audience demanded more and she obliged with three encores accompanied by Bonynge, who abandoned his baton for the surer accompaniment of the piano keyboard.

151

Another concert was given in Antwerp where Sutherland had a nasty fall on the platform which aggravated an existing back weakness. Anne Roughley was with her and next day they travelled to Amsterdam by train. 'That was two hours of hell as far as she was concerned because she couldn't sit, she couldn't stand and she was in agony the whole time. When we got to Amsterdam, the people there were very good to us, and she thought she would try to get through a rehearsal — which she did by the skin of her teeth.' The next day there was another rehearsal and when Sutherland hit a high note, she suddenly lost her place in the score and her voice. Nobody knew what the matter was because she hadn't told them of her intense pain. 'We took her back to the hotel and a couple of specialists worked on her back for two hours. They advised her to cancel the performance, but she said it was too late, they couldn't get anyone else at such short notice, and she was determined to go on.' She eventually sang strapped up in a maternity binder which was not obvious to the audience, but was extremely hard and cumbersome to get into and out of. Anne Roughley remembers, 'She sang, I might say, extremely well. She said she had to alter her breathing a little but nobody noticed. The doctor himself went to the concert because he was so concerned about her and he said he's never seen such courage.'

On her arrival back in London Sutherland stated, 'I have to be very careful about moving a lot. My doctor thinks I should be on my back.' She was advised that the long confined air journey to Australia would be extremely bad for the back complaint which was diagnosed as spinal arthritis aggravated by the Antwerp fall. Consequently she had to cancel the Australian tour. It was a great disappointment for her personally and also for the thousands of concert-goers who had bought tickets to see and hear her. The Australian Broadcasting Commission's general manager, Sir Charles Moses, announced that Maria Callas would be asked to replace Sutherland at short notice, although it seemed to be little more than a forlorn hope when he added, 'I doubt very much if she would be available. In fact, I'd be very much surprised.' The ABC fortunately had a reservoir of leading concert artists that season with the Menuhins, Claudio Arrau, Ruggiero Ricci, Gina Bachauer and Daniel Barenboim.

The news of the reason for the cancellation of her Australian tour prompted sympathetic comment in the press. The Sydney

JOAN SUTHERLAND CRIPPLED

Dobell paintings bring £33,531—P2

Tour cancelled

LONDON, Monday. — Joan Sutherland, the world's greatest

Sun published a leader headed 'A Gallant Australian', the London papers reported Sutherland's indisposition, and the most grotesque headline came from the Adelaide *News* of 27 March. It read, 'Opera Star is Cripple'. Dorothy Kilgallen, in her widely-syndicated column in the United States, reported that record stores were cashing-in on the Sutherland 'retirement' headlines with special advertising banners announcing, 'Yes, we have Joan Sutherland in stock!' and 'Big Specials on *Lucia di Lammermoor!*'

Sutherland was ordered by her London doctor to take an immediate six-week rest, but her schedule was full and there were several engagements that could not be turned down without serious financial loss to the other participants, and so she fulfilled several dates including a concert at London's Royal Albert Hall on 1 April which included the *Lucia* Mad Scene and Queen Marguerite's Aria from *Les Huguenots* by Meyerbeer, and an audience of 6,000 gave her a thirty-minute ovation. 'Miss Sutherland's Night of Triumph', reported *The Times* and added, 'The singing was of the kind that made one feel privileged to be living in the 1960s to experience it'. She planned to complete her Covent Garden performances of *La Traviata* and sing in a new production of *Les Huguenots* at La Scala, vowing that she would sing until she dropped rather than consider retirement.

The demands on her for *Les Huguenots* were greater than ever because of her back trouble and the need to be strapped in a steel corselet. The production was scheduled for March 1962 and promised to be an extraordinary occasion — even by the standards of the house. The work had not been produced in Milan for sixty-three years and the scale was so daunting that very few opera houses could cope with its grandiose concept and the need for seven top singers. Once again Sutherland was following in the steps of Nellie Melba who had performed the work at the Met in New York in 1894 with a cast that featured Nordica, the de Reszke brothers and the famous bass, Pol Plançon. Milan's cast included Sutherland, Giulietta Simionato, Franco Corelli, Fiorenza Cossotto, Giorgio Tozzi and Nicolai Ghiaurov. La Scala planned to present the work virtually complete, including the last scene of the St Bartholomew's Day massacre which had often been omitted in the past. Sutherland had the role of Marguerite de Valois, wife of Henry IV, who attempts to halt the rising storm of antagonism between Catholics and Prostestants which culminates in the massacre.

Sutherland had been forced to cancel her Australian tour on medical advice because of spinal arthritis, but now the news reached Australia that she would be riding a horse on La Scala's stage. There were suggestions that her apparent recovery had been far too swift for the sake of credibility, which prompted a statement from Anne Roughley, 'The extent of Miss Sutherland's horsemanship is a two-and-a-half minute appearance on a docile horse during the second act of Meyerbeer's opera. She mounts the horse from a specially-built platform and the animal, firmly held on the stage by grooms, stands perfectly still throughout her brief appearance on it.' As it turned out the horse proved to be the most temperamental of the large cast, and needed to be reined and steadied during rehearsals of the second act finale, but Sutherland didn't miss a note, retaining control of the tranquilized animal with the help of the two grooms. But the main problem was the all-pervasive stable smells that the animal emitted in the wings while waiting for its big moment. Combined with the heat from the stage lighting and the smell of the greasepaint, it was often difficult for the singers to catch their breath. The *Sydney Morning Herald* announced 'Heroine Joan Sutherland Sings Opera on Horseback'. The dress rehearsal was attended by two of

Marguerite de Valois in *Les Huguenots*, La Scala 1962

La Scala's biggest stars — Tebaldi and Callas — and, at separate intermissions, they individually visited Sutherland in her dressing-room to wish her well.

It was a fashionable international audience which crowded into the theatre to experience one of opera's most notorious works that had once been extravagantly praised, then vehemently denounced, and subsequently unperformed. Although several cuts had been made in Meyerbeer's score, the performance lasted

155

four and a half hours, of which one and a half were taken by the intervals. Sutherland herself thought the role was 'more taxing than two *Traviatas* and two *Lucias* put together' and at the end of the long evening she was called back for eighteen curtain calls, which was the most since Callas had sung *Anna Bolena*. *Corriere della Sera* next day stated, 'Miss Sutherland displayed prodigious technique'. *La Stampa* described her performance as 'stupendous', the London *Times* said Sutherland 'makes the highly ornamental music allotted to her glitter like the jewels of a crown as they catch the light and send radiant beams flashing in all directions', London's *Evening Standard* headlined, 'Soprano Joan Triumphs on a Temperamental Horse'.

Sutherland was often asked to give advice to young people who might be considering a professional singing career and was always happy to do so in the light of her own experiences.

They must be prepared to dedicate their life to opera. That is not a career but a way of life. They would have to be prepared to put their personal affairs completely in the background. Given technical ability, I would tell them that the most important quality to foster is individuality. It is no use listening to recordings of great singers and copying them slavishly. I have admired several singers and indeed taken leaves from their books but I have always been very careful to cultivate an individual style. The great singers have all done this. The result is that you can listen to their recordings without being told who is singing and say, 'That is unmistakably Madame Callas' or 'That is Madame Tebaldi'. Yes, I would tell them that the essence of star quality is individuality.

In late 1962 Russell Braddon's biography of Sutherland was published. He described in such colourful detail her operations and medical problems that some critics thought he was, literally, getting too close to the bone in a sort of narrative *Gray's Anatomy*. This prompted Sutherland to play down the effects of illness on her life. 'I don't suppose my physical difficulties really outweigh anybody else's', she said. 'The sort of book that was written was a general biography, not a particularly musical book. I think some of the critics have forgotten this. They were expecting something a little more glamorous, also perhaps a little more erudite. I think it's a bit too early for a book like that.' She was then aged thirty-six.

In Sydney they still hadn't put a date on the Opera House opening. 'Yes, I've been asked to open the Opera House', said Sutherland, 'but they had better hurry up or I'll be engaged elsewhere'.

Chapter Eight

It was the British public which first accepted us and we know we owe a debt to them. Because of this we are happy to pay taxes but the Inland Revenue Department are trying to tax us out of all proportion.

Richard Bonynge's career progressed during 1962 with his first engagement as a conductor without Sutherland's presence on the same programme. On 31 July he directed the Los Angeles Philharmonic Orchestra with piano soloist Byron Janis in the Overture to *Norma*, Rachmaninoff's Piano Concerto No. 2, Divertissement by Ibert and the Overture to *La Belle Hélène* by Offenbach. The music critic of the *Los Angeles Times* was non-committal about the performances, 'One would like to be generous to a young and obviously untried conductor, but Mr Bonynge's choice of music was so trivial that it was next to impossible to obtain any very definite impression of his abilities'. The local *Herald-Examiner* thought he 'revealed himself as an excellent musical workman. His programme reflected his fascination with music of the nineteenth century, and by and large his readings persuaded the audience to share his interest.' Two nights later a concert with Sutherland on the bill drew 20,000 people to the Hollywood Bowl and caused immense traffic jams in the area. Arias from Meyerbeer, Verdi, Rossini, the inevitable *Lucia* Mad Scene and another one from Thomas's *Hamlet* proved to be so attractive that thousands were turned away at the gates and a repeat performance was hurriedly arranged. The show-business gossip columnist, Hedda Hopper, found Bonynge's conducting 'a mixture of St Vitus' Dance and the Twist' but thought his good looks might land him some Tony Curtis film roles.

157

These concert successes in America by Sutherland prompted some more questions to be asked in Australia, as they were taking place when she would have been performing there on her ABC tour but for its cancellation. The press had queried the true state of her health when the horseback appearance in La Scala's *Les Huguenots* seemed a hazardous undertaking for someone with spinal troubles and that had prompted her to make a statement on arriving by sea in New York. 'Once and for all I want to clear up the state of my health. Two or three hours is the most I can endure sitting still at one time. This means I can only travel by ship or take short rail journeys. Travelling that way I could never have reached Australia in time.' She emphasized that at no point during her illness had she considered ending her singing career. A few days later she received a rapturous reception from more than 20,000 people at an open-air concert in New York's Lewisohn Stadium, before travelling to a Chicago recital and then to the Hollywood Bowl.

Capacity audience at Lewisohn Stadium, New York, for Sutherland's concert

158

At the end of 1962 Sutherland was at La Scala again, this time for a large-scale production of Rossini's *Semiramide*, a spectacularly ridiculous drama based on Voltaire's tragedy, *Sémiramis*. She was playing the Queen of Babylon who, in league with her lover, murders the king. Later she falls for a young man who turns out, to the surprise of nobody, to be her own son. Perhaps for that reason, together with its extreme vocal demands, the work had been almost ignored in the twentieth century; Paris last saw it in 1874, Milan in 1881 and New York in 1895.

During the rehearsals, Sutherland displayed some of the earthy humour that she had learned from her uncle, Tom Alston, back in Sydney during the 1930s and 1940s. Gabriele Santini was the conductor and at one point she turned her back to him on the vast stage of La Scala and was resting her voice a little by singing at less than full volume. He stopped the orchestra and, in Italian, shouted across the pit, 'I don't hear anything at all. All I see is a large English backside' (*culo Inglese*). Sutherland turned around, placed her hands on her hips, looked Santini straight in the eye and remarked, in Italian, 'Australiano, maestro'.

It was an audience suffused with curiosity that filled every one of La Scala's 3,600 seats in the auditorium rising six tiers to its huge chandelier above. At the end of the performance Sutherland received twenty-eight curtain calls and although it had not been a flawless occasion there was little doubt that the patrons went home satisfied with what they had seen and heard. In a breathtaking display, Sutherland attacked her complex and difficult arias with ease, taking triple trills and long legato passages with complete confidence. They heard a thrilling voice combined with acting that was far superior to anything she had demonstrated at La Scala before.

A Sutherland opening in a rarely-heard Rossini opera attracted the international press to Milan. Andrew Porter in the *Financial Times* wrote for his discerning readership,

Semiramide without Sutherland would have been impossible. She brings a great role to life, for she has both the technique for it and the artistic force to use roulades for eloquence. Beyond this there is the thrilling realization that, far from resting on *Lucia*, she is developing new powers, conquering relative weaknesses; and the technique (unlike Callas in her great days) is so secure that there is every reason to anticipate a long series of increasing triumphs.

John Amis in the *Scotsman* was not as impressed as Porter. 'La

159

Top left: Richard Bonynge conducts, 1962
Top right: Amina in *La Sonnambula*, La Scala 1961
Below: *Semiramide*, La Scala 1962

Street poster advertising Sutherland-Bonynge recital, Seoul, South Korea

Taking tea at Nara on tour in Japan

Recital in Nagoya on Far East tour 1978

I Puritani in New York with Luciano Pavarotti

Norma in Sydney with Heather Begg

Scala has revived *Semiramide* expressly for "La Stupenda" Sutherland. After the first performance here, however, the general impression is that, when the statutory four or six performances are over, the corpse will slide quietly back into its grave, unwept because unsuitably sung.' The *Observer* headed its review with the blunt comment 'A White Elephant at La Scala'. Sutherland added her name to the list of famous prima donnas associated with the title role of Rossini's opera — Pasta, Malibran, Grisi and Cruvelli — and later she performed it in America, Australia and on records.

The slowly simmering Sydney Opera House situation continued to amass newspaper comment in Australia. In January 1963 Sutherland stepped off the *Queen Mary* in New York on her way to Washington to represent Australia at a ceremony marking the second anniversary of President Kennedy's inauguration and admitted she was 'stepping into hot water' in criticizing the building as 'too monumental'. She said that from what she had heard and read of the Opera House it sounded 'too monumental on the outside at the sacrifice of being functional on the inside'. Unknown to her, or anyone else, the building's opening was still ten wrangle-ridden years away. But that was of little concern to anyone outside of Sydney as she joined other performers at the White House gala at the Armoury in Washington, including Gene Kelly, Kirk Douglas, Judy Garland, Carol Burnett, Yves Montand and George Burns.

The Bonynges were now spending less time in Britain, although they were more than ever in demand there. By year's end Covent Garden announced that its most popular opera productions for 1962 had been *La Traviata* and *Lucia di Lammermoor* — both with Sutherland. Her income, principally from America, was increasing rapidly and with residences in Britain and Switzerland, the demands of taxation were becoming irritating. 'The way things look today, we may have to sell our Kensington home and leave England for good', Sutherland told the press in early 1963. 'Sometimes I even wonder if I can afford to sing in England ever again. Just because we have that home in Kensington we are subject to British taxes.' During 1962 Sutherland and Bonynge were in England for a total of six weeks and they were understandably annoyed at the large part of their income disappearing in British tax. She thought the Inland Revenue Department was particularly unfair to performers.

161

Royal Albert Hall, London 1962

They have absolutely no sympathy with an artist and they don't seem to know or care about the expenses we incur. They were quite amazed when I said I needed all sorts of clothes to travel round the world giving concerts. And when I said I needed money to entertain people professionally, an inspector said he did not think I ought to spend more than £3 a week on entertainment; a person in my situation should accept invitations, not extend them.

At the time the Bonynges were paying taxes in Switzerland because of residence there and smaller amounts on their earnings in Italy. But it was in America that much of their activity was concentrated and they also paid taxes on everything they earned in the United States. Sutherland pointed out, however, that it was in England where they were penalized the most. The ultimate indignity was connected with income from record sales. 'The royalties are taxed as "unearned income". The other night I came out of a recording studio absolutely dropping with exhaustion and I said to myself "I wish the tax man could see me enjoying my unearned income"!'

Life may have been gloomy in respect of taxes, but her health was on the mend. The arthritis in her back had lessened and she changed with relief to a much lighter support in place of the rigid corselet she had been forced to wear since the Antwerp fall and the subsequent cancellation of the Australian tour. 'I have a lighter corselet which was made for me in America', she said. 'It is comfortable enough for me to wear all the time instead of just on the stage as I did with the other designs. It's a marvellous feeling to be free of pain.' In Milan she had met a woman who was almost crippled with arthritis and who introduced Sutherland to her masseuse from Zurich. 'She gave me exercises and massage for two hours, two or three times a week. I began to notice the difference and when I went to New York I got a Norwegian masseuse who was equally brilliant and continued the same treatment. In London I have a Swedish masseuse who is keeping up the good work.' In New York Sutherland had a special portable table made for exercises and she took it with her everywhere. The treatment was designed to strengthen her back muscles so that they took the strain of support from the spine to relieve the pressures on the vertebrae.

In early March 1963 the Canadian city of Vancouver played a significant part in Bonynge's career, as it had done with Sutherland's *Don Giovanni* in 1958, when he conducted opera in the theatre for the first time with a performance of *Faust*.

Sutherland's fame spread in America following her regular appearances on television — a medium she was at first suspicious about, although aware of its great publicity value. In the early 1960s she was to many Americans the world's number one prima donna because of widespread television exposure, through 'The Bell Telephone Hour' in which she appeared with such guests as the singer Polly Bergen, pianist André Previn, violinist Michael Rabin and the Red Norvo Quintet. In her first appearance on the show in February 1962 Sutherland had presented the *Lucia* Mad Scene. As a guest on 'The Ed Sullivan Show' she sang shorter, more popular arias, usually from Verdi.

One of the most memorable shows in which she appeared was taped for the NBC network for transmission on 17 March 1963 — St Patrick's Day — 'The Dinah Shore Show'. Dinah Shore was something of a national institution, having been a popular band singer during the 1940s and a film star in Hollywood musicals in

Left: An aria from Verdi's *Ernani* on 'The Bell Telephone Hour' 1962
Right: 'The Ed Sullivan Show' 1964

which she introduced a string of hit songs that, combined with her blonde all-American good looks, made her a sweetheart of the forces. Shore bridged the media gap from radio to television very successfully and remained at the top as one of the more durable personalities of American show-business. In 1963 she hosted a series of television 'concerts' in which the top singers and performers of the day appeared in expansive settings and to lush musical arrangements with budgets for each show exceeding the cost of producing most operas at the Met. Sutherland was contracted to appear with Ella Fitzgerald, forming the unlikely trio of a leading popular singer, the undisputed Queen of Jazz and the new operatic superstar performing individually and together. Sutherland was nervous at the prospect because opera can appear stilted and stylized when reduced from its broad theatrical proportions to the small, two-dimensional screen. Combined with popular music and jazz on the same bill, it could result in an uneasy mixture. Bonynge thought the combination would work and provide the sort of publicity that was helpful in keeping Sutherland's name to the fore right across the United States, ensuring that offers of engagements would continue to flow in to their New York agents. Although it was in Europe that most of the artistic accolades were handed out, America was the source of the largest income, with a string of well-funded opera companies around the nation and huge audiences for recitals and concerts.

164

With the thoroughness permitted by large budgets, the rehearsal time for 'The Dinah Shore Show' was as generous as its demands were strenuous. The American network variety shows leave little to chance in their preparations; the reputation of their stars and the interests of the sponsors see to that. Sutherland, of course, was no stranger to hard work in the opera house which had led to a perfection of performance, the envy of her colleagues, and the delight of audiences everywhere. She was always prepared to respect the professional advice of her producers, but the grind of television rehearsals seemed to be a matter of overkill, with too much attention to detail. But behind all the efforts was the single-minded purpose of presenting the best possible product. Shore and Fitzgerald were easy to work with and, in spite of their many years in the business, they took rehearsals very seriously, knowing that the desired result of spontaneous informality was only possible if every moment was fully worked out.

The recording of the show was before a large studio audience and Sutherland's first appearance came as Shore introduced her as 'The fabulous new star of the Metropolitan Opera'. She continued, summing up her career for a television audience who knew little about opera or its personalities,

She's from Australia, she's a soprano, and when she made her debut at Milan's La Scala Opera House, she had to take thirty curtain calls. This is the artist who has critics all over the world calling her a phenomenal singer, possessing a phenomenal voice. She is the most spectacular coloratura ever heard. So I'm proud to invite you now to sit back and — well, pick a word: be thrilled, devastated, knocked out by one of the most magnificent operatic voices of our time. Here to sing for you '*Ah! fors' è lui*' from *La Traviata* — Miss Joan Sutherland.

Such an introduction was the cue for warm applause from the studio audience as Sutherland entered, looking a little nervous and vulnerable in a white dress, and began to sing her aria from the first act of Verdi's opera where Violetta asks herself if she is falling in love with Alfredo. Television performing is very different from opera. In the theatre the audience is within a narrow angle of the stage, and the conductor is reassuringly in front of the singer. But in a television studio, the audience is often to the side and out of sight while all around are the cameras — the eyes for the viewers at home. These conditions make opera very difficult to present satisfactorily in the medium and an unnerving experience when the conductor is unable to be seen against the banks of lights

165

that blaze into a performer's eyes at every angle. Because of the rehearsals, Sutherland knew her technique well enough to overcome the drawbacks of the situation and that, combined with a sure knowledge of the music, enabled her to give a reduced and intimate performance of the aria which fitted neatly within the confines of the small screen. She overcame the problem that had faced so many other opera singers on television — that of giving too 'big' a performance both in vocal delivery and gesture.

In the middle of the show the unlikely trio of Shore, Fitzgerald and Sutherland sang 'Three Little Maids From School' from *The Mikado* and the audience warmed to the opera singer as a diva with the common touch. Then it was time to introduce some substantial material. Shore presaged it with a fine edge. 'This is a torch song about a woman who is separated from the one she loves due to circumstances beyond her control. And she's quite put out by the whole thing!' Sutherland sang Tosca's aria in the second act of Puccini's opera in which the heroine laments her fate — '*Vissi d'arte*'. This was the most serious contribution from her in a show that demonstrated to the millions that she was a handsome, warm-hearted human being with girlish qualities that belied her thirty-seven years.

The end of the hour-long show brought the star and her guests together again in the time-honoured show-business tradition of a rousing finale. This had been a problem for the producers. It was fine to assemble three vastly different singers in a Gilbert and Sullivan romp, but the closing needed an extra dimension. Obviously Shore and Fitzgerald could sing together in virtually any American songs but what about Sutherland? Bonynge's flair for theatricality came to the fore once again. At home in Australia they had both seen many of the musicals presented with high-quality casts principally by the J.C. Williamson organization which, since the late years of the nineteenth century, had dominated the music and theatrical scene in Australia and New Zealand. Sutherland was fond of American musical comedy and she and Bonynge had plans to record an album of British, Viennese and American material. Consequently it was no problem to select for the television show a number from that repertoire which all three of them could comfortably encompass. A special arrangement of 'Lover Come Back To Me' from Rudolf Friml's *The Desert Song* was made. It was a show that had seen many successful stagings and revivals in Australia and had been, during the 1920s and 1930s, the backbone of musical comedy there. For television the director devised an effectively simple staging for the number. In an 'infinity' set, Shore and Fitzgerald stood together beneath a microphone suspended from a large studio boom, while Sutherland in the foreground sang without the apparent need of electronic aids. Each verse of the song was treated in the participant's own style; Shore sang in typical American musical-comedy fashion, Fitzgerald veered into jazz and eventually bop, and Sutherland played it operatically, attacking and sustaining a succession of high notes that Rudolf Friml certainly never wrote and no musical-comedy actress could have hoped to reach. It was thrilling, funny and thoroughly entertaining at the same time — a prime example of the way time, money and effort could combine to produce a notable result. On the strength of this performance alone, Sutherland could have continued guesting on American television for many years, but the demands of the medium conflicted with her own plans. The long rehearsals and the necessity to be either at the West Coast television studios or in New York, made it impossible to fit such appearances into her busy international opera schedule. She would continue to be an occasional performer on television throughout her career, but never again in variety.

With Ella Fitzgerald and Dinah Shore on 'The Dinah Shore Show' 1963

'I wish there were more tenors today who were tall and big so that we could have a more balanced stage situation, especially when I am playing a "fragile" part.' Sutherland was expressing a problem that recurred in nearly all her roles. Her size, although now acceptably slim, was often emphasized by the small stature of the men she sang with. However romantically the music and settings combined to create an emotional moment, the sight of a strapping Violetta confessing her frail, but fervent love to a small, stocky Alfredo, is a difficult convention for modern audiences to accept. Sutherland came to fame principally on the strength of her voice and there were few regular tenors with whom she established an exciting stage presence. The top male singers were as much in demand as she around the world and seldom were their paths to meet on the same stage, except in recordings. Sutherland was realistic about the situation. 'Of course, in operas like *Norma* the height of the tenor really doesn't make any difference. In fact the shorter he is, the more heroic I look! And that's 5 feet 8½ inches of heroism!'

Memory was another flaw in her professional armoury. She needed to spend longer than most in memorizing a part, and for concerts she invariably had her music on a stand in front — a practice frowned upon by some members of the audience — but Sutherland was pragmatic about her memory lapses in opera. 'Of course I've forgotten my lines on occasion. Usually the prompter comes to the rescue. Otherwise if I'm singing in England I work in something like Italian. For obvious reasons, of course, I couldn't do that in Italy. If I forget my lines there, I strike a good vowel sound and hold it.'

There wasn't, however, constant praise for Sutherland. In *Gramophone* of July 1963 Desmond Shawe-Taylor, who was also the music critic of the *Sunday Times*, was highly critical of the singing on her latest records. He claimed she was showing signs of vocal deterioration and accused her of artistic immaturity, weak enunciation and a monotonous 'droopy' tone. He blamed this on 'over complacency, lack of comparative rivals and artistic negligence'. He stated, 'Many of those who most admired Joan Sutherland's work at Covent Garden in pre-*Lucia* years and who delighted in her sensational and well-earned triumph in Donizetti's opera have felt a certain disquiet at the subsequent trend of her singing'. Shawe-Taylor admitted that Sutherland was capable of fine performances in surroundings such as La Scala, but in the more exacting ambiance of the recording studio, her presentation was 'technically uncertain and artistically immature'. He admitted that Sutherland had the field to herself, being in constant demand in every operatic centre of the world. 'It must therefore be almost impossible for her to believe that there can be anything seriously wrong with her singing.' Most of the criticism centred on the release of the 'Command Performance' album and he was not alone in voicing reservations. Andrew Porter, previously a staunch supporter, wrote, 'I feel I want to stick a pin into her or Bonynge and tell them to stop being so affected about it all and for heaven's sake just get on and sing the piece'. A Decca spokesman in London noted that Sutherland's records were selling in huge numbers, in fact better than ever, and the press attention given to the adverse critical comments proved to be a help rather than a hindrance to sales. Sutherland said little; 'It's their opinion. I would never enter into any discussion with the press as to whether they are right or wrong.'

To a singer's public, how their idol performs and, above all, how she sounds, are most important, and yet the very act of producing sounds that makes a prima donna stand apart from the chorus is extremely difficult to comprehend. Sutherland, while she was still a child, paid a visit to a doctor in Sydney to find out if the removal of her tonsils might improve her general health. He advised against it, and during the examination of her throat, noticed how impressive her vocal cords were. However, they are only one link in a chain of organs and tissues that combine to determine how one sounds. The cords are, in fact, membranes, more similar to a reed than a cord, and they vibrate when air from the lungs causes them to come into contact with each other. The sound produced can be on several frequencies and the articulation of it — the combining of these sounds — makes basic notes that become speech or singing. It is a process taken for granted by most people because it is to all but an unfortunate minority a reflex action as normal as breathing, sleeping or walking. Few need to think of the many components and actions that must combine to form human sounds of communication. These include the moving articulators: the jaw, the lower lip, the tongue and the vocal cords themselves. The sounds so formed by these moving parts are 'bounced' off the fixed sections of the head: the gums, the upper lip, the upper teeth, the hard and soft palates and the larynx. Then there is the particular nature of the sounds produced, including the volume, which is directly related to the amount of air from the lungs forced past the vocal cords. A trained singer can conserve the volume of air expelled so that each lungful results in a given strength for much longer than that of an untrained person. There is also the question of pitch which comes about principally from the tension and length of the vocal cords so that, again with training, a singer can control them to move more easily from octave to octave as with a musical instrument. The other element that determines the individual characteristic of a voice is the quality — or its timbre — which brings together the loudness and pitch and puts them through the various resonating chambers in the throat, head, chest and mouth.

The description of all these elements and how they combined to form Sutherland's voice can be outlined in physiological language, but it is virtually impossible to explain in aesthetic terms. The inexact nature of vocal training makes for some exciting, as well as disappointing, results and in attempting to describe vocal quality beyond the simple judgements of range and individual characteristics, vocal terminology has to be used — the language the composer uses to tell a singer how the music should be sung. How that is interpreted is then a matter of a personal taste allied to artistic training and vocal technique. Sutherland was now noted for her mastery of all aspects of vocal technique and in a 1963 American radio discussion with Birgit Nilsson, the celebrated Swedish singer who was the leading Wagner soprano of the day, she demonstrated with vocal illustrations what she had learned about the art of singing. Nilsson was of the opinion that every effort should be made to carry out the composer's wishes but pointed out that sometimes tradition made that difficult. She gave the example of how a great and popular singer of the past could please audiences by treating a phrase or even a note in an idiosyncratic way and ignore the composer. Today's public might expect the same treatment because that was the one they were familiar with. Sutherland replied, 'Yes, that's quite true, Birgit dear, but of course in the bel canto repertoire we have a great deal of freedom. Every composer of the nineteenth century and even earlier, beginning with Mozart himself, made it clear that we were to take over on our own in any way we pleased. This applies not

170

Lunch with Birgit Nilsson, New York 1963

only to singers, of course, but to instrumentalists as well in their own pieces.'

Nilsson replied that it was mainly for interpolated parts where a singer made up her own music, such as in the unique Sutherland vocal fireworks. Sutherland went on, 'But apart from the inter-polations a composer will very often write over a phrase the two words *"a piacere"*, which means roughly "at the singer's pleasure". Though the notes and the tempi are generally indi-cated, we sing the particular passage in whatever way we feel best conveys the dramatic intent. Most conductors tell me I always sing *"a piacere"*!' That was to be a matter of declining importance in the future because Sutherland would increasingly sing under the direction of her husband — and he would make sure it was '*a piacere* Bonynge'.

Sutherland's professional relations were invariably good and most of the top singers who worked with her were impressed by her capacity for endless toil and tension-breaking high spirits. The leading baritone of the Metropolitan Opera, Robert Merrill, gave an insight into her personality. Merrill had experienced a rather stormy career at the Met, having been fired by Rudolf Bing in

171

1951 when he failed to honour his engagements with the company because of filming commitments in Hollywood. He was later re-instated and continued his career. He recalls,

I first met Joan at a reception after the Metropolitan *Lucia* and I fell in love with her. I think she's a natural lusty girl who likes singing. Of course, I had to kid around a little in a recording session sometimes, and we got along fine. She's a great colleague and I find that compared to other prima donnas that I've sung with, she is very easy to work with. She'll do a take over and over again when you ask her, and that's unusual for a soprano. I believe temperament during a performance is fine. It lends itself to a performance. But after it's over — that's for the birds. You read about some prima donnas and their behaviour is an act — not natural temperament but artificial temperament. Sutherland creates an aura that's all her own.

A notable example of this aura was demonstrated during October 1963 when for the first time she sang in the theatre with Bonynge conducting the orchestra in Bellini's *Norma* with the mezzo Marilyn Horne and tenor John Alexander. The season of five performances for the Vancouver Opera Association was sold out well in advance and the gross of $85,000 allowed for Sutherland's fees in the neighbourhood of $15,000. The ten-day period of performances was very satisfactory for all concerned, the local press basked in the fame of such a distinguished production in their small city and the British magazine *Opera* reported that 'Richard Bonynge has without question arrived as a talented, intelligent and serious conductor'. *Norma* would be one of Sutherland's greatest and most-repeated roles. Another seventeen months would pass before Sutherland created a new role again because her time was taken up with repeat performances from the repertoire she had already established, many concerts and recitals and spending as much time as possible at their Cornwall Gardens home in London with Adam, who was now seven.

The new house was decorated to their specifications and was just along the street from their previous smaller apartment. 'I seemed to watch the work go on for years, feeling "so near and yet so far" ', Sutherland said. 'Now at last we know it's there to come home to.' Much of Bonynge's growing inventory of paintings, books and scores were moved in during 1963 while the decorators were putting the finishing touches to the furnishings, and

Opposite: *Norma*, Vancouver 1963

thoughts of leaving England evaporated for the moment with the pleasure of spreading their belongings throughout the roomy Victorian house. Adam was able to play in the private gardens of the leafy square and a separate music room made the long rehearsal periods more bearable.

The year 1964 started in fine style for Sutherland in New York during a season of *La Traviata* — her first Verdi role at the Metropolitan. Harold C. Schonberg in the *New York Times* thought she sang it with a prodigality of tone and with convincing acting. 'It would be idle to pretend that Miss Sutherland is a great actress', he wrote. 'Temperament is not her forte. As an intelligent artist and a hard worker, though, she has mastered the mood and basic character of Violetta to a point where the interpretation is entirely feminine and believable.' A few days later, this hard worker was given one of the highest accolades the Met can offer — a gala evening to herself with the full company and orchestra at her disposal. It was the first time in the memory of New York opera-goers that one singer had been accorded such an evening so early in her career — more notable since it was barely two years since her debut there. To the cheers and shouts of a gala benefit audience, Sutherland sang arias from *Traviata*, *Sonnambula* and *Lucia*. At the end of the year she would appear in another glittering gala with three other famous sopranos at the Met — Schwarzkopf, Tebaldi and Della Casa — singing Act I of *La Traviata*, the sleep-walking scene from *La Sonnambula* and the mad scene from *Lucia*.

In March 1964 Sutherland was invited to attend London's annual opera ball, one of the highlights of the social scene. Almost everyone was in fancy dress including the Earl of Harewood as Caesar in toga, satin drapes and a laurel wreath, and Lady Harewood sporting a sari and claiming to represent Titania. Sutherland agreed to be one of the five judges of the costumes which was made difficult by the inclusion of five Mark Antonys, four Cleopatras, six Caesars and twelve Aidas. She herself wore a formal gown for the occasion.

The thought of returning to Australia became an increasing preoccupation in the minds of Bonynge and Sutherland. It was now fourteen years since he had left Sydney and Sutherland's absence was only a year less. There had been sporadic family contacts in that time but it was not the same as going home. Soon

With Joan Hammond (on Sutherland's left) and the Australian Prime Minister, Sir Robert Menzies, London 1964

after the cancellation of her ABC concert tour, the J.C. William-son organization approached Bonynge about the possibility of a future concert tour or an opera season in Australia along the lines of their successful collaborations in the past with Melba. The Bonynges were interested, but their bookings were already extending for two years ahead, and there was Sutherland's recurring back problem which made flying long distances difficult. John McCallum, managing director of Williamson's, and his actress wife, Googie Withers, had talked about the prospects in New York in late 1962 and then in mid-1963 Sir Frank Tait, the head of the company, discussed the proposal with Bonynge in London. Mid-1965 seemed to be an ideal time for all parties and it was agreed that an opera season should be mounted starring Sutherland and with Bonynge as artistic director and chief conductor. Tait found Bonynge extremely demanding, 'Costs and expenses get higher every day and there is little I can do to avert it'. This was said against the background of the last independent opera season, backed by his organization in 1955, which ended with a £55,000 deficit. The Sutherland-Williamson International Grand Opera Company, as it was to be cumbersomely called, was a far more ambitious operation and might, if not carefully managed, endanger the financial solvency of the whole business.

175

Bonynge had a tremendous bargaining advantage because Sutherland was in such great demand everywhere and it was understood that she would accept a lower fee for Australia than she was receiving in America. He, quite naturally, wanted to present her in the best possible package which meant good design — Tonina Dorati, the younger daughter of the conductor Antal Dorati was chosen, the top producers — Martin Scheepers and Norman Ayrton and, above all, the singers — they included Margreta Elkins, Elizabeth Harwood, Monica Sinclair, Lauris Elms, Joy Mammen, Morag Beaton, Luciano Pavarotti, John Alexander, Richard Cross, Robert Allman, Clifford Grant, Alberto Remedios and Spiro Malas. The make-up of the company, comprising 150 people, included twenty-one principals, a chorus of thirty-six, orchestra of forty-four and a ballet of twelve. The estimated cost was a minimum of £500,000, with £70,000 coming as a subsidy from the Elizabethan Theatre Trust. It was a vast logistical operation to take so many people to Australia, link them with a local chorus and orchestra, and attract enough money into the box office to justify the effort of the enterprise. It would be the last grand operatic gesture on such a huge, virtually unsubsidized scale.

Much of the initial organization took place across the world in a barrage of detailed letters and long international telephone calls between Williamson's head office in Melbourne and wherever Bonynge happened to be. In September 1964 Bonynge went to Australia to organize the chorus and the orchestra. In two weeks he auditioned more than one hundred singers in Melbourne and Sydney with an eye and an ear to the highest possible standards. 'There is a tremendous shortage of tenors in Australia, and not too many mezzos and contraltos', he observed, 'but I have heard basses and baritones who are very good and first-rate sopranos'. He thought the opportunities for professional singing in Australia were limited, forcing too much diversified work. He was determined not to have any dead wood in the chorus. 'I want every singer, to the last member of the chorus, to have a voice and a personality, to be an individual who can give something to the whole production.' He added, 'I will compromise if the singer has good dramatic talent and the voice needs to be built up, or if there is a good voice and the acting can be built up. The season will be a new experience for them — it is mostly Italian and more specialized in bel canto.'

Relaxation on Sydney Harbour

The beach house on Sydney's northern beaches

At a Sydney press conference Bonynge cut quite a figure at the end of the Australian winter with his deep suntan, and grey flannel suit complementing his grey-flecked dark curly hair. He was asked some leading questions and he replied with direct answers. Was opera a dying art form? 'No. The centre of opera is no longer in Italy — although La Scala, Milan, still radiates its influence — but this does not mean that opera is any less virile in its more modern centres of activity around the world.' Could opera pay its way? 'Operas starring my wife are likely to show a profit, otherwise it is necessary for subsidies, support and some-times financial losses, to allow the freedom of artistic expression.' How was Miss Sutherland's back? 'My wife is in splendid health. She is no longer in pain and is quite able to undertake the long tour.'

The next year was shaping up to be a very important and extremely busy period in Sutherland's career, perhaps the most significant in her thirteen years of professional singing. At home, too, there were changes of plans that would also alter the Bonynges' way of life. The continuing burden of paying taxes in several countries was partially solved by concentrating their finan-cial affairs in Switzerland and in early 1965 they registered two companies in Luzern — Joan Sutherland A.G. and Richard Bonynge A.G. Their rented mansion on Lake Maggiore had provided a splendid escape from the constant pressures of touring, performing and recording, with many relaxing holidays spent there. Gradually it had become as comfortable and lived-in as their house in London but when they tried to buy the property, to make it a permanent base, the owners named an impossibly high price, which precipitated another search.

On one of their trips from England to the United States on the *Queen Mary* they had met Noël Coward and a friendship grew as Sutherland and Bonynge were added to Coward's circle of famous friends. He admired her singing and was particularly taken with her modest, no-nonsense attitudes. Coward had moved away from Britain at the end of the 1950s, escaping taxation and the climate, and had gone to live in a large chalet in the sleepy village of Les Avants, high above Lake Geneva in Switzerland. There, in the fresh mountain air, he spent most of his summers and then flew to his property in Jamaica to escape the worst of the European winters. Coward heard of the Bonynges' house-hunting and invited them to stay with him so that they could look around his area for available properties instead of in the far south. 'Don't think about getting a house down there', Coward had told them, 'it's so awkward to get at'. That was true. The international airports of Milan and Geneva were a considerable drive away from southern Switzerland, particularly in winter conditions. Coward said, 'You must come and live near me if you're looking for a house'. Certainly his location was much more convenient — scarcely more than an hour away from Geneva airport in good conditions and with plans for an expressway direct from Montreux, just eight kilometres away, to the airport terminal. Coward lived in a rambling chalet-style mansion, built at the turn of the century with little turrets and large overhanging gables suggesting it had been designed more as a parody of a typical Swiss house than as a functional residence. The exterior combination of bleached wood and pink stucco added to that impression and its situation, with an imposing snow-capped alp in the background, a view of the lake far down the valley, and a dense pine forest rising behind bisected by an impressive waterfall, looked just like an archetypal illustration for a Swiss National Tourist Office calendar.

The weekend was thoroughly enjoyable with the exception that there seemed to be nothing suitable for sale. There were a few large and expensive lakeside estates on the market but nothing of a manageable proposition and within their price range. This was an area that had attracted many wealthy residents, particularly film stars, and within a short radius there lived Charles Chaplin, the Nivens, the Richard Burtons and James Mason. Just as they were leaving after what had seemed to be a fruitless search, Bonynge noticed the house next door to Coward's, looking unloved and rather ramshackle, tucked away on the edge of the forest. He asked about it. Nobody knew if it was for sale but Coward promised to find out. It proved to be available and Bonynge bought Chalet Monnet, as it was called, with an eye to extensive renovations and rebuilding to make it their permanent home. Coward was delighted. He told Sutherland, 'We'll leave a gap in the hedge so I can pop over and borrow a cup of flour when we run out'.

Coward planned to be in Jamaica during the early part of 1965 and he invited the Bonynges to stay with him for a well-needed holiday after engagements in the United States where she taped a television special, sang *Semiramide* for the first time in fifty years in America, and made her debut as Marguerite in Gounod's *Faust*. Sutherland's biggest television show to date was taped in the studios of WGBH in Boston during the *Semiramide* season there. Called 'An Hour with Joan Sutherland', it was for transmission on the National Educational Television network. The programme was scripted and introduced by Terry McEwen, their friend and Decca associate from their earliest days in London, who was now living in New York and working for London Records, Decca's American label. McEwen's soft but authoritative Canadian voice, together with his boyishly rotund appearance and a highly literate script, was the springboard for several Sutherland display pieces interspersed with some homely conversation between McEwen, Sutherland and Bonynge and duets with Marilyn Horne and John Alexander. The result is an exciting and revealing reference point showing how Sutherland's style, both visually and vocally, had developed to this high point in her career. In both areas she appeared relaxed and comfortably within herself, while still displaying a disarmingly girlish delight that so much was happening to her and around her.

It was the complete opposite to 'The Dinah Shore Show' of two years earlier in form, style and content. In the Boston studio the orchestra took most of the space against a neutral setting with a youthful-looking Bonynge on a small podium wearing a dark lounge-suit. For the singing, Sutherland, wearing a full, dark formal gown, stood slightly to his left with a music stand in front. McEwen's introductions took place against a rather awkward set decorated with opera prints and antique furniture. 'In the last century, Joan Sutherland would have been called a prima donna assoluta — the rarest of musical birds.' McEwen went on to refer to her arrival in London,

Joan was an aspiring young dramatic soprano singer singing a different kind of music from that we are used to hear her singing nowadays. Her first teacher had been her mother, who had a beautiful mezzo-soprano voice and naturally believed that her daughter had the same vocal range. And it wasn't until later, when Joan and Richard began working together and married, that they discovered the joys of the bel canto repertoire — of Rossini, Bellini and Donizetti.

179

There were arias from Handel, Ricci and Meyerbeer, a song by Paisiello and duets with John Alexander and Marilyn Horne. It was a dazzling display of vocal art and the show remains an invaluable record of three great singers at the peak of their performing careers — two of whom would be singing in Australia later in the year.

The Bonynges enjoyed a few weeks of complete relaxation at Blue Harbour, Coward's rambling estate, together with his biographer and confidant, Cole Lesley, and Anne Roughley. It was a secluded and stimulating interlude of relaxed living with the sea and the sunshine and the company combining to make an idyllic interval in the busy lives of all of them. There was the opportunity to practise some of Coward's songs for a planned recording of Sutherland singing Coward, and frequently in the heat of the Jamaican afternoon, the bitter-sweet words and melodies sung by a great soprano voice and accompanied on the piano by the composer, would waft out through the broad open verandahs of his house, Firefly, and down to the palm-fringed shore. There were afternoons of Sutherland singing, dinners with Peter Sellers's patter, and always the witticisms of 'the Master'. (Sellers and his wife, Britt Ekland, were holidaying nearby.) One morning Sutherland appeared with her hair more beautifully bouffant than usual for a series of photographs taken by Sellers for the *Australian Women's Weekly*, which prompted the remark from Coward, 'Joan darling, you're looking magnificently like the MGM lion today!'

They left Blue Harbour to return to London for a season at Covent Garden which included a revival of *Lucia di Lammermoor*. It was another triumph for Sutherland and at the end of the first performance the stage was deluged with spring flowers — daffodils, primroses, jonquils and bluebells. But it was not such a happy night for Bonynge, who received some boos from sections of the audience as he took his call, and the next day the critics referred to his 'slow dragging tempo' (*Daily Express*), 'the impression of disjointedness' (*Daily Mail*) and his conducting as being 'correct but unimaginative' (*Guardian*). The same treatment was handed out by a small section of the audience on the first night of *La Sonnambula* three weeks later. A Covent Garden spokesman remarked that it occurred only after the first performance and

180

was limited to a 'silly-minded minority'. It prompted the columnist Bernard Levin to comment,

In the audience of 3,000-odd there weren't more than five or six demonstrators, but the ugly sound of booing can be heard above almost any amount of applause. It has long been apparent, at performances of operas in which she has sung and he has conducted, that there is a small gang that has a mad and implacable grudge against Mr Bonynge, and is determined to boo him whatever the quality of his musical direction.

They both ignored the fuss. Bonynge's mind was now concentrating on the forthcoming Australian season for which he stated, 'I intend to have a finger in every pie — singers, music, programmes, publicity, the lot'.

Chapter Nine

When I left this country fourteen years ago Australians were much more interested in foreign artists than their own. I wasn't sure what sort of reception they would give us.

Opera on a full-time, professional basis is a relatively recent occurrence in Australia but it has a history going back almost to the start of permanent European settlement. The first known performance was in 1834 with *Clari, The Maid of Milan* by Henry Bishop with its famous song 'Home, Sweet Home'. After that productions were scattered but during the nineteenth century Sydney and Melbourne saw such works as Rossini's *La Cenerentola*, Weber's *Der Freischütz*, Auber's *Fra Diavolo* and Donizetti's *Roberto Devereux*. It was not until the turn of the century, however, that opera became a popular entertainment with the power to attract houses large enough for commercial success in a country that could not yet supply its own leading singers and which imposed the demands of rigorous touring over long distances to reach the largest possible audiences. Opera became established with reasonably frequent seasons of touring companies from abroad. In 1900 the Musgrove company toured thirteen German and Italian works, playing to packed houses with some of the highest seat prices ever demanded — 2s 6d to 7s 6d. The next year, which saw the federation of the Australian states into a Commonwealth, Musgrove's rivals — J.C. Williamson — presented the finest opera season yet seen in the country. It was under the musical direction of Roberto Hazon and they nearly had a young tenor with the company called Enrico Caruso; he declined to go to Australia at the last moment in favour of engagements in Europe, including singing with Nellie Melba in early 1902 in Monte Carlo. Hazon presented six operas including the first local performances of *La Bohème, Cavalleria Rusticana* and *I Pagliacci.* Musgrove returned to the operatic scene with a German season in 1907 including *Lohengrin, Die Walküre* and *Tannhäuser.* The 1911 Williamson season combined with Melba for her first presentation of opera in her native land. The great tenor John McCormack was also in the company, which used an Australian chorus and orchestra. Melba, now at the age of fifty, agreed to appear three times each week during the tour, which was double her normal performing frequency. The following year, the Quinlan Opera Company came from London bringing their complete force of two hundred people, hundreds of costumes and tons of scenery. One novelty they presented was Puccini's *The Girl of the Golden West* which had premiered in New York less than two years previously.

Companies arrived, flourished and departed Australia's shores regularly for the first three decades of the century, including another Melba-Williamson season in 1924 which also included a pretty newcomer, who soon became an audience favourite — the Italian soprano Toti dal Monte. There was, in fact, no opera company in Australia during 1926, although in faraway America the issue of *Time* magazine for the first week in November, when Sutherland was born, featured as its cover story the long-standing director of the New York Met, Giulio Gatti-Casazza, and Melba's farewell to Covent Garden was widely reported in the local press. 'Goodbye is of all words the saddest, the most difficult to say', a tearful Dame Nellie told her devoted London audience at the end of a highly-charged evening in which she bowed out of the house that had been her 'home' for thirty-eight years. Melba made her farewell to opera in a matinee at Melbourne's His Majesty's Theatre during the Melba-Williamson 1928 season. On 27 September, at the age of sixty-seven, she sang the third and fourth acts of *La Bohème* and the Prayer Scene from *Otello* to a packed audience with all the proceeds going to charity.

Melba's final silence was echoed in fewer opera productions during the 1930s. The Depression caught up with the medium and by the time economic conditions were beginning to right themselves, the Second World War put paid to much activity until J.C. Williamson organized an Italian season in 1948 with twenty-five singers selected from various Italian opera houses under the musical and artistic direction of Franco Ghione. They played fourteen works including such box-office favourites as *Aida*, *Butterfly*, *Bohème*, *Trovatore* and *Carmen*. Another six years were to pass before a similar season was organized, when Ermanno Wolf-Ferrari, the nephew of the composer, was musical director.

In the meantime, separate local companies had been formed and were struggling to survive in Melbourne and Sydney. Eventually they amalgamated under the banner of the Elizabethan Theatre Trust — funded by federal government subsidies — which presented its first season, of four Mozart operas — *Così fan tutte*, *The Marriage of Figaro*, *Don Giovanni* and *The Magic Flute* — in Adelaide in 1956, just a year after an international competition selected Joern Utzon's designs for the Sydney Opera House. In their first season the Company travelled 8,000 miles and performed to more than 168,000 people. During the 1950s and early 1960s, the Trust's opera company under various names kept the art alive and made it flourish by presenting seasons in the principal Australian cities, and country centres as well, with such singers as Joan Hammond, Elsie Morrison, Sylvia Fisher, Rosina Raisbeck, Ronald Dowd, Constance Shacklock and Raymond Nilsson, and conductors Karl Rankl, Walter Stiasny and Charles Mackerras. But the event that led to opera as a permanent, vital force in Australia was the last great commercial opera enterprise, the Sutherland-Williamson season.

The number of works to be performed was finally settled at seven. J.C. Williamson had wanted less and Bonynge had hoped for more:

From Joan's point of view I naturally chose *Lucia di Lammermoor* because it was the opera which first made her famous. I chose *La Sonnambula* because it is my favourite role for her. She is a great Bellini singer and the one singer today who has really studied the style of this composer and understands it. *La Traviata* is her favourite role. She does *Faust* because it is not only a lovely role for her but because we wanted to do it as a homage to Dame Nellie Melba. *Semiramide* she does because it is her great bravura role and I think I can safely say that there is nobody else in the world who dares to try to sing it.

All the operas required a minimum of learning for Sutherland, being part of her recent repertory, and *Faust* was a brand new role which she had just performed in Philadelphia. The two additional operas in which she didn't sing were Donizetti's *L'Elisir d'Amore* and Tchaikovsky's *Eugene Onegin*. 'We chose them to make as much contrast as possible in the repertory. But the whole emphasis of the season is on the bel canto period', Bonynge added.

It was a very different Australia to which Sutherland was about to return after her absence of fourteen years. One of the few unvarying aspects was the continuing rule of the prime minister, Robert Gordon Menzies, who had been in power since 1949. Almost everything else had changed dramatically. The face of the cities now featured glass-walled skyscrapers reaching ever higher, urban expressways and the turnaround in status of formerly run-down inner-city suburbs which were becoming transformed into the habitat of an upwardly mobile affluent society. Nearly a decade of television had helped to erode the traditional insularity and had virtually killed off the cinema as a medium of mass entertainment. Delicatessens, espresso bars, continental restaurants and wine drinking proliferated, but they were only kinks in a continuing conservatism — the sunshine and beer mentality was still a great levelling force and continued to stifle much individuality. Away from the cities a mining boom was underway with Japan an eager customer for coal and iron ore. Young men were being conscripted for the armed forces with the prospect of fighting in Vietnam, Australia placed sanctions on trade with Rhodesia and Op Art arrived. The newspapers reported the rampage of the Red Guards in China's cultural revolution, while high above it all the Russian, Alexei Leonov, was walking in space.

In the face of all this domestic and international activity, a stranger might have been forgiven for assuming the principal subject of concern to Australians in mid-1965 was opera — or more specifically, opera as personified by Joan Sutherland. For more than four months the press had a field day, reporting every minute detail of the Sutherland-Williamson season in thousands of column inches and hundreds of photographs.

It began in earnest with a correspondent at Kennedy Airport in New York asking about the price of tickets for the tour. Sutherland and Bonynge were making a ninety-minute stopover there on their way to a brief Honolulu holiday before arriving in Australia. 'I am astonished they have been put up so high', she said, 'I think the organizers are being unreasonable in making the prices so high for my performances. I think there should be an even, flat price for the series.' This published statement prompted Sir Frank Tait to respond, 'We calculate our costs very carefully and make our prices as reasonable as we can. Everything is expensive nowadays but the public apparently accept our prices as shown by the overwhelming demand for tickets.' That demand was, however, overwhelming for the five operas in which Sutherland was performing. J.C. Williamson was getting worried at the lack of booking support for the remainder of the season.

Sutherland and Bonynge arrived in Sydney on a Qantas Boeing 707 from Honolulu via Fiji on the morning of 17 June, ninety minutes late. Awaiting them were hundreds of fans, together with several relatives and a group of senior prefects from St Catherine's, Waverley, Sutherland's old school, who had been at the airport since the chilly dawn. Sutherland, wearing an enveloping chinchilla coat which made her appear larger than her normal size, followed by a steward carrying her mink coat, came down the steps of the aircraft and strode with Bonynge to the terminal, waving to the cheering crowd. It was like a royal occasion mixed up with the frenzy of a pop star's arrival but, although she was back in her home town, there was no time to linger. Their connecting domestic flight to Melbourne had already been held for thirty minutes to wait for them and in the crush and excitement of the arrival, it was further delayed. They were whisked through Customs and then airline officials had to clear a path through the throng so they could get from the international to the domestic terminal. On the way the press took photographs and attempted to obtain interviews on the run. Did she feel nervous about her return? 'Of course, wouldn't you feel nervous returning home after fourteen years?' What did she most want to do in Australia? 'Please the people. That's what I want to do — please the people.' Her two sisters who had waited for so long to greet her were confused. Mrs Nancye Baker said, 'I haven't seen Joan for fourteen years. After all this time I hardly got a chance to see her, let alone say hello. There was so much confusion I'm not sure Joan recognized us.' The other sister, Mrs Ailsa Hargraves, shook her head in disbelief at the scene. At home in suburban Strathfield, 'Uncle' John Ritchie, now 86, listened to reports of the arrival on his radio and was proud that his £1000 'investment' of 1950 had paid such handsome dividends. 'I got it back in fame and pride', he said.

LARGEST AFTERNOON PAPER SALE IN N.S.W.

THE SUN

"ABOVE ALL" "FOR AUSTRALIA"

18,253 THURSDAY, JUNE 17, 1965   Phone 2 0944.   Price 6d.
Registered at the G.P.O., Sydney, for transmission by post as a newspaper.   Jones Street, Broadway, Box 506, G.P.O., Sydney.

A

● Lotteries: No. 5544, P. 36; No. 5545, P. 42   ● TV, P. 62   ● Finance, P. 55   ● CITY FORECAST: Fine, cool

Enter Joan Sutherland

The Mad Scene

12 MINUTES OF PANIC

WORLD-FAMOUS Australian opera star Joan Sutherland flew into Sydney this morning and after 12 minutes of airport turmoil, flew out again.

In her brief hectic stay Miss Sutherland was rushed from a Qantas jet through Customs then back to the tarmac to a Melbourne-bound Viscount, which had been waiting 35 minutes for her arrival.

Between planes Miss Sutherland (pictured) was mobbed by welcoming fans and relatives interviewed by dozens of Press, radio and TV reporters and temporarily separated from her husband Richard Bonynge.

Surrounded

Out of breath and surrounded by reporters and cameramen, all Miss Sutherland could say was, "I don't believe I'm back."

Plans for a well organised reception and welcome to the great star on her first visit to Australia since she won "The Sun" Aria 14 years ago went adrift when her plane from overseas arrived at Mascot 90 minutes late.

It had been intended that she would be welcomed home by a group of prefects from her old school, St. Catherine's, Waverley, and J. C. Williamson officials, before giving a Press interview and boarding a plane for Melbourne.

However, as son as the gangway was put into position alongside the Qantas jet Miss Sutherland, wearing a magnificent full-length chinchilla coat, was hurried into Customs.

● CONTINUED PAGE TWO

Miss Sutherland in another mad scene — on stage, in her most famous role as the tragic heroine of Donizetti's opera.

This scene from "Lucia di Lammermoor" which she first sang at Covent Garden in 1959, brought the house down . . . and overnight fame to Australia's prima donna.

The Viscount aircraft arrived an hour late at Melbourne's Essendon airport and Sutherland sprinted across the tarmac to escape the chilly winds of Victoria's winter. 'Crikey it's cold and I'm dead tired', she exclaimed, as she met the assembled J.C. Williamson executives who would be responsible for every detail of the forthcoming tour. After a short rest there was a press conference the same day at the Southern Cross Hotel and she recovered sufficiently to sparkle for the large turnout who wanted to question her. How did it feel to be in Australia? 'I don't know, I haven't had time to find out. Ask me in a week's time.' She was asked about the extra cost of first-night tickets. 'Personally I would never go to the first night because singers are never in top form. People all over the world go for the social aspect.' Did she admire Callas? 'I used to think my large voice was incapable of singing those roles. Callas showed me this was not so. She sang them and this fact indicated that I could too.' There was a question about whether she was unhappy that Adam had not been born in Australia. 'You should see him playing football. Then you could see if he is really so un-Australian.' What about the Sydney Opera House? 'They were talking about that when I left — that and the Snowy Mountains Scheme. One has progressed faster than the other.' It was a successful performance that reaped a fine spread of publicity for the season in the Melbourne and interstate newspapers.

After the conference it was back to the house they had leased for their Melbourne stay in the fashionable suburb of Toorak with the prospect of rest and privacy. The Sydney *Sun-Herald* of 20 June reported that Sutherland, during her tour, would 'live like a recluse at secret addresses'. It added that the address and telephone number of her Melbourne two-storey mansion were the most closely guarded secrets in show-business. But the press would often prove to be persistent to the point of provocation where privacy was concerned. The *Australian* had already described their home as being 'a secret hideaway in Toorak', stating that it was a big two-storey mansion in Tintern Avenue with quiet surroundings suitable for peace after a performance — 'cream and red brick nestling under the trees', it added. On that description it was not difficult to pinpoint exactly where the Bonynges and their staff were staying, but the weekly newsmagazine, the *Bulletin*, with a complete disregard for personal privacy, went further and published an article a few weeks later signed by their anonymous contributor 'Batman' which began, 'The Richard Bonynges are living at No. 1 Tintern Avenue, Toorak'. This style of journalism, often cloaked in anonymity, would increase during their tour and be a cause of concern and irritation.

The next three weeks were a continuous round of rehearsals to mould a company from the disparate group of performers who were coming together for the first time. The weakest link in the whole enterprise was the orchestra, which had to be assembled from scratch, mostly from a limited pool of local theatre musicians. Bonynge, as supremo of the whole operation, needed to pay particular attention to that department for it to match the standards of the singing.

Mail bookings had been open for some time in Melbourne but when the box office opened to the general public there was a queue of three hundred people waiting to snap up the remaining Sutherland seats and some of them had been there all night.

Young Adam arrived on 5 July to join his parents during the break from his schooling in London. It was, of course, the first time he had seen their homeland. 'It'll be great fun to see his reactions to the country he has heard so much about', said Bonynge.

John McCallum hoped the first night would be a special occasion. 'We are making no special requests', he stated, 'but we expect most men will wear evening dress or dinner jackets. In New York recently I was one of half a dozen in a dinner jacket at a first night. I sat next to a young man who wore a red sweater. I don't mind but I know the artists mind.' There was little need to fear red sweaters or the like at Melbourne's gala opening. All seats were sold and there was a spirit of determination to make this the most glamorous social occasion Melbourne had known for many years. The rush of opera-goers to buy new dresses and take family jewels out of safe-deposit boxes at the banks was paralleled by a widespread curiosity about the events that was fired exclusively by the press; there was no way of persuading Sutherland and Bonynge to appear on radio or television. The mass-circulation magazine, the *Australian Women's Weekly*, included in its edition to coincide with the Melbourne opening a comprehensive booklet giving historical details of each of the works to be performed, casts, an act-by-act synopsis of the plot and a pronunciation guide so that no operatic gaffes would be committed at genteel afternoon tea parties. 'Loo-CHEE-ah dee LAHM-maw-mohr', it instructed, 'Say-mee-RAH-mee-day' and 'Lah Son-NAHM-boo-lah'. A rival women's magazine announced they had arranged a party on the Opera House site in Sydney with Sutherland as guest of honour to present the *Woman's Day*-Joan Sutherland scholarship.

Opening night, 10 July, was a gala occasion more brilliant than any since Melba's farewell in the same theatre thirty-seven years before, and the huge and unique venture would become a reality with the curtain rising on *Lucia di Lammermoor*. That reality, however, was tinged with an air of fantasy. None of the Australian

190

theatres in which the Bonynges would be performing had anything like the audience capacity or the stage areas of their European or American counterparts. The seven operas, all in completely new productions, were to be presented during a fourteen-week season in four cities, thousands of miles apart, in an exercise that would tax the ingenuity of the best tour managers. It was a season logistically, financially and artistically beyond the capacity of most of the world's great opera houses — and yet here it was about to happen in Australia as a commercial enterprise, virtually unsubsidized. It was as if the clock had been put back to the Melba years.

The guest of honour for the occasion was the Administrator of the Commonwealth, who was accompanied by H.R.H. Princess Alice, Countess of Athlone. Extra police were on duty to control the huge crowd of sightseers outside the theatre in Exhibition Street, while bewigged flunkeys in eighteenth-century court dress acted as footmen for the patrons arriving in a motor show of new and expensive models. Inside the narrow foyers there was an even greater human congestion as people jostled each other to see who was there — or not there — in a society scrum. One story circulating at the time claimed that a number of wealthy people had been slow off the mark in applying for their Sutherland seats and, rather than face the shame of admitting to missing out, fled north to the sunshine of Surfer's Paradise. In Sutherland's dressing-room, a red rose from the garden of Bonynge's parents in Sydney stood behind the statuette of the Madonna of Monserrat.

At this stage the box-office statistics were both interesting and worrying. They showed that 97 per cent of the bookings were for the Sutherland nights, while the remaining 3 per cent of takings had to cover the five out of every eight times when she wasn't performing. This prompted comment from the general manager of the opera company, Mr Syd Irving, 'Australians should be ashamed of themselves for their complete lack of enthusiasm. When some of these Covent Garden singers return and say they had as few as three hundred in the audience it will be quite laughable.' John McCallum said, 'Many people are regarding this as a Sutherland season when it is not. Every singer brought here is a great singer in his or her own right.' J.C. Williamson, in their advance publicity, had promoted Sutherland almost to the exclusion of anyone else and it was not really surprising that her

191

performances were outselling all others. But McCallum was right in his assessment of quality, for this was no makeshift season using well-worn stock scenery and a pick-up cast. By 10 July it had become a fully-integrated company on a high international level. However, the opening coincided with a statement from the Elizabethan Theatre Trust, who were assisting Williamson's season and who had cancelled most of their own opera productions for 1965. They concluded that audiences in Australia had increased during the past ten years only in proportion to population growth. Rather gloomily they stated that there was no public for opera as such — only for a handful of twelve or fifteen works guaranteed to bring in audiences who were usually influenced by the appearance of a few stars such as Sutherland. Their report seemed to be endorsed by what was happening at the box office.

Few in Her Majesty's Theatre that Satuday night, except Williamson executives, were concerned with such statements. They were there to enjoy themselves. And they did. 'It was for every opera lover in the theatre one of the great operatic experiences of a lifetime', wrote the *Herald* music critic, John Sinclair. 'It was by international standards a first-rate performance, superbly staged, finely sung and raised to the point of greatness by Joan Sutherland's magnificent performance.' Felix Werder in the *Age* stated,

The opera was an occasion of festive splendour and Pompeiian triumphs for the cast. *Lucia* is very much a heroine's opera full of prodigious vocal acrobatics, machinegun-like bravura effects and feats of virtuosity and not a few good tunes; in fact it is a score into which only a Sutherland could breathe life. She has a glorious voice which she promenades with easeful fioritura that soars like a lark above the ensemble to produce a heart-rending vocal characteristic of the fragile Lucia.

John Cargher in the *Bulletin* wrote, '*Lucia di Lammermoor* was an auspicious start for the new opera season and if this standard is kept up, Mr and Mrs Bonynge may yet convince Australia that opera is a good night's entertainment — and to hell with culture'.

At the end there were twenty curtain calls for Sutherland, who was excited and relieved at the reception. 'It was as great musically and greater personally than any of my performances at Covent Garden, the Met or La Scala, because it was coming home after fourteen years.' Norman Ayrton was as amazed as anyone in

Opposite: Opening night of Sutherland-Williamson season, Melbourne 1965

the cast. 'I've never seen anything like this in my life before', he exclaimed excitedly.

Sutherland was singing three times a week which, with preparation and rest, left little time for other events. There was the inevitable Lord Mayor's reception, a handful of official luncheons and dinners, but little else. A link with Australia's operatic past was the presentation to her of a slim gold-plated pen used by Melba when she sang Violetta in *La Traviata* in Melbourne in 1924. She had used it all over the world and on her death it had passed to her niece, Miss Helen Patterson, who gave it to Sutherland. It was added to a fan and a hairpin box of Melba's which she already owned. Coincidentally during the Melbourne *Traviatas* she was wearing a necklace of gold camelias once owned by the great actress Eleanora Duse and lent to Sutherland by an admirer. Sutherland and Pavarotti in Verdi's masterpiece proved to be a great soprano-tenor combination and gathered acclaim as the season progressed. Kenneth Hince writing in the *Australian* about *La Traviata* stated,

I have never before heard a pair of voices like these, soprano and tenor, on the Australian stage. Only Max Worthley and Sena Jurinac in *Don Giovanni* come close to them. There is an inevitable temptation to speak *ex cathedra*, and say that we will never hear this evenly matched excellence again. Perhaps we may: but it will be one chance in tens of thousands.

'Richard Bonynge directed a version of the opera with all the usual cuts restored and in a sympathetic and flexible way that did him and Verdi honour', wrote Roger Covell for the *Sydney Morning Herald*, 'Since I know how badly the company's orchestra can play, I must give Bonynge unstinted credit for subduing it to a polite murmur and for securing from his string players a surprisingly creditable attempt at the high, exposed writing of the first and last act preludes'.

Not everything was going well on the musical side of the production. Some of the cast were perplexed by the verbal brutality of Bonynge's treatment of Sutherland at rehearsals. The number two conductor for the season, John Matheson from Sadler's Wells in London, disagreed with Bonynge's artistic imperialism and resigned from the company. 'I came here to play music', he said at the airport as he left, 'not to twiddle my thumbs'. The 37-year-old conductor had agreed with J.C.

Williamson not to disclose the nature of the row, merely to say that it was an 'artistic disagreement'. He left, his fourteen weeks' salary paid, without giving one public performance. 'We have four other conductors as well as Mr Bonynge', Williamsons stated. But very soon there was one less when Georg Tintner, going home from the theatre on his bicycle after a rehearsal, was hit by a car and broke two bones in his left leg. 'My bike was not damaged', he said phlegmatically, 'but I was'. He hoped to be conducting again, from a seated position, in a couple of weeks.

As the Melbourne season progressed the bookings improved for the non-Sutherland nights. Early on there had been a depressingly small audience of barely three hundred for *L'Elisir d'Amore* in a production that was hailed by the critics as among the best in the season. But later there were full houses for Elizabeth Harwood's *Lucia* and standing room only for Joy Mammen's *Traviata*. For Sutherland, *Semiramide* was one of the highlights of the Australian tour and that too, although unfamiliar to local audiences, was well-received. 'Her performance was the most staggering show of singing heard in Australia for decades', wrote the *Australian* critic. 'She put her voice through acrobatics that could hardly be imagined, let alone thought possible. Passages of rapid detached notes — like a violinist's spiccato — poured from her with the ease of thought. The theatre was flooded with incredible grace-notes with trills in every part of her register.'

Left: Sutherland-Williamson season: *La Traviata*
Right: *Faust*

195

The final opera of the seven-work repertory was Gounod's *Faust* and, with Sutherland partnered by John Alexander, it emphasized the singing strength of the company. Roger Covell wrote, 'A company that has two tenors of the calibre of Alexander and Pavarotti is fortunate indeed; and the voices of Sutherland and Alexander in the final prison cell trio sounded gloriously assured and unstrained'. He was not, however, happy with the orchestra conducted by William Weibel. 'Some of its string players have manifestly never heard of vibrato and several of them give the impression of managing to play out of tune for an entire evening.'

At the end of the Melbourne season Sutherland was given a riotous send-off. Women in evening dress stood on their seats cheering, the stage was deep in streamers and flowers. After nine curtain calls, she thanked the audience for being so kind and attentive. 'Never anywhere have I had a reception like this.' And still they stayed and cheered. At the twentieth curtain call three members of the chorus trundled a piano on to the stage, Bonynge sat down at it and played the introduction to 'Home, Sweet Home', which Sutherland then sang to a hushed auditorium.

Sir Frank Tait went backstage, congratulated everyone and was concerned at the strain the season was putting on Sutherland. He personally escorted her to her car through the cheering crowds outside in what was to be his last visit to a theatre after a lifetime in show-business. The next day he wrote to Williamson's offices in London, New York, Auckland and Sydney about the last night and the season in general. Part of his memorandum read,

Joan Sutherland was really fagged out after all of this and departed for Adelaide on Sunday showing signs of fatigue, naturally, and with still a big programme ahead of her. I only hope she will be able to stand up to it all, but apart from her glorious artistry she is a truly wonderful person and I am confident that only complete fatigue will prevent her from carrying through, but it is obvious that she needed a week's break after this very strenuous five weeks plus four weeks' rehearsals.

A week later he was dead at the age of eighty-two. When they heard the news, Sutherland and Bonynge were greatly saddened. They wrote to his widow, Lady Tait, 'Sir Frank was a really great man and contributed more to Australian culture than anyone else we knew. His death is a terrible blow and the only consoling thought is that he lived to see in Melbourne, his home ground, the big success of this opera season.'

Top left: Part of the audience at the conclusion of *La Sonnambula*
Top right: Last night of Melbourne season 1965: *La Sonnambula*
Below: 'Home Sweet Home' at the end of the Melbourne season

Sutherland and Bonynge took the evening flight to Sydney after the Adelaide season on Saturday 28 August, planning a quiet family reunion at the airport and afterwards at their apartment. There was a small group of relatives waiting to greet them as Sutherland came down the steps of the plane wearing a black woollen suit with a black bow in her hair and clutching two hand-bags. A hostess followed behind carrying her mink coat. In addition there were about a hundred fans and a large flock of journalists and photographers who blocked the way from the aircraft to the waiting car. Bonynge made a gesture for everyone to move back, but to no avail. In the bustle the red rose she was carrying shed its petals symbolically as Sutherland's and Bonynge's tempers shortened. There were demands for statements about the season and requests for photographs. The quiet family gathering that had been anticipated quickly turned into a noisy scramble for pictures and comment. The Bonynges couldn't believe what was happening, particularly after their requests for privacy. The press, on the other hand, had been informed by Williamson's Publicity Department of their arrival and consequently they were annoyed at the effort of going to the airport on a Saturday night and the prospect of getting nothing. Bonynge made it clear that he didn't want photographs taken and escorted Sutherland out of the terminal. It was not an auspicious prelude to the official press conference less than twenty-four hours away.

The next morning the *Sunday Mirror* was on the streets with a large story headed 'JOAN BLOWS UP! Amazing Sydney Welcome' together with a picture of a very stern Sutherland. Frank O'Neill, the paper's senior features writer, reported that he had asked if she would kindly answer a few questions but that she had pushed past him with the comment, 'There is a press conference tomorrow'.

They gathered at a Kings Cross restaurant named The Four Canoes for the conference, with more than a hundred of the city's reporters and photographers. The proprietor of the establishment, Peter van Brunik, a long-time fan of Sutherland, wanted to create a dish in her honour and at first he had in mind a confection rather like Peach Melba but, on hearing that she was not fond of sweet things, he quickly changed it to a fish sauce which, he told the press, he was keeping under wraps until the prima donna herself was informed of it. A red carpet was placed on the steps of the restaurant and a basket of flowers made ready for a presentation.

Sutherland and Bonynge arrived forty minutes late. Almost immediately Bonynge got into a heated exchange with some journalists about why he hadn't allowed photographs the previous evening. He replied, 'We were greeted by a herd of orang-outangs. We do not believe in the divine right of the press. We want to be treated with courtesy — and we demand it.' Somebody said, 'Don't be silly' and one of Sydney's leading journalists, Ron Saw, muttered a disparaging remark, whereupon Bonynge grasped Sutherland's arm — she had not said a word yet — and left the restaurant followed in hot pursuit by van Brunik. Outside, he dropped to his knee grasping Sutherland's hand and kissed it saying, 'Please Joan, come back. I love you and there are a lot of people here who love you.' Bonynge said, 'I don't know if we can do that now. We didn't come here to be picked at or insulted. I don't mean to accuse all the press of being orang-outangs, probably only 5 per cent of them are. But they are the ones who have given the Sydney press such a stinking reputation.'

'It's true', Sutherland added, 'and I feel very disillusioned about it. Neither of us has been treated so badly and so downright rudely by pressmen anywhere in the world as we were last night at Sydney Airport. It has shaken me. I was always the one to defend Sydney press when friends criticized it to our faces overseas. Now I find it is true. I really don't know if I want to have any more to do with any pressmen in this city.' Van Brunik and Williamson officials asked them again to consider returning inside. Sutherland turned to Bonynge, 'What do you think?' He shrugged his shoulders. 'Well perhaps we could go back in there and see what the others have to say. It is true that they can't all be as bad as that mob at the airport.' He took her arm, 'Well, if you feel up to it...' 'All right', Sutherland sighed and they returned.

Bonynge addressed them again. 'I would first like to say a few words. We are very happy to speak to you at any time. Some people might get the impression that we do not like the press. We are happy to speak to you at any time.' An onslaught of questions followed, many of them about publicity, because they were more familiar with celebrities seeking personal attention than rejecting it. Bonynge replied, 'We realize the press helped once. We are, for example, especially grateful to the *Sun* Aria, but Joan would have been great anyway. I feel my wife has an obligation to herself. She

Cartoon by Rigby in the *Daily Mirror*, Sydney

has none to the public except to perform as best she can on stage. The public don't own her.' Sutherland added, 'There are times when one really wants to be alone.' There were also questions about retirement, which was curious considering she was only thirty-eight and at the peak of her career. 'As long as she pleases her audience', said Bonynge with restraint, 'she will continue to sing to full houses. If she does not please her audience she will retire.' 'I am surprised I am still on top today', Sutherland added modestly, 'I didn't think I would last that long'.

There could be little doubt that Sydney's own prima donna was back home. The newspapers the next day were full of Sutherland reports including Ron Saw's petulant account of the conference in the *Daily Mirror* which described Bonynge as Sutherland's head-waiter. The rival newspaper, the *Sun*, published a large picture showing Bonynge, arms folded, talking to the press with grim-faced officials from the opera standing by while Sutherland clutched a battered bouquet of flowers. The headline read 'Tarzan and his Mates'. Rigby's cartoon in the *Mirror* two days later, immediately after the first night, depicted Sutherland hovering in the wings dressed in her *Lucia* costume while an opera official tells her 'You'd better be good tonight — the Gentlemen of the Press are out front!' The auditorium is filled with large anthropoid apes holding peeled bananas.

The Sydney opening on Monday 31 August was fourteen years, four months and ten days since Sutherland's farewell concert at the Town Hall. The prices then had been 7s 6d, 5s and 3s. A mile away at Her Majesty's the 1,650 members of the audience had paid £10 10s and £7 7s for the privilege of hearing her. It was a low-key occasion with only a few policemen on duty while drinkers from the Crystal Palace Hotel opposite the theatre stood on the footpath and watched the dressy audience arrive. They raised a cheer when a truck loaded with cabbages on its way to the nearby city markets got caught up in a traffic jam with the taxis and hire cars of the opera patrons.

The performance itself was at first politely received. There was no applause for Sutherland on her first appearance and a mild burst only after '*Regnava nel silenzio*'. But by the end of the evening there were seventeen curtain calls and both she and Bonynge felt relieved and happy at their homecoming as she returned to her newly-decorated dressing-room with its lilac walls and ceiling and grey carpet. The next day Ron Saw in his column in the *Daily Mirror* wrote under a large headline, 'LA STUPENDA INDEED! — She can call me an orang-outang': 'It was her night and nothing — not even the most tactless tantrum of her husband — could have taken it away from her.'

La Stupenda indeed!

• *Joan Sutherland takes a curtain call last night.*

In terms of tiaras and tailcoats, and for those who counted curtain-calls, the evening was disastrous.

She can call me an orang-outang

By Ron Saw

Ron Saw's comment in the *Daily Mirror*, Sydney

201

Sutherland and Bonynge reflected on the press reports with a rueful amusement. 'I must learn to keep my trap shut', confessed Bonynge. 'At least until we know all the facts', added Sutherland. They thought the reporting of the Sunday press conference had not been unfair. 'You know', she said, 'you can't beat a good old Australian pressman letting his hair down in print. The way they hit back at us was really very well done. And that cartoon of Rigby's had me in stitches.'

The Sydney season was successful and a last-minute rush for seats changed plans, adding a week in Sydney and cutting back the Brisbane performances to just one week instead of two. The tour was a particularly arduous one for both of them. Bonynge had the constant responsibility for all the artistic decisions and Sutherland was singing three times a week which, over a fourteen-week season, was a more taxing schedule than she had ever faced. But at least in Sydney she was stimulated by the experience of being at home, seeing family and friends and working in a generally relaxed atmosphere. The casual manners of the Sydney audience were highlighted at a Saturday night performance of *La Traviata* when a well-dressed man in the audience was seen to insert a transistor earpiece to get the dog racing results from Wentworth Park as, on stage at the end of the second act, Alfredo has called back the guests from supper and in front of them throws his winnings at cards at Violetta's feet in a gesture of paying for her former favours.

After so many *Traviatas* during the tour Sutherland one night, for fun, added thirteen staccato notes on the high C as Tetrazzini had done on an old record. Bonynge said, 'We had played the record about three years before at a party and Joan didn't make any comment. She was doing her needlepoint and wasn't interested and I didn't even realize it had gone into her head. And then three years later it came out to everyone's surprise on stage in Sydney.' Sutherland remarked, 'I just felt a bit devilish that night. I felt good, otherwise I would never have attempted to sing thirteen top Cs, especially at the end of "*Sempre libera*".'

At a reception arranged by the state branch of the National Council for Women, Sutherland met her old headmistress at St Catherine's School and reminisced about the days when she sang hymns in the school chapel every morning. 'I was laughed at when I said I wanted to be a great singer. I think they thought I had a lot of nerve.' Mrs Isobel Hall, the headmistress, commented, 'At school Joan was just like any other pupil with nothing to indicate her great talent. All girls at a certain age want to be prima donnas, air hostesses or models.' Sutherland was bothered by television lights and noisy cameras during her rather nervous speech to the gathering and at one point she stopped speaking, looked up and said, 'That's all, gentlemen. I've had enough.'

Other engagements in Sydney included a sentimental return journey to her old school, and the presentation of the Sutherland scholarship to a 25-year-old baritone, Tom McDonnell, at a cocktail party on the Opera House site. The growing shell-like roofs of the building and the giant cranes towered above the three hundred guests and after a short speech on a makeshift platform she quipped, 'I may be too old to sing in this opera house when it's finished, but at least I've performed in it first'. She hadn't been told that Paul Robeson had sung several songs there fully five years previously, when the structure seemed to be only slightly less advanced.

Another brief encounter with the press occurred at her civic reception in the Town Hall. There was so much shutter noise from a bank of unblimped television cameras and such a glare from the extra lighting that she could hardly make herself heard above the din or see the prepared notes she was reading. In mid-speech she turned to the cameraman operating a particularly noisy machine and commented, 'I can't hear myself think, let alone talk'. That quietened the proceedings for a little but after the speech, the press and invited guests crowded around and she remarked to Norman Ayrton, who was accompanying her, 'I will never come back to this city. Never. I couldn't hear myself speak.' She turned to the Lord Mayor, Harry Jensen, and told him, 'I love your company and I love your people but I can't stand this sort of treatment. I'll have to leave.'

This latest confrontation generated two prominent editorials. One, in the *Daily Mirror*, read in part,

We are grateful to Miss Joan Sutherland for bringing a touch of excitement into our drab little lives. We now realize for the first time that what we have been missing all these years is the authentic prima donna flounce.

Every day or so Miss Sutherland gloriously reminds us that the function of the diva is not only to sing but to put on a ojlly good show of temperament.

The newspaper's proof reading seemed to match the quality of its journalism. The national daily, the *Australian,* wrote its leader couched in schoolmistress-like terms.

Joan Sutherland must control her petulance. She is a famous lady now, and entitled to the occasional show of theatrical temperament that seems to be part of the great actress's equipment.

But she must learn to act like someone famous when she is off stage; she must learn to handle with dignity and quell with charm the little imbroglios that an excited Press and public create when she appears.

'I cannot stand this sort of treatment', she cried in her latest outburst, at a reception at Sydney Town Hall on Tuesday, meaning she objected to the rather frantic background of TV cameras and flashbulbs.

Apparently it upset her so much she threatened never to return to 'this city' (although yesterday she seemed to be changing her mind about this).

'This city' is where she was born and got her first break — thanks to one of its newspapers. This is the first time she has been back to it, or Australia, in fifteen years; and now she is getting the kind of star treatment she deserves, and must expect, since she is what she is.

And it is inexcusable that she should reprove our newsmen and cameramen — a timid lot by world standards, in fact — who are naturally interested in photographing and questioning the world's leading opera singer for the benefit of her Australian admirers who may not see her again for another fifteen years.

It is all very unfortunate and very unnecessary. What she and her husband should do now is call another Press conference, shake hands and call it quits. Even Maria Callas has made up with the Press before.

Exactly four months after their arrival, Sutherland and Bonynge left Australia without any publicity. There was a final performance in Brisbane on the October Saturday night, a flight to Sydney on Sunday morning and a quiet day at leisure before some private family farewells at Sydney Airport. Their journey took them back to London by way of stopovers in Honolulu and New York. The season lost £24,000 which was split equally between J.C. Williamson and the Elizabethan Theatre Trust. It was a gratifying result for such an ambitious undertaking.

Chapter Ten

You're really only judged by your last performance. It doesn't matter how many superlatives are behind you, you still have to think of what you must get through in the future.

Sutherland's reception at Covent Garden just before leaving for the Australian tour had been rapturous for both *Lucia* and *Sonnambula*. Her next visit there nearly a year later stirred up a storm of reaction that, once again, made her the talking point of London's opera world. Donizetti wrote seventy-five works for the stage, and the next for Sutherland performance was one of the slightest and yet most appealing of those that survive; it was among Jenny Lind's favourite roles, and in the twentieth century Lily Pons kept it on the boards of the Metropolitan for many years. Mendelssohn, in a rebuke to some of the work's detractors, said, 'It's so pretty. You know, I would like to have written it myself.'

The opera in question was *La Fille du Régiment* and it gave London audiences the first opportunity to see and hear Sutherland in a non-tragic role: Marie, the tomboy who grows up in a French regiment and falls in love with one of the soldiers, Tonio. When it is revealed that she is, in fact, the niece of a countess, she is forced to leave the army and learn genteel manners. Eventually, after a military confrontation, she returns to her Tonio. The first performance was given at the Opéra-Comique in Paris in 1840 and this storming of the bastion of French entertainment by an Italian resulted in some organized hostility to the production and a decidedly cool first-night audience. Later the same year La Scala saw it in an Italian version. Berlioz was outspoken about the score, 'It is one of those things that one writes by the two dozen each year'. But the initial audience resistance in France was soon eroded by the infectious good nature of Donizetti's music and the patriotic plot, and more than forty performances were given during 1840 at the Opéra-Comique alone and that had totalled to more than a thousand by the end of the century. London first heard it with Jenny Lind in the main role in 1847, but it was not performed again in the British capital after 1876 until this new version, which in its casting was rather like a reunion from the recent Australian tour with Pavarotti, Sinclair, Malas and Sutherland getting together again.

Bonynge's view of the work was entirely in tune with Sandro Sequi's, the producer. 'The great point about *La Fille*', Bonynge said, 'is that it must be a "fun" evening for everyone. It is charming musically, and, although it is a mixture of gaiety and real pathos, it must sparkle. It is not my business to educate, but to entertain the public.' Sutherland began working on the score during December 1965 and it was hard going for her because Bonynge added many difficult roulades for decorating the reprises, so that remembering them was a strain. When it came to the rehearsals, she found it very tiring to carry out the physical demands of the role — the movement, the drum beating, and the dance lesson — on top of the vocal demands. She had never liked 'marking' — holding back — during a rehearsal, preferring to sing in full voice almost all the time. But she had enough spirit in reserve to play a few jokes. On one occasion she heard that it was Edith Coates's birthday. Coates was playing the role of the Duchess of Krakentorp, Marie's intended mother-in-law. She had an entrance to a waltz melody and at the dress rehearsal, unknown to Coates or to the invited audience, Sutherland arranged for the orchestra to play a different melody. As she came on to the strains of 'Happy Birthday to You' it stopped the show and Coates, surprised and delighted, had to wait until the applause of the cast and audience died down before she could repeat her grand entrance.

The producer for the new production was Sandro Sequi, who accepted that it was almost operetta — a landmark on the road toward Offenbach — and he was determined to use the original French which he thought was less confusing than the more familiar Italian version. Sequi set the action not during the Napoleonic wars, but in an earlier conflict. 'Donizetti's war is a crazy war with a funny army', he said. He believed the Napoleonic connection would add inevitable overtones for present-day audiences. He emphasized that it was vitally important to get the style right; not '*opera buffa*' denoting Italian comic opera with its humorous subject played by comic characters drawn from everyday life, but '*opéra comique*' — the French style — depicting amusing episodes and characters within a framework of comment about society and standards. Sequi had worked with Sutherland in Venice on *Sonnambula* some years before and for *Fille* he worked up a tomboy character for her that she found vastly enjoyable to play. It was a new light-hearted Sutherland, swaggering across the stage wearing red baggy trousers and expertly beating her side drum. She began to learn the basic technique of this during recording sessions. Invariably her microphone position was behind the orchestra close to the tympani, and between takes she would get some lessons on how to create the right military sounds. Reg Barker, the tympanist with the Covent Garden Orchestra, taught her the finer points of drumroll. 'I was told by him to practise two beats with each stick — Mama...dada, mama...dada — and I practised the rhythm on my knees saying it in quick succession.' First night, which was a charity performance in aid of the Royal Opera House Benevolent Fund, was attended by the Queen Mother together with a celebrity-studded audience including Rudolf Nureyev, Margot Fonteyn, Danny Kaye and Julie Christie and it created a great deal of comment.

The British press generally enjoyed Sutherland's romp and the virile support given her by Luciano Pavarotti as Tonio, although there were some reservations about what was considered a rather vulgar production. Sequi had gone too far some thought. Many of them chose to ignore what was obviously an audience-pleasing performance and behind headlines such as 'Sutherland Clowns Her Way to New Triumphs' and 'La Stupenda Hams It Up — Brilliantly!' there lurked the taint of exhibitionism and poor taste. Sutherland enjoyed herself in the broad comedy role and after the final curtain she was still smartly saluting the cheering audience for twenty-minutes while the pile of flowers at her feet grew ever larger. She said, 'We all had a hell of a lot of fun doing it. And there is no doubt that the audience had as much watching it. They are the critics in the matter. Unfortunately for their own enjoyment some of the London critics are the most inhibited creatures

La Fille du Régiment, Covent Garden 1966, with Spiro Malas

on God's earth.' Certainly some of them put a sharper edge to their pencils than usual. 'An opera about a camp follower — in a superlatively "camp" production', wrote Phillip Hope-Wallace in the *Guardian*. 'What could be more fashionable just now? The audience at Covent Garden seemed to love it: really, they must ask Miss Sutherland to do *Annie Get Your Gun*.' Andrew Porter, who also thought that she should be tackling heavier dramatic roles, stated in the *Financial Times*,

Often we have thought her self-conscious on the stage; now the barriers are down and her huge high spirits bubble over in the least inhibited performance of her career...the opera, heaven knows, has but a slender charm, and precious little of it could survive this broad execution. On the level of belly-laughs it seemed to be a success with the public. I will not conceal my opinion that I consider this particular *Fille* thoroughly inartistic and a waste of everybody's time.

Others took a different view. Peter Heyworth in the *Observer* noted,

Miss Sutherland is not one of nature's actresses, and ever since Zeffirelli devised a passable stage manner for her in *Lucia di Lammermoor*, she has clung to it for dear life and played sweet, silly Lucy through a dozen quasi-tragic roles. Yet somewhere beneath all that preposterous swooning there has been a real-life Aussie tomboy screaming to get out and in Sandro Sequi's production of *La Fille du Régiment*, she has at last made good her escape from all this too artful artifice that has for years encased her. For this relief, much thanks.

'I think we sometimes take our careers too seriously', Sutherland commented. 'This opera, and also the lighter music of Coward and musical comedy, require good singing. But I certainly don't think I could do musical comedy on stage eight times a week. Opera for me is enough at three times a week.' *The Times* put the production into the sharpest focus in its review,

... A different Joan Sutherland, not the languishing tragedy Queen but the gay, good humoured, unsophisticated tomboy that her friends have told us about. She enjoys herself immensely with the jaunty back-slapping, the military boots and knee-breeches, the uninhibited laughter and comically aggrieved grimaces; and her enjoyment is infectious. The song-lesson scene stopped the show several times last night, and the dancing lesson was skilfully judged, too. But the role is there to be sung, and the strength of this production was the vivacity and accuracy, the nuance and modulation of timbre of Miss Sutherland's singing in the gay numbers (hearing her anybody must be proud to be called a canary fancier) and the unforced artistry that she brought to the pathetic solos '*Il faut partir*' and '*Par le rang*' particularly. But nothing that she did was more admirable than the weight and balance of the delicious trio in the second act when Marie and Sulpice are reunited with Tonio. This was a tiny triumph of style for Miss Sutherland and Luciano Pavarotti and Spiro Malas and the conductor Richard Bonynge and the orchestra. The ensembles in the opera are glorious — we expect this from mature Donizetti. One can forget how brilliantly Donizetti keeps a slender plot going so that both acts seem completely worth while, full of musical if not dramatic eventfulness. Mr Sequi's production includes a vividly dotty Countess in Monica Sinclair, protesting, floridly hatted, Mr Pavarotti is fierce but vivacious in his high notes, beautiful to listen to in his plea, '*Pour me rapprocher*', atrocious in his French which might as well

209

be Serbo-Croat… The settings are ugly and poorly painted. But the production strikes a powerful, pleasurable blow for the cause of French opera. Welcome home to the Daughter of the Regiment!

The Bonynges now thought about the welcome to their new home at Les Avants. Before they left for the Australian tour, Anne Roughley went to Switzerland to supervise the moving of their possessions from Rocca Bella to Chalet Monnet. Most of the material had to be left in packing cases and trunks while waiting for the extensive renovations to transform the old-fashioned holiday chalet into a modern, comfortable house. Bonynge had plans for a large music room to be built over a double garage at the back, a tower to be added and inside, the installation of new bathrooms, a modern kitchen and central heating. The climate in that part of Switzerland, above Lake Geneva at an altitude of 1000 metres, is highly changeable and rarely very warm. Before the renovations were completed, visits there were largely confined to holidays during the summer months. At the end of their Adelaide season, they had taken on a new member of the staff, Chester Carone, to be Bonynge's personal secretary. Carone came from Sydney and, after several years in show-business in which he had been everything from a cinema projectionist to a singer in J.C. Williamson musicals, he gained a place in the chorus for the

Lakmé on 'The Bell Telephone Hour', 1967

Australian opera season. An engaging buffoon when prompted to be, he also knew music and singing together with such useful down-to-earth activities as carpentry and domestic odd jobs. He and Adam's former nanny, Ruthli, made several journeys to Les Avants to get the place in order between his commitments on tour with Bonynge and her need to be in London for housekeeping duties during term time for Adam's schooling.

The year 1967 began in a busy way for Sutherland with the role of Donna Anna in *Don Giovanni* at the Met with Karl Böhm conducting and then in Boston Bonynge took over the baton. Back in London, Sutherland's next big production at Covent Garden was also produced by Sandro Sequi — *Norma*. She had first sung the role more than three years previously in Vancouver but now there was much more attention given to this performance at the Royal Opera House. Bonynge had no doubts where the work stood for him,

I think *Norma* is the greatest work of Bellini, and all operas of the period must have great singers, they don't really work if you have just nice singers — they must be great because they were written, as in the case of *Norma*, for the finest singers of the day — Pasta and Grisi. Bellini, of all composers, understood the human voice.

The Bonynges prepare for *Norma* at Covent Garden 1967

After the critical dismay of some of London's music writers at Sutherland's lapse into levity with *Fille*, it might have been assumed that a return to one of the great romantic bel canto operas would be more acceptable to them, but there was now added criticism of both Sequi's direction and the lack of Sutherland's enunciation. Sequi had stated, 'With this opera you have to work within a formal structure of arias, duets and ensembles which can sometimes be rather static. But it can be a great mistake to give a more modern view of this kind of opera.' The plot is set in Roman-occupied Gaul about 50 B.C. against the background of a Druid revolt. Norma, in love with the proconsul Pollione, is abandoned when he leaves her for a young priestess, Adalgisa. The plot then meanders its way to a climax of mutual immolation. Sequi explained:

Drama does exist in the plot and it can come out while respecting the structure of the opera itself. That is why I produce it in a romantic way, trying to follow the Bellini mood. The private personality of Norma is most important. She is a priestess, but she is in love with somebody and she is a mother. Being Italian I know how important this is and the personality of Joan Sutherland fits the role perfectly because she is, in fact, a very warm person. I didn't want to get anything of a Medea quality in the title role.

Norma, Covent Garden 1967

Bonynge agreed with him. 'Norma is not just a great statue on stage, neither is she a virago; she is a woman who also has her faults and weaknesses. It is not a realistic opera but there are moments of great theatre.' The question of Sutherland's enunciation arose in several of the press reviews while the record critics, who are often the same writers, continued to comment about the subject with almost every new release. Covent Garden's audition report of 1952 commenting on good diction seemed a long time ago. Bonynge stated his views on the matter.

The emotion must come from the musical score — the sounds of the voice. If one over-enunciates the words, as in the big ensembles, they can only get in the way of the music. They frequently get right in the way of the music and spoil the line. In fact, I frequently ask the chorus not to enunciate so much because I do not want to hear the words. When we go to the theatre we must hear every word that is spoken throughout the piece, but not in opera. I think when one goes to certain performances in English one hears the singers spitting out the words in a most ghastly manner; it has nothing to do with the music. They destroy opera and I'm very anti spitting out words except in recitatives where they should be heard. The recitative is to tell the story. The music is to carry on the emotion, not the words.

This was a very busy production year for them. In April, Sutherland and Bonynge were back on the American West Coast

Lakmé, Seattle 1967

in Seattle for another premiere performance — Delibes's *Lakmé*, a role Sutherland had to learn during the preparation of her role in Haydn's unfamiliar *Orfeo ed Euridice* at the Vienna State Opera in May. Memory was still not a strong point. Her technique for learning a part was to study the music and the libretto together. 'I find it difficult to learn the music apart from the words', she said, 'because it has so much influence on them. The two, when the opera is well-written, go together. I study the words separately in order to memorize them, but I tend to sing along with them.' She received a stencilled note with her name written on it from the San Francisco Opera. It read, 'Please note, we will not be using a prompter for the 1966-67 season'. Sutherland wrote to the director, Kurt Herbert Adler, 'Please note, I'll not be singing without a prompter'. The post was re-instated. Sutherland explained, 'It's comforting to have that little man down there when you're working. He relieves some of the strain — although a bad prompter is worse than none.'

For the next three years work continued in a stream of engagements that were so varied in their content and location that they would quickly become in retrospect a jumbled confusion of passing time to both of them. Sutherland's health was much improved as she approached forty, although she still needed to have regular back massage and found long periods of sitting uncomfortable. 'I am coming up to forty at the end of the year', she admitted with little concern. 'People are suggesting that I ought to be changing over to more dramatic roles. But my voice is still far more suited to the lyrical parts I am singing now. Dramatic roles are more satisfying; they have more emotion and feeling. But, after all, one can sing the Marschallin at sixty.' It would be a long time, if ever, before an opera house would see her in that role as the Princess von Werdenberg in Strauss's *Der Rosenkavalier*. Bonynge, summing-up his wife's voice, said, 'I call her a soprano and only a soprano because she sings all the repertory that a coloratura sings, most of the repertory a dramatic soprano sings and all the lyric repertory as well. So what else can you call her but a soprano? It's a heavier voice than most coloraturas, however; it just has a broader range.'

Her voice and stage technique had now reached their peak and there seemed to be no reason why the Bonynge team shouldn't continue to prosper under the benign eye of devoted audiences on

Left: *Orfeo ed Euridice*, Vienna 1967

Right: *La Traviata*, Buenos Aires 1969, with producer Sandro Sequi

Below: In Vienna 1967

three continents. There were a few incidents, some slight and amusing, others potentially hazardous, that ruffled the otherwise smooth professional progression. In March 1968 while singing in *La Traviata* in Boston, she found herself flat on her back during the Casino scene in the third act. Violetta's irate lover, sung by Anastasios Vrenios, threw his gambling winnings in her face and pushed her away from him. She was to reel back and collapse into a chair, but one night she missed it and fell heavily to the stage. As if part of the action, and still in character, Sutherland, on the right music cue, got to her feet, smoothed her skirt, rearranged her hair and continued to sing. It was reminiscent of a lighter incident nearly ten years previously when she was singing at the San Carlo opera house in Naples. 'I didn't realize that anything was happening until I looked down and there was a frill of white at my feet.' She had lost a white underskirt during her performance of *Lucia*. She stepped out of it, the leading man bent down, picked it up, tucked it under his arm in a display of gallantry that was more Italian than Scottish, bowed to her and made his exit.

Work had been proceeding at a varying pace over the last three years at Chalet Monet, as it was now called. One 'n' was deleted to make it sound more artistic, suggesting perhaps that the celebrated French impressionist painter had lingered in this part of Switzerland. But he had not. The early days of rooms full of packing cases, a minute kitchen which was Ruthli's horror, and family gatherings around a single oil heater when the fuel for the central heating system was not delivered, had given way to a comfortable and striking Swiss chalet with a rapidly improving garden nurtured by Sutherland whenever she could find time.

Les Avants, the village where they now planned to establish their permanent residence and give up living in London, was originally developed around the turn of the century for the visiting English, who could take the new railway from lakeside Montreux to alpine Les Avants in a spectacular ascent of twenty minutes. The scenery was dramatic, yet friendly, and a funicular from Les Avants to the top of the hill at Sonloup, meant that winter sports of a gentle nature could be enjoyed without the inconvenience of travel to distant and remote villages. In spring the vivid green pastures were flecked with white narcissus and the valley echoed to the flat chiming of cow bells; in summer the days were warm, the nights cool and the vegetation remained lush. In autumn the pine forests on the higher slopes took on a golden tone as the first chill winds blew down the valleys from the north, scattering the leaves and heralding winter's long blanketing of snow which showed off the landscape to picture postcard perfection, overlooked during all seasons by the brooding, rocky peak, the Dent de Jaman. In the early part of the twentieth century, three large hotels had been built in the village and, together with two inns, they catered for the tourists who flocked to the winter skiing or summer tennis amid the tranquil permanence of the rural scene. By the late 1960s when the Bonynges began moving in, most of the foreign tourists had gone, deterred by the ever-hardening Swiss franc. One of the hotels had burned down many years before, the second was functioning as an exclusive finishing school and the third was deserted and boarded up. The two inns satisfied the needs of visitors. There was, however, an intense sense of village pride, and the residents made it their duty to see that Les Avants remained as one of the prettiest communities in the Vaud canton. It was an ideal spot for getting away from the scramble of touring, a place to withdraw to and do your own thing, sharing it sometimes with the famous neighbour, when he was home.

'I wish we'd had a tape recorder going; he was so funny; so entertaining, so charming and kind.' Sutherland enjoyed the company of Noël Coward. 'You might think he was bitter or sarcastic from his writing', she adds, 'but he wasn't at all. He was a wonderful neighbour.' From 1969 they began a tradition of spending Christmas together at Les Avants, visiting each other's houses, exchanging presents and generally relaxing from the pressures of their equally busy worlds. Then, after the break, Coward would be off to Jamaica and the Bonynges back into the round of recordings and opera and travel. 'I remember the very last Christmas he spent in our house', she says,

My housekeeper had the dearest little baby and he was dangling her on his knee, the flashbulbs were popping and Rachel just sat there, completely unconcerned, with her big eyes wide open, not even blinking. Noël turned to her mother, raised an eyebrow and intoned, 'Oh Ruthli, what have you done? You've created a star. She's not even turning a hair — she's even posing. You've made a rod for your own back, my girl!' And he was right!

In March 1973 Coward died at his Jamaica home of a heart attack and Christmases at Les Avants were never quite the same again.

In 1968 Sutherland's successes began to attract academic notice.

Judging by the characters that we originally transported to Australia we could not complain, no matter who they sent back to us, but instead of retaliating they have been sending us one virtuoso after another — culminating in our present graduand as their supreme effort, and we are all grateful to Australia and welcome this opportunity to acknowledge it.

The words of the oration at Aberdeen University for Sutherland's honorary doctorate of laws, heralded a similar award the same year. In July she went to the University of Leicester to receive another doctorate, this time for music. There, the oration was more personal:

I'm afraid the prima donna has not always borne a character beyond reproach. The term should be one of honour but we apply it quite commonly to anyone who is temperamental and vain. 'If a singer may not be indulged in her humours', one of them was made to say in Handel's time, 'I am sure she will soon become of no consequence within the town'. Miss Sutherland has never indulged in her humours to become a prima donna in that sense...

Academic honours at Aberdeen University 1968

The new personality of Chalet Monet shone through in Bonynge's realized designs for the layout of the house on its three floors and a basement area leading out to a broad terrace. The rich, heavily-patterned wallpapers set off the huge collection of pictures, books and display cabinets containing their bewildering multitude of porcelain. 'It's rather like living in the nineteenth century', is how Bonynge sums it up. Sutherland's touches were obvious in the furniture and the furnishings with the emphasis on greens and blues in the curtains and the cushion covers and seats, many of them made by her in needlepoint during endless journeys and at rehearsals and recording sessions during 'other people's bits'. Against this background of antique furniture, patterned wallpapers and drapes, is a functional, modern house that makes the nineteenth century seem remote.

Collecting was part of Bonynge's way of life long before the rewards of their successful careers were able to be displayed so fully. 'Collecting is a disease from which I suffer very badly', he admits. It began, modestly enough, with stamps when he was a young boy in Sydney. Usually that is as far as the urge goes in childhood — with the exception of hoarding comics. This he did also, building up a library that made him the envy of his school-friends. After arriving in London, with a small allowance to live on, he began to make excursions to the junk and fringe antique areas of Portobello Road and Shepherd Market. In the early 1950s with the Festival of Britain focusing attention on contemporary design and its place in a new world, there was only limited interest in the paraphernalia of the past. Objects that are now rare and valuable could be picked up very cheaply. 'I'd spend my allowance on prints and pictures and china — things which cost a few pence then but which are very expensive today.' By the time the Bonynges moved to their first London apartments in Aubrey Walk and then to Cornwall Gardens, the burgeoning collection was already in evidence. Over the next few years it grew in proportion to their income so that at the time of the move to Chalet Monet there was need to start a methodical listing in an attempt to keep track of possessions and purchases. 'Collecting is a great change of pace from working', Bonynge explains. 'Wherever I am I just go out and roam around the shops and find things here and there. And when I'm home I have all the fun of getting them together and cataloguing.' On tours he will be eager to slip away from the demands of the press and the technical discussions of performance, to head for the local antique district. Probably more purchases can be credited to his wife's need to spend long hours with hairdressers to prepare for her performance because during those times Bonynge has made some of his most spectacular finds. In cities as widespread as Seoul, Denver, Stockholm, Tokyo and Munich, the normal pressures on a visitor are to go sightseeing. But Bonynge's simple demand is invariably, 'Take me to the antique shops'. Then with the keen eye of a hunter he will search out old books, prints, jewellery — anything of quality that catches his attention. 'My wife frequently threatens to throw me out of the house together with all the stuff. But I think she's getting used to it now.'

Sutherland takes little part in the collecting and is reluctant even to discuss what is much more than just a hobby to her husband. It is a professional safety valve he can use when the pressures of performance build up too much. 'Richard's always saying that one of these days he's going to open up a shop', she quips.

I'm never quite sure if it's just a ruse to placate me so that he can go on collecting without my protests. He used to spend his last bob on something if he had to have it for that collection of his. In Portobello Road he would snap his fingers to indicate that I should give him some money because he had just used his last pound and couldn't miss some great find he'd just come across. A lot of it I frankly can do without, but he gets so much pleasure and satisfaction out of it. Sometimes he's bought some music — the occasional old score — and later found out that it was, in fact, the original version of an aria. I learned a different version, so I have to learn the new, original piece in its place. That rather upsets me, but he's tickled pink.

On the walls at Chalet Monet is an extensive range of prints and paintings with an equally wide variety of quality. There are portraits of famous singers of the past including Benedetta Rosamunda Pisaroni, an Italian who excelled in Rossini roles and who is known as the first Italian contralto; Emmy Destinn, the Czech-born soprano who sang with Caruso in the first London performance of *Madame Butterfly*; Giuditta Pasta, the almost legendary creator of *Norma*; Giulia Grisi, the creator of Adalgisa to Pasta's *Norma*; Maria Malibran, another renowned *Norma*; and Jenny Lind, the so-called 'Swedish Nightingale'. In the entrance hall is a portrait of Verdi. Elsewhere are stacks of scores, theatre prints and antique postcards, while in the sitting room with its view over the balcony to Lake Geneva far below, a Winterhalter portrait looks down on two fine settees that were once owned by Talleyrand. But perhaps the best quality is in the Staffordshire figurines, of which Bonynge has collected many hundreds. Some of them are unique and others, such as the figures of Malibran, Jenny Lind and others from *The Daughter of the Regiment*, are within the general theatrical theme of the whole collection.

Sutherland comments,

His collection started off as basically music and ballet and then it branched out into pretty well every field that is vaguely allied to theatre. He now really has a splendid collection of theatrical memorabilia. He can sit in his study and read stage reports from the *Illustrated London News* of the 1840s, for instance, and be oblivious of everything that's going on round him. We call him for lunch and he just doesn't appear and so we have to send someone down to drag him away.

For her, gardening is one of the most relaxing activities when she's at Les Avants. In spring frequent forays are taken with Ruthli and Asta, the family Bernese Shepherd dog, down to the village where, between the stacks of freshly-cut logs beside the railway tracks, the local growers display pots of seedlings with their promise of a summer riot of colour. Geraniums, particularly, flourish in the climate, but a whole range of temperate plants add to the beauty of the short spring and summer season. Sutherland orders a vast number of plants to be delivered to the house. She says, 'One of the greatest joys of Les Avants is deciding what else I can put into the garden'. She remembers her love of flowers and plants from childhood.

I am really not much of a northern hemisphere gardener — but I like to read my gardening books and plan where to plant new shrubs and flowers. I ask the gardener to do all sorts of things in my poor French, and I'm never really sure if he understands what I'm after. Occasionally I get out there and plant four or five hundred bulbs and hope I'll be home during the following spring to see them come up. Unfortunately, it doesn't often happen that way — for me, not the bulbs!

The rest of the time, when Sutherland is not learning a new opera with Bonynge at the piano in the music room or revising a part from several years ago, Asta takes her for a daily walk down the hill, dragging her through the village. There are regular visits to Montreux for shopping and for back massage, and short drives along the Lake to Vevey for more extensive shopping. From the kitchen Ruthli, who admits she didn't even know to how roast a joint of meat when she first joined the Bonynges in London, produces some splendid meals with the accent on the Swiss-German cooking her family eats at home in Basel. There are steaks, goulashes, potatoes and fish regularly on the menu and a salad and cheese is served with most meals; Chester sometimes contributes an Australian pavlova or an ice-cream cake. Bonynge has a cellar of fine wines but for everyday drinking they prefer the excellent crisp whites of the region bottled under the Vevey and Montreux labels. He tried to add to his French, German and Italian vintages with a supply of wines from Australia but the effort of shipping and the high tariff barriers and taxes made the venture cumbersome and pointless. At first they spent up to ten weeks a year at Les Avants, with visits home by Adam who was attending a nearby school.

He's at an English boarding school in Switzerland and I think that's a good thing because he's an only child. We started taking him around a little, but it was almost impossible to cope — he wasn't terribly obedient. And all the ladies came out with, 'The darling, he doesn't realize what splendid parents he has'. With all this nonsense being poured into him, we sent him back to school.

In Philadelphia, at the beginning of 1970, President Nixon attended a birthday concert in honour of the Academy of Music's 113th anniversary and also the seventieth birthday of Eugene Ormandy, who was then in his thirty-fourth year as music director. The President presented him with the Medal of Freedom, the nation's highest civilian honour. At the concert the tenor, Placido Domingo, and Sutherland and the pianist, John Browning, presented several works including 'O beau pays' from Les Huguenots sung by Sutherland and 'Ah! Verrano a te sull'aure' from Lucia with Domingo. Wherever she went Sutherland retained a proud Australian identity which was not always to her advantage, especially when she was asked to play the role of unofficial ambassador for her country — a part she accepted willingly.

One event with home connections was a Salute to Australian Television, organized in New York by the National Academy of Television Arts and Sciences at the Hotel Roosevelt in February 1970. Sutherland and Cyril Ritchard were asked to co-host the programme whose guests included Dame Judith Anderson, Zoe

222

Caldwell, Lana Cantrell, Rod Laver and Merle Oberon. None of them, with the exception of Lana Cantrell who sang regularly on a Melbourne variety show, had any connection with Australian television, and in the case of Miss Oberon a national link was even more tenuous. Cyril Ritchard told the gathering he thought the most impressive thing about the medium in Australia was its reception, which was vastly superior to that of the United States. Both Ritchard and Sutherland assumed the invitation was just for dinner, but instead they had to sit through a film of unrelated sequences taken from a variety of shows featuring entertainer Rolf Harris, artist Russell Drysdale, Skippy the kangaroo and, inexplicably, a segment on the 1956 Melbourne Olympics. Then they were expected to make speeches to the audience. Sutherland was not happy about this and instead her part of the proceedings turned into a question-and-answer session with the President of the Academy, Ted Cott. He asked her, 'What is your husband's name, how do you spell it, and what does he do?' 'His name is Richard Bonynge', she replied rather curtly, 'and it is spelt BONNINGE — um...ah...I mean, well, you know it's Irish! He's a good musician and conductor.' Cyril Ritchard was asked what he did before he became an actor and he replied, 'Nothing'. As if that wasn't enough, they had to be introduced to and photographed with a live kangaroo which was registered with a local talent agency and hired out for $300 for two hours plus limousine fees.

In June 1970 the opening date of the Sydney Opera House was finally set — for March 1973. There was a general assumption that Sutherland would be the guest of honour at the first concert. But she was saying nothing about returning home. In the meantime performances went on at the same hectic pace as before with holiday breaks in Switzerland.

In November 1970 Sutherland sang all four soprano roles in Offenbach's *Les Contes d'Hoffmann* at the progressive Seattle Opera. The composer had died before the work was completed and the scoring was completed and some recitatives added by Ernest Guiraud. For this new production Bonynge went back to the original play and retained only Offenbach's music with the spoken dialogue. This was not destined to please Sutherland very much who still disliked dialogue. 'I do not sing as I speak', she explained, 'and I find I have to do a gear change. In fact, I usually

223

try to persuade the producer to drop as much of the dialogue as possible.' Sutherland excelled in the roles of Olympia the doll, Giulietta the Venetian courtesan, Antonia the consumptive German opera singer, and Stella the prima donna. Bonynge regarded his performing version as a return to the composer's original concept, but he didn't please everyone. Harold C. Schonberg, the music critic of the *New York Times*, went to Seattle to see the performance and returned to the East Coast praising the operetta as a whole but unimpressed with the musical direction. 'If only the conducting matched!' he wrote. 'But Mr Bonynge was sloppy — the same old story. He has all the knowledge in the world, but not the baton technique to put it into effect.'

In early 1971 she was rehearsing *Semiramide* in Chicago with Marilyn Horne and the two of them began musing with Bonynge about the future. Horne said she was looking to extend her repertoire and was 'dabbling in Wagner'. Sutherland commented, 'My dear, maybe we can do Brünnhilde and Sieglinde together and really shock 'em!' Bonynge said he didn't want to touch the symphonic repertoire, or Wagner, or the moderns. 'But that still leaves a lot of music', he added. 'French music, particularly Massenet, attracts me and so I have enough to last me out, I'm sure.' Sutherland commented, 'Ricky is fast becoming a French opera nut!', and said she wanted to get back more into the Mozart repertory. 'Since I branched out I seem only to have sung *Don Giovanni*.' 'You can't keep getting into new fields', Bonynge pointed out, 'it's much better to keep on doing what you're best at. There are dozens of Rossini and Donizetti operas still to do — not to mention other works of the bel canto repertoire.'

The opening night of *Semiramide* was followed by one of Chicago's social events of the year, the Lyric Opera's annual ball. Sutherland was tired after the performance and she was made to wait before the nine hundred guests in the Conrad Hilton Hotel were seated and ready for the traditional march of the opera stars. 'I want to sit down, I'm tired and hungry', she complained. But still the singers were kept waiting. She waited to make her entrance with Marilyn Horne and immediately it was over, stormed out of the hotel with Bonynge.

Opposite: *Semiramide*, Chicago 1971, with Marilyn Horne

224

Sutherland sang in a new production of *Lucia* at the Hamburg Opera early in 1971 which was a tremendous personal success for her, although Bonynge was less well received. He found it difficult rehearsing the orchestra; they didn't want to follow his instructions and a tension grew up as the opening night approached. The audience at the end of the performance gave Sutherland a warm welcome, but some of them booed Bonynge as he came on stage to take his bow. Shaking her fist in fury, Sutherland walked off the stage and refused to take any more curtain calls. The following day she was greeted by a huge crowd in a Hamburg shipyard as she attended the ceremony to launch the 21,000 ton vessel, *Columbus Australia*, the second of three ships for the Hamburg-Sudanische line on the container run to and from the American West Coast from Australia and New Zealand. Bonynge declined to attend.

At the time a widely-syndicated press agency report stated that if an American opera house now wanted Sutherland, who was described as the prima donna with the most box-office magnetism in the world, then it must take her conductor-spouse as well. It was pointed out that, lacking the European subsidies, American houses could not afford to gamble on the obscure bel canto operas that he constantly demanded for her. The report added, 'As musicologist, Bonynge has made himself the outstanding authority on the bel canto operas. As a conductor of them, he hasn't been accepted with any notable enthusiasm by opera audiences and critics.' His thoughts on the matter were simply to shrug off the criticism and the reference to his recondite repertoire, 'One finds that the operas that were very famous last century, even if they've been on the shelf for a while, are usually worth doing again'.

In May 1971 the Sydney *Sun* was confidently stating that Sutherland would appear at the Sydney Opera House opening and receive about $140,000 for fourteen, as yet undefined, performances. Edward Downes, the newly-appointed musical director of the Australian Opera, confirmed that negotiations had begun with her to head the opening season.

The San Francisco Opera staged Sutherland's debut in Donizetti's *Maria Stuarda* in November 1971. 'I was intrigued with the role at the outset', she said 'because of the association with my Scots forebears. I've always had a soft spot for Mary Stuart and I rather thought she was put upon too much — she was a very much misused woman. It gives me the greatest pleasure to,

Left: *Lucia*, Hamburg 1971

Right: Cleopatra in *Giulio Cesare*, Hamburg 1971

Below: Arriving to launch *Columbus Australia*, Hamburg 1971

227

as it were, throw the book at Queen Elizabeth in this production.'
The version used by Bonynge was the most complete since its first
staging, and was based on Malibran's 1835 La Scala performance,
although nobody knows with any certainty what was the original
because Donizetti's score is lost. Sutherland had another successful role to her credit, in not so much a coloratura part, but one
requiring more middle voice than had been heard from her for a
long time.

At the end of the year Sutherland's memory was brought into
question once again during a recital at the Kennedy Center in
Washington. In between songs, a small grey-haired woman in a
trouser suit jumped to her feet and shouted out, 'I'm sorry, I love
your voice but...why do you use music?' Sutherland replied in a
matter-of-fact way as if she always chatted to her audience during
recitals, 'I have a rotten memory. If I don't use music, I don't
sing.' The audience cheered her for the reply, the grey-haired
woman sat down and the music continued.

The beginning of 1972 saw Sutherland and Bonynge busy in a
medium they had shied away from for several years. They were in
London taping the first two shows of a television series aimed at
popularizing opera and intended primarily for the American
market. The project, to be called 'Who's Afraid of Opera?' was
announced in London during the previous October and it
revealed an ambitious plan to feature Sutherland in the leading
role of several famous operas, cut down to thirty minutes each and
featuring a trio of puppets named Sir William, Billy and Rudi.
She was to chat with them about the plot of each opera and it was
intended that the camera from time to time would concentrate on
their reactions to the proceedings. The casts were to include some
of the top singers available in Britain, amongst others Monica
Sinclair, Spiro Malas, Clifford Grant, Ramón Remedios and Tom
McDonnell (who had won the Sutherland-*Woman's Day* scholarship in Australia in 1965) and Bonynge was to record the music
with the London Symphony Orchestra. 'Richard really did some
smart talking to get me to do them', Sutherland admitted. 'First of
all, I'm terrified of television. When you're out on the operatic
stage, you know the audience is out there but it's so dark you get
absorbed in your role and forget about the people. When you do
television there are so many distractions, you can hardly keep your
mind on what you're doing.'

The producer/director of the series, Nathan Kroll, stated that the idea was to create a wider audience for opera. 'Opera on TV is a dirty word', he stated. 'By taking away the feeling of pomposity and the secondary plot line, we have a fighting chance to prove we have something terribly exciting.' He had plans for a total of twenty-six mini-operas but two were to be recorded first for transmission over the 210-station PBS network in April 1972. The large corporation General Telephone and Electric had given a grant of $160,000 for the first two shows — *The Daughter of the Regiment* and *The Barber of Seville*. Sutherland said, 'I didn't even like the idea. I thought it would never, never work, me talking to puppets. I was also very much afraid how I was going to look. I just thought the whole idea was silly and doomed and I told them so.'

Bonynge, indeed, did some smart talking and convinced her that it was worth proceeding and, of course, she did. 'I was wrong', she admitted. 'Once I started to work, I loved telling the story to the puppets. I could just feel it was coming off well. When I saw the show I was satisfied with the way I looked. I hope we can do more of these.'

With the puppets for 'Who's Afraid of Opera?', London 1972

The number of programmes in the series depended on the result of the audience reaction to the first two. There were press advertisements announcing the transmission and the newspaper critics reviewed the show extensively. Staff writer Irving Lowens in the *Washington Evening Star* saw it on his local PBS channel, WETA. He wrote,

The general idea behind the gimmick is that the byplay between the singer and the puppets, when combined with arias and ensembles in the original Italian or French and scraps of recitative in English, will somehow add to the pleasure of the uninitiated. The show isn't intended to be educational — horrors, no. 'It's a format I think both children and adults can enjoy. I want to entertain an audience, not educate it', Miss Sutherland insists. 'This new format allows me to bring the essence of what I do in opera houses to vast television audiences, and that's been a dream of mine for years'... I found the format patronizing and distracting. The single consistent virtue of the special is Miss Sutherland's expert singing. As an actress, she is strictly from hunger, and I didn't find the sight of her horsey, smiling face sufficient compensation for the inferior sound that comes out of television sets. PBS gets brownie points but this approach isn't likely to win friends and influence people unless they're already hooked on opera. And I have the sinking feeling that there's an equally good chance that these campy half-hours may alienate the affections of a fair number of intelligent individuals (both young and old) who haven't yet discovered the genre.

Harry Harris in the *Philadelphia Inquirer*, with an apology to Sutherland, stated that she was too old, too big and too plain to fit most children's concept of a beautiful heroine. 'Although Miss Sutherland kept smiling gaily amid the mugging and the slapstick as if it were all great fun', he wrote, 'the brightly-coloured proceedings seemed to be suffering from a bad case of fallen archness'.

Six more productions were made: *Lucia di Lammermoor, La Périchole, Rigoletto, Faust, La Traviata* and *Mignon*, all under the supervision of Piers Haggard, Herbert Wise and Ted Kotcheff and scheduled for transmission the following year — 1973. There was not enough sponsor interest for PBS to back any more productions and sales of the programmes outside the United States were not good. 'Who's Afraid of Opera?' remains the only permanent visual record of some of Sutherland's finest roles and a unique document of otherwise unseen public performances of Thomas's *Mignon* and *La Périchole* by Offenbach.

In July 1972 the journal *Opera* came out with an article by Michael Scott which was subsequently much quoted around the

La Fille du Régiment, New York 1972, with Luciano Pavarotti and Ljuba Welitsch

world and gave an insight into the fees being demanded by the top singers. Scott had attempted to run an unsubsidized opera in Britain, the London Opera Society, but it had failed financially. He suggested that the world's principal houses should form a cartel to limit the size of fees being paid to some singers. In a table of the most highly paid performers (given in American dollars), Sutherland and Beverly Sills came out on top charging, according to Scott, between $5,000 and $10,000 per performance, followed by Monserrat Caballé ($4,000 to $7,500), Renata Tebaldi and Carlo Bergonzi ($5,000 to $6,000), Alfredo Kraus, Nicolai Ghiaurov and Mirella Freni ($4,000 to $6,000), Marilyn Horne ($3,000 to $6,000), Placido Domingo ($3,000 to $5,000) and Boris Christoff ($3,000 to $4,000).

Also in 1972 Sutherland and Bonynge received academic recognition for the first time in the United States when Rider College in Trenton, New Jersey, awarded them honorary doctor of letters degrees. Bonynge's critics thought that Master of Operatic Archaeology might be more appropriate! Soon after, they appeared at the Metropolitan to farewell another of the world's great opera administrators, Rudolf Bing. (It was two years after a similar occasion at Covent Garden when another great figurehead, Sir David Webster, had been cheered into retirement at a gala performance to mark the end of his fifteen influential years as general administrator of Covent Garden. But he was now dead, his retirement having lasted less than a year.) Bing was born in Vienna and he had spent a lifetime associated with music, including managing Glyndebourne for ten years, helping to found the Edinburgh Festival where he was director for two years, and holding the post of the General Manager of the Metropolitan since 1950. His term of office in New York had established him as one of opera's most flamboyant and persuasive personalities. His memorandum to the performers at his farewell on 14 April was couched in a style typical of the man. Under the heading, 'To all those artists who are so generously participating in my Farewell Gala', it read,

This is a request to help speed up the happy proceedings during the Gala. Will all artists please accept their applause after finishing their number and, indeed, allow that applause to develop to certainly deserved proportions, but once they leave the stage as directed by the Stage Director, please do not return. For very obvious reasons, we cannot have duplicating bows and if for no other reason, because we all wish to get home before breakfast! Thank you very much! Rudolf Bing.

It was a thirty-item gala with Sutherland and Pavarotti bringing the first part to a close with 'Sulla tomba' from *Lucia*.

Far away in Sydney, word was getting around that despite the talk and the expectation, Sutherland would not, after all, be in the 1973 opening season of the Sydney Opera House. She explained,

They asked me to the opening and I was delighted. We juggled the New York Met dates, and the Met were very helpful. They then changed the date and the Met again helpfully juggled their dates. Now they've changed the management in Sydney and it has all changed again and is all up in the air. I'll certainly go, but it will now be in 1974.

The Opera House opening concert featured Birgit Nilsson instead of Sydney's own prima donna. Audiences would have to wait until the following June before they could see Sutherland performing at home again, and in their brand new temple of culture for the first time.

In the meantime, the 1970 Seattle production of *Les Contes*

Les Contes d'Hoffmann, New York 1972. Top left: Olympia, top right: Giulietta, bottom left: Antonia, bottom right: Stella.

d'Hoffmann was proposed for production at the Metropolitan in New York. The new general manager, Schuyler Chapin, who had succeeded Bing, was anxious to get the financial backing to enable his theatre to stage the work. But there were two problems to overcome; the first was to find $110,000, and the second was one of the rare occasions when Sutherland was involved in a situation of prima donna rivalry. Beverly Sills, the American soprano with a huge reputation and following in America, was soon to be making her long-awaited debut at the Met after attaining her stardom with the New York City Opera. Sills had duplicated much of Sutherland's repertoire on stage and records and it was suggested that *I Puritani* was the ideal vehicle for the debut. Chapin did not know that Sutherland had been trying to persuade Bing to produce the same opera for her over the past ten years.

233

Word got around New York singing circles about the plans and Chapin was quickly informed by Sutherland's New York manager, Anne Colbert, that if Sills got *Puritani*, the Met might lose Sutherland. When Sills heard of the situation she agreed to relinquish her claims to the Donizetti work. That was one problem solved. The next was the money for *Hoffmann*. If it could not be raised it would mean that the Metropolitan would be without Sutherland for the first time in over twelve years, and it would also have been the first season she would have missed at the Met's new home in Lincoln Center since the 3,800-seat opera house opened in September 1966. There was a good cast available, including Placido Domingo and Huguette Tourangeau. Finally, a sponsor was found and the original Seattle production, much expanded for the huge New York stage, went ahead. Sills eventually made a triumphant Metropolitan debut in an unfamiliar Rossini opera, *The Siege of Corinth*, and honour was satisfied all round. In September 1980 Sutherland and Sills sang together for the first time at San Diego, alternating in the roles of Rosalinda and Adele in Tito Capobianco's production of *Die Fledermaus*.

Rodelinda, Holland Festival 1973

Chapter Eleven

I never thought of myself as an actress. But whether I'm one or not doesn't matter. It's the feeling of electricity and atmosphere during a performance that keeps me going.

After an interval lasting nine years Sutherland and Bonynge returned to Sydney in June 1974. They managed to arrive unnoticed by the press on a Saturday and there was the opportunity of spending a quiet weekend before facing rehearsals for *The Tales of Hoffmann* in the Opera House. By now the Australian Opera had become well-established as a full-time permanent company based in Sydney but undertaking extensive tours to all the major Australian cities. The musical director was Edward Downes and there were two permanent orchestras to ease the logistics and the expense of touring — one based in Sydney and the other in Melbourne. These, managed by the Elizabethan Theatre Trust, alternated between seasons of the Opera and the Australian Ballet. Since the Opera had become an autonomous company in 1971 the repertoire had become larger and more adventurous. There were eleven productions staged in that year including *The Rape of Lucretia* by Benjamin Britten as well as standard repertoire leaning heavily on Verdi — *A Masked Ball*, *Nabucco*, *Otello* and *Trovatore*. The opening production in the Opera House during 1973 had been Prokofiev's *War and Peace* which was also shown on television to large audiences throughout Australia and Britain. In 1974 there were nineteen productions listed for performance ranging from Wagner to Verdi, Puccini, Janáček and local composers Peter Sculthorpe and Larry Sitsky, and the Opera had become a leading repertory company based on a fine chorus and a roster of experienced Australian principals

235

supplemented by guest singers and conductors. The signing of Sutherland and Bonynge was seen as a considerable coup for the company and a significant boost to its increasing prestige. It may have been a quiet weekend in Sydney for them but by Monday word had got around that La Stupenda was in town and the press greeted her in force at an informal meeting in the forecourt of the Opera House beneath the soaring white roof shells that had become a city symbol more famous than the Harbour Bridge. Other cities had bridges, many of them grander and vastly more interesting than the steel 'coathanger' spanning the narrow channel between Millers Point and Milsons Point and looking suspiciously like a copy of New York's Hell Gate Bridge, but no city had a building like the Opera House, seeming to float as if moored on the edge of the bustling blue harbour. Sutherland, wearing a brown coat with a collar of red fox fur, posed for pictures against the background of both symbols — the old and the new — as she parried questions and gave brisk answers that matched the chilly winter breeze.

As she stood before one of the most striking modern buildings in the world surrounded by the Sydney press and television, she might have mused on the twenty years of disputes, exhilaration, despair and triumph that had accompanied its birth and uneasy development. It began almost exactly twenty years before in a state of euphoric confidence when the New South Wales Labor government decided to build a cultural centre at Bennelong Point, a prime waterside site near the city centre, surrounded by the waters of the harbour on three sides. It had been used for many years as tram sheds, but after the last tram shot through to Bondi in an emotional and, some thought, premature farewell, there was much discussion about the future use to be made of the magnificent but narrow location. A building to display the city's growing cultural status was the answer. An international competition was organized for a structure to house a dual-function auditorium seating between 3,000-3,500 people and capable of presenting concerts as well as opera and 'pageants', together with another hall seating about 1,200. The complex was to be named the Sydney Opera House, in spite of the fact that its prime user would be the Sydney Symphony Orchestra which had been built up to a high standard by its conductor, Sir Eugene Goossens, one of the prime movers for a new auditorium to replace the acoustically indifferent Sydney Town Hall as the orchestra's home.

The competition attracted 223 entries from all over the world and the winner selected by the judging panel, headed by the eminent American architect, Eero Saarinen, was a little-known Dane named Joern Utzon. His entry broke most of the rules because it was barely more than a series of sketches whose proportions did not fit the site. But his concept of a unique structure surmounted by a seemingly random collection of thin concrete 'curves in space geometrically defined' was so exciting in its combination of concrete and glass that it won, invoking a mass of local comment — everything from 'poetically imaginative' to 'a vast Danish pastry'. Utzon himself called the creation, which being on a prominent peninsula site was to be seen from all sides, a sculpture. The functions of the interior working spaces were to be expressed in the size and form of the decorative roof shells faced with glazed white ceramic tiles.

With few buildings to his credit, but imbued with the spirit of contemporary architecture from personal contacts with such international giants as Le Corbusier, Frank Lloyd Wright and Mies van der Rohe, Utzon translated his sketches into plans and the plans began to become concrete reality. He saw Sydney as a dark city in spite of its frequent sunshine. There was too little white in the buildings around the waterfront to reflect the sun and dazzle the eyes as he had experienced in the Mediterranean. And so his roof shells would be brilliant in sunlight during the day and softly glowing under floodlights at night. But there was no known way of constructing such vast shapes and it would take nearly three years of computer calculations and experiment to come up with a structurally secure solution — taking segments of the same sphere to allow the orderly pre-fabrication of the concrete roof sections, although that also stiffened the profile from its previous free-form shape. All this work, on the frontiers of technology, delayed construction and forced costs to rise dramatically. The original opening date, planned for Australia Day 1963, came and went with nobody prepared to say when the structure might be completed. By the mid-1960s, when Sutherland attended her cocktail party there during the Williamson tour, there was growing friction between Utzon and the government over the delays and the mounting costs — although an Opera House lottery was paying for most of the construction. The estimated cost in

November 1965 was close to $50 million and that was already seven times the figure for the building's completion at the time of the competition. The final cost would rise to more than $100 million before the Sydney Opera House opened.

A change of government in New South Wales brought matters to a head in 1966 and while the community was taking pro-and anti-Utzon sides over 'the Opera House affair', as it was called, Utzon in sheer frustration at the political pressures being forced upon him was virtually made to resign from the project and he left Sydney with his creation a recognizable shape but with no definite plans for the interiors. In March 1966 a cable was sent to the new Minister in charge of the construction expressing the greatest concern that Utzon would not be completing his project. It was signed by many of the world's leading architects including Niemeyer of Brazil, Kenzo Tange of Japan and Gropius of the United States. It was never made public and was to no avail.

By this time the building's original function had come into question and under pressure from the Australian Broadcasting Commission, who had the interests of their Sydney Symphony Orchestra at heart, the dual-purpose hall, in which Utzon could not seat more than 2,000 people for opera, was changed to a concert hall with 2,800 capacity and the second theatre was adapted as the opera/ballet hall with seating for 1,500. This change of direction resulted in the scrapping of $3 million worth of stage machinery which had been designed and manufactured in West Germany to fit the specific dimensions of the major hall. It was virtually useless when the plans were revised and it was taken in its crates to an industrial wasteland near the Parramatta River and left to rust away as the rains rotted the cases and the weeds grew up through the steel frameworks — an expensive monument to a compromise. The large void left by the stage lifting areas was eventually utilized for a small group of theatres not in the original concept.

A team of Australian architects completed the interior designs, tackled and solved the problems of anchoring large areas of glass windows to the concrete, and accepted defeat on the proposed underground car park because of environmentalists' and unions' refusal to cut down a small group of old fig trees that would have been necessary for its construction. Eventually, the building was officially opened by Queen Elizabeth in 1973 and Utzon declined to return to Australia to see his creation. He remained as either an absent hero or the villain of Bennelong Point, depending upon one's point of view and, as a pathetic tribute to his brilliant architectural concept, a dull, featureless street of low-income housing was named after him in one of Sydney's western suburbs.

By now it was agreed that the lack of wing space in the opera theatre, the number of seats with poor sightlines and the small orchestra pit militated against the effective production of large-scale opera. Yet somehow the ingenuity of designers and producers combined to make a performance there a night to remember.

The Opera House was the main topic of discussion at Sutherland's press conference and she had made only a brief initial tour of it that morning before a *Hoffman* rehearsal.

It is quite obvious that the opera theatre is not large enough; the orchestra pit is far too small and I really don't see how we can possibly hope to fit a full orchestra into it for the season... No, it is unlikely I would ever settle in Australia; I am too European geared... Our home in Switzerland is a chalet, not a chateau... I'm getting too long in the tooth to think too much about the future.

That evening the *Sun*, with a continuing fixation about her retirement, came out with a front-page story boldly headed 'Our Joan May Quit'.

Front page of the *Sun*, Sydney

The season of eight *Hoffmann* performances had been sold out long before her arrival and it was reported that up to $500 was being offered on the open market for first-night seats which were originally sold at $30. The opening on 13 July was the success predicted by everyone and six hundred red roses flown from Holland for the occasion made a colourful climax to the evening. While they were in Sydney, Sutherland and Bonynge had discussions with the Opera's management about future plans and by the time they left in August, the chairman announced that they would be returning as guests in 1976, 1977 and 1978. A new pattern of life was being established by them with an axis of activity based more on the Pacific than the trans-Atlantic region.

Over the years Vancouver had been one of their regular places of performance and now that association, extending back sixteen years in Sutherland's case, was formalized when Bonynge was made artistic director of the Vancouver Opera Association for three years from July 1974. He had already conducted five works for them — *Faust*, *The Marriage of Figaro*, *Norma*, *Lucia* and *Lucrezia Borgia* — and two had been debut performances for Sutherland which they later took to other opera houses. Bonynge had plans for repertory seasons in the fall and the spring although, because of previous commitments, Sutherland would not be appearing there until the 1975-76 season. Bonynge's challenge in Vancouver was considerable, but certainly no greater than the assembling of an entire touring company that he had supervised for the 1965 Sutherland-Williamson season in Australia. Vancouver, however, had no permanent orchestra or singers, and they needed to be brought together for the two seasons each year and then disbanded again. He soon discovered that money was short, suggested a private fund-raising campaign and quoted the example of the Australian Opera which was underpinned by Federal government subsidies as well as private sponsorship. 'I come from a country', he said, 'where the government finances opera for the whole year'. A secondary challenge was the Board of Directors in Vancouver, described by Bonynge as 'charming people who don't like change very much'.

Meanwhile, Sutherland's remark about Bonynge becoming 'a French opera nut' was manifested in the production of Massenet's *Esclarmonde*, one of the lesser-known of his twenty-seven operatic works. Its premiere with Sutherland in the title role was in San

Chalet Monet

The village of Les Avants

Northern hemisphere gardening

Vevey market in Switzerland

Domestic duties in the kitchen at Chalet Monet

Francisco during October, in the same state in which the originator of the role was born. Sybil Sanderson, a soprano, charmed Massenet, who wrote *Esclarmonde* and *Thaïs* for her with high Gs in the score for the vocal fireworks she was particularly good at. She died in Paris at the early age of thirty-seven. When the Metropolitan saw Sutherland in the role the *Herald-Tribune* writer Herbert Breslin wrote,

Miss Sutherland is the supreme soprano of this century. She may be the greatest soprano of any century but we have no way of judging. We do know that she is the only person in the world who can sing *Esclarmonde*. It is a fiendishly difficult part that demands a combination of every vocal skill. Only Sutherland can do it. She is the phenomenon for whom this opera was revived.

It was a relatively short-lived revival on stage after thirteen performances at the Met, but the complete recording of the work released in 1976 is a permanent record of a great vocal performance.

On Christmas Day 1974 the northern city of Darwin in the Australian tropics was almost flattened by a cyclone named Tracey that swept in from the Arafura Sea and completely shut down the city, killed dozens of its inhabitants and generated the biggest human airlift ever seen in Australia. Relief poured in from many sources including a hastily organized midnight gala at Covent Garden on 25 January 1975 which was arranged by Sutherland and Bonynge and their friends. All proceeds went to the Darwin Fund, including royalties from a recording of the concert and the television coverage.

Record sleeve for Darwin benefit concert, London 1975

241

In January 1975 Sutherland received recognition in an unexpected way with the issue of a set of stamps by the Central American republic of Nicaragua. It was titled 'Fifteen Greatest Opera Singers of Our Time' and the opera stars depicted had been selected by forty-eight international experts and critics whose votes seemed to be reflected in the face value of the stamps. On that basis, Caruso came out on top, with Chaliapin second and Callas third. Sutherland came down the list in order of value, dressed as *The Daughter of the Regiment*, between Ezio Pinza and Giuseppe de Luca. Others represented were Melba, Lauritz Melchior, Rosa Ponselle, Kirsten Flagstad, Lotte Lehmann, Birgit Nilsson, Giovanni Martinelli, Tito Gobbi and Jussi Björling.

Il Trovatore, San Francisco 1975, with Luciano Pavarotti

Another honorary degree was added to her tally in 1975 — a doctorate of music from the University of Liverpool in England — and then in mid-year it was announced that Sutherland had received the highest award in the new Australian system designed by the federal Labor Government to replace the British honours that had traditionally been announced twice a year, at the beginning of January and again at Queen's Birthday in June. She was made a Companion of the Order of Australia (AC), together with the Nobel Prize author Patrick White, for 'eminent achievement and merit of the highest degree in service to Australia or to humanity at large'. The system was not a great popular success as only the two Australian states with Labor governments adopted the scheme. The other four continued to recommend their honours direct to Buckingham Palace.

Sutherland was always being invited to appear at special functions and to take part in a wide variety of events wherever she happened to be. In 1975 she was asked to be a judge in the Miss Nude America contest in Chicago, joining the nightclub comedian George Jessel on the panel. Along with most of the other invitations it was politely turned down.

In spite of previous protestations to the press about returning to Australia to live, the Bonynges now intended to spend more time back home. In 1976 he was appointed musical director of the Australian Opera. Being based in Sydney, this position enabled them to relocate part of their operatic work to a place where they enjoyed living for some of the year. The disadvantages were the need for Sutherland to make two or three long flights from Europe or America each year and Bonynge several more. But she admitted that the home-town pull was considerable,

As I grow older I'm becoming more and more partisan. I think Sydney has the most wonderful harbour in the world and it's one of the most beautiful cities, if not for me *the* most beautiful. Every time we come back we're flabbergasted at how beautiful it is. Richard and I are absolutely enchanted by it all and we spend what time we can just looking at it.

This they could do at any time of day or night from the apartment they acquired in 1976, situated at Potts Point, on the edge of bustling Kings Cross, but far enough from its curious mixture of cosmopolitan sleaziness and hubbub to be quiet and free from interference. It overlooks the Garden Island naval dockyard and looks across Double Bay to Point Piper, where Sutherland was born. It is uncommon enough for artists of their calibre to be able to spend much time in their birthplace — even rarer to have the opportunity to carry on a professional career. 'I come back after spending so much time away and feel as if I never left', Sutherland says. 'It is very gratifying to be able to come back and work in the same fashion as we do elsewhere in the world — except that here we have the added advantage of being surrounded by familiar places, faces and family as well.' Bonynge echoes his wife's sentiments, 'We've had our careers for many years abroad and it's wonderful to come back to our own country where we have a very good opera company. I like to live in Australia. I love the climate, I like the people and I feel very much at home here.'

The apartment is a group of rambling rooms on the top storey of a building constructed down a steep hillside. It was built in the 1920s when Sydney was going through a phase of Californian Spanish decoration which, together with a local version of Art Deco, can be seen all around the area in houses and blocks of flats, adapting much better to the Mediterranean-type climate of the city than many of the later buildings from the 1930s using dark bricks and capped by red tiled roofs. Each apartment covers an entire floor with car parking on the roof, which is the street level. An elegant cage-type elevator is used either for surfacing or going down to one's apartment. Inside, the Bonynge style is immediately evident with a spacious, but dark, hallway dominated by a large portrait of the young Nellie Melba which he discovered and bought in London many years ago. The walls are crowded with paintings — including a fine Sidney Nolan — theatre prints, photographs and portraits of Sutherland, which in total would amount to visual chaos, if not displayed with such an obvious touch of theatrical flair. The furniture is dark wood and comfortable, the draperies rich greens and reds and outside, through the windows, is the ever-changing panorama of Sydney Harbour. This would be too mannered, too stylish if it were not for the workaday touches of a baby grand piano stacked untidily with scores, a top quality high-fidelity system and the latest video-cassette equipment used for playback of their television performances.

The return visits to Australia mean that the Sydney Opera House now sees more stagings of operas with Sutherland than any other single venue in the world. After *Hoffmann* in 1974, she sang

Left: *I Puritani*, New York 1976, with Luciano Pavarotti
Right: *Suor Angelica*, Sydney 1977

Lakmé in 1976, *Lucrezia Borgia* in 1977 together with a debut in *Suor Angelica*, *Norma* in 1978, her debut as Elettra in Mozart's *Idomeneo* in 1979 together with *La Traviata* and another debut in 1980, Verdi's *I Masnadieri*. These, together with summer seasons of *The Merry Widow* and *Lucia* in the converted Concert Hall, have made Sutherland seasons in Sydney as regular as those in London and New York in the 1960s.

In November 1976 she turned fifty and wasn't at all worried by it. 'I was dreading it', she admitted, 'but fifty turned out to be a terrific age. All the beastly hurdles one has to overcome in youth are behind me. I've had a splendid career and I would not mind settling down to grow a few roses.' There seemed little prospect of that with engagements stretching ahead for the next few years and the voice as good as ever. 'Actually, I'm slowing down a bit', she confessed, 'I need my glasses for reading and needlework and I wouldn't dare open a telephone book without them.' Sutherland claimed that she continued to be unconcerned about critical opinion of her performances, 'At fifty I can only do my best and reading reviews isn't going to make me a greater or lesser singer.' And she promptly went back to work.

245

'I don't think the public realizes the amount of work that goes into the preparation of a new production', Sutherland says. 'It is usually mooted for a couple of years and casting, designs for costumes and sets have to be submitted a long time in advance. Models have to be made of the stage sets to see how workable they are — and very often something doesn't work, so they have to be redesigned.' She has an interest in all facets of a production and, although the preparation of her own role is always uppermost in her mind, she retains an interest in the activity that goes on around her.

Sometimes the costumes turn out to be too expensive and so eliminations and changes have to be made. It all takes an infinite amount of time and patience behind the scenes. Then there's the musical preparation of the orchestra and the singers — slogging away in a production room getting all the loose ends tied together. I think the audience feels sometimes that the singer knows the opera, whether it be *Traviata* or *Norma* or *Lucia*, and just comes on and sings it her way. But it's not like that because you do *Norma* with a producer in England, with a different producer in the United States, again in Holland and Australia — and each of them has a different idea of how it should be realized. You often find that for a particular scene, the last producer had you downstage right and then the new one wants you upstage left. I find when I'm repeating operas, stage directions get put into a mental pigeonhole and sometimes I take the production from another pigeonhole and get completely mixed up. And so it needs rehearsing and rehearsing and that way you find out all sorts of new things about a role you've been doing for maybe fifteen years.

In 1978 Sutherland played *Norma* in Sydney and Sandro Sequi, who had directed her at Covent Garden eleven years before, was again her producer. 'I think *Norma* is the greatest role I try to portray', she says, 'I adore the character and the music and it is such a challenge — both musically and mentally. The great thing is when it gets all together and is up there on the stage with costumes and orchestra for the final dress rehearsal. That's the culmination of everything so many of us have striven for over such a long time.'

Sutherland's professional quality is most obvious at this point. After so many years in the business and countless performances, she is completely in command on stage often giving a 'big' performance at the dress rehearsal when other divas prefer to save their voices for opening night. In Sydney the final dress rehearsal is sometimes ticketed for the Friends of the Opera and that tends to ensure a full performance from her. If there are stops and starts for technical or artistic reasons she often breaks the tension and fatigue of the moment with laughter. Sutherland usually doesn't 'mark' her role at rehearsal because she needs to prove to herself that she knows the part well enough by singing to full capacity. Bonynge knows she is confident when she saves her voice — as with the new *Lucia* in Sydney in 1980. At one of the dress rehearsals for *Norma* she was handed by the High Priest the ceremonial sword to cut the stage mistletoe. The real sword was not ready and they used a small and unimpressive toy dagger in its place. She brought the house down with an un-Bellini-like recitative which went, 'What on earth do you expect me to do with this? It wouldn't even cut a piece of string let alone make any impression on the damned mistletoe!' She was hastily assured by the designer that a more effective implement would be available for the opening night. 'I should think so!', she exclaimed. Her innate sense of fun was also in evidence during the duets with mezzo Margreta Elkins singing Adalgisa — or 'Analgesia' as they referred to her. A complete absence of pain was evident as they sang the music they had performed together so many times before, while eyeing each other, attempting a send up and almost breaking out into laughter. During costume fittings Sutherland's sense of the ridiculous came to the fore, querying whether she'd trip on the hem of her gown during the first entrance and suggesting that the appliquéd buckles on her shoes would be sure to fall off. 'Bet they do', she told the designer. But they didn't.

It is indicative of Sutherland's desire to be 'one of the team' that very few special privileges are sought by her. The seasons of the Australian Opera are played in repertory and the leading sopranos use the same modest dressing-room whose only claim to fame is that it is closest to the stage entrance. During rehearsal days Sutherland can often be seen in the canteen sitting having a cup of tea with members of the cast and during actual performances she reads her mail in the dressing-room and sometimes continues her needlepoint while waiting for calls. On the opening night of *Lakmé* in 1976, a stop-work meeting delayed the start of the first night in front of a dressy Sydney audience. The musicians were protesting at a decision to dismiss twenty-four players from the Sydney and Melbourne orchestras because of budget cuts. The VIPs wandered out into the foyers to have a drink and Sutherland stayed in her dressing-room reading a book until the musicians went back to work and the performance started forty minutes late.

In August 1977 the *Sydney Morning Herald* quoted a 'New York magazine' which had recently announced that 'Joan Sutherland, the great Australian coloratura can no longer reach high F'. Bonynge replied to the *Herald*, 'Indeed she can't, but she's only ever hit it occasionally *in rage*'. He added that the Queen of the Night in Mozart's *The Magic Flute* was one of the few roles where there is a need for such a high note.

When Maria Callas died in September 1977, Sutherland was in Vancouver and she commented in memory, 'She gave me the inspiration to join her at the beginning of my career and she never failed to encourage what I tried to do'. Callas's career had been in eclipse for the past decade and her passing caused no sudden performance gap; instead there was the realization that her absence had left a silence. Sutherland and Callas had met only briefly during the past twenty years but they were constantly linked by the press for comparative judgement and Sutherland knew and understood the pressures that could build up in a prima donna's career leading, with Callas, to the renouncing of so many modest things before she finally and unexpectedly renounced life in her Paris apartment. In 1958, the year before she visited Sutherland's dress rehearsal of *Lucia*, Callas had stated while at the height of her fame, 'I am only a woman and I am only an artist. I am not a voice alone — I cannot give the public an athlete's way of displaying vocal muscle.' Being a myth was a hard role for anybody to play constantly. 'I really feel that I am wasting my energy, wasting my life just for the sake of celebrity', she admitted. Because of the immense publicity surrounding her life, Callas held the popular image of prima donna — glamorous, demanding, enjoying the social whirl that surrounded her. But behind that apparently confident facade was a lonely woman with little private life and few personal satisfactions. In 1965, still in her early forties, she retired from the operatic stage realizing that she couldn't continue to play the living legend much longer. 'The voice is not what it was twenty years ago', she admitted, 'nor does it pretend that. It's natural; the audience knows it, I know it. But you can be more than you were twenty years ago — you can be a better musician, more passionate.' Sutherland had the same pressures thrust upon her during her career but for a number of reasons she was able to avoid succumbing to most of them. Not least, was the basis of a continuing happy professional and

domestic partnership with Bonynge and the satisfaction of a child
— things that were absent from Callas's life of professional fame
and personal anguish, so that at her death her friend and colleague Franco Zeffirelli described her as 'literally the most chaste
person I ever met'. Sutherland was often asked about her impressions of Callas, but there was little she could add to what was
already known. 'I was supposed to have tea with her a few years
ago', she remembered some years before Callas's death, 'but it was
at the time her marriage was breaking up. She sent me a pathetic
little note explaining why she couldn't make it, and we haven't
had tea yet. We have friendly relations, but we are not great
friends.'

It was difficult to get beneath the veneer that Callas had
acquired since her first major role in *La Gioconda* at the Verona
Arena under Serafin in 1947 to a nervous come-back concert tour
with Giuseppe di Stefano in 1973, but the face of opera in the
second half of the twentieth century was changed because of her.
Endowed with a voice that was not one of the loveliest in the world,
and a shortsightedness that stopped her from being able to see the
conductor during a performance, she was, however, blessed with
a great musical and dramatic talent that kindled a new public
interest in the works of bel canto. Her great range of style and
technique encompassing everything from Wagner to Donizetti led
to immense acclaim and an acceptance of hitherto forgotten
works by Rossini, Donizetti, Bellini and Cherubini. Her finest
roles were perhaps *Medea*, *Norma* and Violetta in *La Traviata*,
but her greatest monument is the wide public acceptance of a
repertoire that she opened up, allowing many of the great singers
who followed her, including Sutherland, to explore and present
many operas from the whole sweep of the nineteenth century that
otherwise might have remained gathering dust in museums and
archives.

In December 1977 Britain was coming to the end of a year of
celebrating the silver jubilee of Queen Elizabeth's accession to the
throne. At that time the newspapers were noting another jubilee
— Sutherland's twenty-five years at Covent Garden to be marked
by new production of *Maria Stuarda*. Few people had taken much
notice of the large, slightly awkward singer who played the small
part of First Lady in *The Magic Flute* on 28 October 1952, but the
season of *Maria Stuarda* was fully-booked out long before the

actual performances. Sutherland suggested that her days of entering a new repertoire were probably over and that there were some roles she would definitely like to drop — such as Amina in *La Sonnambula* and Gilda in *Rigoletto*.

I feel a bit long in the tooth for some roles. Yet Lucia is something else. So many places still haven't seen it and people insist that I do it. And I think I can still get away with it because I don't think my style of singing is going to radically change. The voice becomes a little heavier, not quite as thin, not quite as filigree as it was. There's nothing I can do about that. Age is going to take off maybe some of the height. The middle of the voice has always been rather soft-grained. The placing has to be handled carefully, even at this stage. I never stop being conscious of technique.

Bonynge agrees with this but considers the middle voice to have become richer with maturity.

A concert was given at Covent Garden in late November 1978 by the Australian Musical Foundation in London at which Sutherland was the principal singer and she and Bonynge gave their services free. It was attended by Prince Charles who joked afterwards with Sutherland and Barry Humphries who turned up for the evening in his Dame Edna Everage outfit of green silk chiffon, pearls, diamond-framed spectacles and a tiara. The concert raised a considerable amount of money for its cause but was criticized both in Britain and Australia for the high cost of seats. Most of the time Sutherland and Bonynge were able to ignore press comments but this was too much and he was moved to reply.

We don't like to appear paranoid but the media have been giving us a hard time lately. Like the reporters who claim the prices we charge for our concerts are out of sight. What most don't mention is that many of these events are for charity, like the $85 top tickets in London in which all proceeds went to the Australian Musical Foundation.

At the concert Sutherland sang '*Casta Diva*' and the first-act duet from *Lucia*, 'Vilja' from *The Merry Widow* and Ophelia's mad scene from Thomas's *Hamlet*. Finally there was the sextet from *Lucia*. Barry Humphries as Dame Edna threatened to upstage everyone, but the evening was triumphantly Sutherland's in spite of an impeccable reading by the Australian-born guitarist John Williams of a Rodrigo concerto. The London critics commented on Sutherland's voice and most found it to be as impres-

Opposite: *Maria Stuarda*, Covent Garden 1977

251

With Prince Charles, Covent Garden 1978

sive as ever. Edward Greenfield in the *Guardian* wrote that it 'remains as rich and glowing as ever', and Alan Blyth in the *Daily Telegraph* stated, 'The passing years hardly marked her full, round tone or the surety of her line and technique'. William Mann in *The Times* thought that she started 'a shade throaty in her lower register as if England's cold snap had caught her in the chest coming from Australia's summer'. By the *Hamlet* mad scene, however, he noted 'radiant tones, marvellous agility and phrasing to melt the heart'.

Sutherland seemed to make news almost by default, so that what she considered to be routine matters such as future repertoire, sometimes got distorted beyond all recognition. An example of this occurred in 1978. The Metropolitan asked her to sing Constanze in Mozart's *Il Seraglio* for their 1978-79 season. She had never performed the role on stage, although many years before she had auditioned for it at Glyndebourne and they had told her she was too big for the part. Subsequently she recorded the aria '*Martern aller Arten*'. She and Bonynge began preparations for the role, including extensive work at the piano, in Sydney during 1978. 'Richard and I went over it for weeks and weeks until I discovered I should have done it fifteen years previously. The music for Constanze doesn't go above a high D, but it lies much higher than *Lucia*.' Sutherland could have made all the notes and

252

Bonynge had no doubt about her ability and stamina to succeed but she knew her voice was heavier now and the role might lead to some forcing, which she had never done before. 'I finally decided I didn't want to stand on the Met stage with my reputation and appear uncomfortable. So I respectfully turned down the part.' Sutherland had not asked for the Mozart role in the first place and she was giving plenty of notice for any change of plans. The Met countered with the information that if there was to be no *Seraglio* then they wouldn't consider producing *The Merry Widow*, tentatively scheduled for the following year. There was also some confusion about the prospects of a possible *Semiramide* with Marilyn Horne. 'I didn't know the Met considered I had a package deal to do both the Widow and Constanze', said Sutherland, 'that would be quite a package indeed!' This behind-the-scenes manoeuvring was picked up by the New York press and the story was represented as a full-scale conflict between the Bonynges and the Metropolitan Opera House. Sutherland was prompted to admit, 'I love singing there but now, for the first time, they have hurt me. *The Widow* was a promise, and since I die at the end of so many operas it would have been so much fun to do this.' One Sydney newspaper came out with a prominent front-page story which screamed 'Our Joan Sacked' and everyone knew that the mysterious, eruptive world of opera in-fighting was active once again. The result of the events was that Bonynge continued to conduct at the Met in his own right, including Massenet's *Werther* on three successive visits. *Seraglio* was staged there with Edda Moser singing Constanze in October 1979 to little effect, and Sutherland commented, 'This kind of thing happens in opera all the time. I am definitely going back there to sing Donizetti's *Lucia* in 1982 and *Daughter of the Regiment* in 1983 — a fairly old daughter by then!' Bonynge estimates that the two leading singers in that production — Sutherland and Alfredo Kraus — will have a combined age of 112 years.

While news of the wrangle with the Met was still simmering, Sutherland and Bonynge were in New York for a new venture, a concert in Lincoln Center's Avery Fisher Hall with Luciano Pavarotti. Since the 1960s they had sung together on stage in Britain, America and Australia, but more recently their careers had gone separate ways as Pavarotti's fame rose to equal Sutherland's. Fortunately they were both contracted exclusively by

Donna Anna in *Don Giovanni*, New York 1978

Decca/London for recording and by the time they appeared at Avery Fisher Hall, they had participated in eight recorded operas together, the Verdi *Requiem*, and a joint recital disc that became a classical best-seller. The New York concert in January 1979 was planned for television as well as being a public concert — although there was little that was fancy about it as a television show. The cameras for the live transmission on the PBS network dwelled on the two singers — Pavarotti formally dressed, holding a white handkerchief, Sutherland in a variegated green gown — with occasional shots of the orchestra behind and the audience in front. The simplicity of treatment added to the effect because the excitement of the occasion was captured far better than in a complete opera where the sense of scale and projection is often ineffectively conveyed on television. The cost of the production was underwritten by the oil giant Exxon. Sutherland relaxed as the long evening progressed, overcoming her natural reticence to performing on television — for although it was essentially a public concert, the extra lighting needed for the cameras turned it into a two-and-a-half hour video marathon. The evening began with a duet from *La Traviata* and progressed by way of Verdi, Massenet,

254

With Luciano Pavarotti, New York press conference 1978

Thomas, Ponchielli, Balfe, Meyerbeer, Bellini and Giordano, to end with a duet from *Lucia*. 'This is what Italian opera is all about', wrote Harold C. Schonberg in the *New York Times* the next day, 'a maximum of words coupled to musical taste, and it is given to very few singers of any generation to have it. There have been reports that an official of the Metropolitan Opera has said that the house could very well do without stars of the Sutherland/Pavarotti type. If that is a true statement, the man who said it is out of his ever-loving mind.' The success of this presentation and its nomination for a 1979 Emmy award — the highest accolade of the American television industry — led to a similar concert with Sutherland and Marilyn Horne at Avery Fisher Hall the following October and discussions about a future Sutherland/Pavarotti/Horne recital.

In spite of cheers in New York, in Vancouver Bonynge's position of artistic director of the Opera Association was showing signs of severe strain. The executive director, Barry Thompson, the husband of the mezzo Huguette Tourangeau, had left the company in early 1978. Bonynge agreed to remain as consulting artistic director until the end of his contract in June 1980 but he saw his contributions as being minimal. In December 1977 the Association announced a deficit of $225,000 and the Board scrapped Bonynge's planned productions in favour of three popular low-budget operas spread over a performing period of eight months. Thompson had wanted to cast as many Canadians in as many roles as possible, but to Bonynge it was a matter of standards rather than nationality. Sutherland's first production with Bonynge as musical director generated some of the worst press reviews of her career for *The Merry Widow*. They were mostly on the theme that it was a terrible waste of talent to have her perform such trivial music.

The music critic of the *Vancouver Sun* on 23 April 1976 stated, 'Sutherland turning her talents to *The Merry Widow* is the vocal equivalent of Charles Atlas attending to the problems of opening a new jar of pickles. And to speculate as to how her voice is weathering on the basis of the singing she is required to do in the role would be to judge the contents of a jewel box after looking at its exterior.'

Whatever the critical reception, *The Merry Widow* brought Bonynge's first season in Vancouver to a close with a complete sell-out for all eleven performances of Lehár's work. The production costs were high, but so were seat prices. Some critics maintained that Bonynge's predilection for expensive productions of little-known operas such as Massenet's *Le Roi de Lahore* had been the main reason for the deficit, but the Association was working on quite small budgets for first-rate productions with a limited government subsidy — for the 1977 season the Canada Council grant was a modest $168,000. Bonynge could rightly claim that he and Sutherland had put Vancouver on the operatic map with first productions in Canada of *Semiramide*, *Mignon*, *Ballo in Maschera* among others but, as often happens in provincial cultures, the forces of pragmatism are rarely satisfied with the cost of such recognition and so their association with the city was severed. Bonynge left, having completed casting for the 1978-79 season, but was unable to be in Vancouver for the productions. He says he was lured by promises but little money, so that a relatively modest production cost of $75,000 for *Le Roi de Lahore* was considered as 'breaking the bank'.

The honours continued to pour upon them — both academic and national. Bonynge had been awarded the C.B.E. in 1977 and

Rehearsal in the Music Room at Les Avants

Curtain call of *Lucia*, Sydney 1980

in the Queen's New Year Honours for 1979 Sutherland was finally made a Dame. In terms of protocol it is a lesser rank than the Companion of the Order of Australia she received in 1975 but in international recognition it holds immensely more prestige. In an editorial under the heading 'Dame Joan', the *Australian* stated, 'Perhaps the best news for Australia in the New Year honours is that soprano Joan Sutherland — La Stupenda — has become the third famous Australian singer to be made a Dame of the British Empire'. Melba was the first; Joan Hammond the second, although she was, in fact, born in Christchurch, New Zealand. The editorial added, 'Yet in spite of her international stardom Dame Joan has taken great pains to avoid becoming one of those celebrities Australians have to travel abroad to see. And this in spite of the sometimes quite extraordinary — and unjustified — personal criticism her performances and contracts have drawn.' It was the same newspaper that in the next few months would publish considerable speculation about Sutherland's association with the Australian Opera and Bonynge's role in the disputes that were simmering behind the scenes and threatening to injure reputations and standards. In a weekly arts gossip column headed 'Marietta' there were regular reports of an artistic power struggle. Marietta tended to criticize Bonynge, and at the same time dwelt on the date of Sutherland's retirement and the size of her fees.

Most of the problems were rooted in power play within the Opera's twenty-person Board which is made up principally of businessmen and society women, enjoying the glamour and status that guiding the affairs of a large opera company can bestow. Nowhere in the world is opera a smoothly-running enterprise unsullied by frictions and jealousies. There are too many egos at play to allow for tranquillity. Several leading houses have, however, with a strong and able chief executive such as Bing at the Metropolitan, Webster at Covent Garden and Adler in San Francisco, kept most of their internecine squabbles out of the limelight. The Australian Opera, funded each year by more than $3 million of federal and state subsidies, could look back on a dismal record of administration with a turnover of six general managers in eleven years, reflecting a general rapid turnover of executives in Australian arts administration. The person who looked as if he might end this transience was Peter Hemmings, a former general administrator of the Scottish Opera for fifteen years, who was appointed to the Australian Opera in late 1977. But soon after taking up his post rumours and speculation began to circulate about disagreements on repertoire with his musical director, Richard Bonynge, although the relationship between the two men was, away from the newspaper reports, civilized to the point where Hemmings had been a guest at Chalet Monet to discuss future repertoire. Certainly Bonynge's desire to stage his favourite operas for Sutherland was well-known and, although there was continuing unfounded comment about obscure repertoire, the economic facts of the matter were that she could attract sell-out audiences to every performance whatever role she was singing, and critics had to admit that many works now considered standard repertoire would have remained unperformed were it not for the promotion of them by singers such as Callas, Sills and Sutherland herself.

It was also known that Hemmings was championing Wagner's *Ring* cycle for performance in Sydney during 1980. Bonynge thought it sheer madness to consider such an undertaking in the limiting venue of the Sydney Opera House and with so much money needed to finance it. They disagreed about that and many other points of repertoire. Hemmings had suggested at one stage that Sutherland might sing the title role in Britten's *Gloriana* and the lead in Janáček's *The Makropoulos Case* — both roles for an ageing woman. She politely but emphatically declined. The chairman of the Board admitted that the relationship between Hemmings and Bonynge lacked a spirit of co-operation and it was reported that both men were prepared to resign at one stage, but then a repertoire committee with powers of veto was appointed and the disagreement was patched up. Sutherland then found herself singing the short but difficult role of Elettra in Mozart's *Idomeneo* with more time off the stage than on. 'Oh well', she sighed, 'I'll be able to sit in my dressing-room and get a lot more needlepoint done.'

The polarization into either Bonynge or Hemmings camps threatened to harm the reputation of the Company and also to cloud the real seat of the problem, the functioning of the Board as if it were an exclusive club instead of a multi-million dollar business with 60 per cent of its operating revenue coming from ticket sales. In August 1979 the Board decided that Hemmings would not be offered an extension of his three-year contract when it expired in September 1980 and he began, not surprisingly, to think about his future. At that time, the Victorian Ministry for the Arts and the Victorian State Opera were considering the formation of a national company based in Melbourne in an attempt to break the Sydney-based monopoly of subsidies. Hemmings was invited to discuss the possibility of becoming a consultant to advise on the establishing of the company to perform in the new 2,000-seat state theatre due to open in 1982. The Australian Opera Board heard of this and considered his action to be in breach of contract and decided tq terminate the appointment there and then. In October 1979 Hemmings left Sydney for the United States and Britain to consider other job offers and the Australian Opera faced the task of appointing its eighth general manager in thirteen years. The chairman announced that Hemmings proposed to stay out of Australia for three years in return for a portion of his severance money. The federal Minister for Home Affairs stated that no subsidies would be taken away from the Australian Opera to finance a rival Melbourne company, Peter Hemmings landed the job as manager of the London Symphony Orchestra, and Sutherland wished him every success in his new position in his own country. It was rather like the last act of one of the Opera's own productions with confusion and calumny running riot. Hemmings and six previous general managers were gone, Sutherland and Bonynge remained, but they were unhappy about a situation that intruded into their desire to perform to the best of their abilities in their home country and spend as much time as possible enjoying the pleasures of Australian life.

Whatever the full facts of the case — and one cannot know Hemmings's side of the story because his contract prevented comment on any matters concerning his position during or after his term of engagement — the Australian Opera continued to see Sutherland as its main drawcard. In its press advertising for the 1980 Sydney season, a drawing of her as *Lucia* stood beside the headline, 'It's Sheer Madness Not To Subscribe' and the explanation,

If you don't subscribe to our magnificent 1980 season, you stand an excellent chance of missing one of the great operatic experiences of the century — Joan Sutherland as Lucia di Lammermoor. We know you'll be enthralled — the Sydney Opera House Concert Hall transformed into the gloomy Scottish castle of Lammermoor — and a passionate, outpouring of golden sound from beginning to end, culminating in the famous Mad Scene, one of the great theatre experiences of all time.

Chapter Twelve

Maybe one day we'll uproot ourselves completely from Europe and live in Australia. I don't know. It remains to be seen how long I keep on performing and how many calls are made on our services in Europe and America.

The Pacific Ocean's deep blue swells, unimpeded by thousands of miles of travel, come rolling onto the glistening brown rocks of a beachside community just north of Sydney and break in a froth of dazzling white. The seagulls wheel overhead and warm, humid, northerly winds alternate with cooler southerlies throughout the year. In summer the residents, both permanent and temporary, are imbued with a primal sense of well-being and in winter the days are often clear and dry with a chill in the air whose briskness gives a sharper edge to personal awareness.

The Bonynges' beach house started out to be an occasional escape from the city and Potts Point while they were performing at the Opera House. In 1978 they found and bought a neglected cottage on one of the fashionable beaches about twenty miles and forty minutes drive from the heart of the city. It had been used as a weekender and little care and attention had come its way over the past decade, but the block of land was outstanding, extending from the road in stepped ledges to a cliff edge where the Pacific is ever restless. The position was ideal because it couldn't be built out, there was a fine sandy surf beach nearby and the views of a distant headland and the broad expanse of ocean extended for a panoramic 180 degrees from each room. Sutherland says, 'We bought our little house as a getaway for the weekends. It started off as just that and the more we saw the place, the more we actually wanted to live in it.' Over the period of a year builders renovated the house, extending the exterior spaces, constructing a large stone open fireplace and adding balconies to the upper floors and a terrace for the lower level. A large swimming pool was installed and the whole complex in its dazzling Mediterranean white and bright blue gives the impression of a much larger house than the three bedrooms and open-plan sitting area behind its expansive facade. 'Very few people know how to get to us', Sutherland says, 'they don't know how to reach us by telephone and we can go to and from the house quite privately. It gives us an immense pleasure being there because the views are spectacular, it has a lovely garden and a nice pool.'

What started out as an escape begins to look like something much more permanent, but for various reasons — not least the necessity to retain Switzerland as their place of residence for business purposes — Sutherland and Bonynge are non-committal about their future plans. Adam, however, decided to live in Australia to continue his career in hotel management. His mother says only, 'While we are working with the Australian Opera it is great to have a home of our own here'. There is no doubt about the delight provided by their latest acquisition. It is not unusual for them to fly direct from Europe or America to Australia, arriving early on the morning of one day, resting overnight at the Potts Point apartment, and then driving to the beach house to spend four or five hours beside the ocean before returning to the city to work with the Opera for the rest of the week.

To most Australians, for whom leisure is an essential part of life and the weekends sacred, these fleeting visits might appear to be eccentric. But quick changes of scene for a few hours of intense enjoyment are indicative of the life they have led since 1959. So much of the time is taken up with preparations for performances and moving on, that these moments away from aircraft seats, recording studios and opera houses give a heightened sense of pleasure. Sutherland has sewn most of the curtains herself, Bonynge has transferred shelves of books and some prints from Switzerland and Potts Point to adorn the walls, and Chester with his flair for organization has established an efficient kitchen in quick time for the house that is now named after their first home in Switzerland.

Sutherland says,

261

I think it's very exciting to come back after all those years abroad when there was very little happening on the local scene in opera and to find a really going organization like the Australian Opera. I think it is one of the last remaining repertory companies in the world and certainly it is amazing the number of performances a year that they do. I don't think people abroad realize the standard of the performances that the company gives — and it's wonderful that such an organization has come out of these early days around the time that both Richard and I left the country.

Sutherland has gradually moved back into Australian life, not only domestically and professionally, but also in accepting social and official engagements that previously she tended to turn down.

Return visit to St Catherine's School, Sydney 1979

There have been visits to her old school, the opening of a music festival in one of the southern Sydney municipalities called 'Sutherland', accepting academic invitations and fund-raising functions for the Opera. In fact, Sutherland-as-celebrity occasions occur most frequently now in her home town. Earlier, when she was performing in one place for a length of time, such as London or New York, the demands for public appearances were very much greater and, although always reluctant to face an audience away from actual performance, when she did, there was frequently displayed the ability to put people at ease, to make them laugh and to deflate any feeling of formality. She cannot explain

262

this herself, but it has something to do with her forthrightness combined with a delightfully old-fashioned approach in speech and manners. She gives the faint impression of someone from a time just passed — perhaps of Australia in the 1940s when life was based more solidly on family relationships, people were more resourceful and speech patterns were different. All of this tinged with a sense of propriety and mixed with a touch of Australian larrikinism was taken away intact when she left Sydney in 1951 and, while things changed quite rapidly back home, Sutherland retained these characteristics of another time and place. 'A woman's place is in the home and I have no patience with women's libbers. I'd like to live in just one place and do lots of normal things like cooking and gardening', is how she explains her personal position.

One of her extra-opera activities was accepting the invitation to take part in a seminar on Italian Opera as part of the degree course in the Italian Department of the new University of Wollongong. On a fine winter's day Sutherland travelled the fifty kilometres of tollway and freeway south of Sydney to reach the steel city on the New South Wales south coast, fronted by the blue Pacific and backed by dark green hills. She had last visited the city thirty years before but there was no chance this time of her arriving in anonymity. Looking every inch the prima donna in a navy blue dress on which was pinned a dazzling diamond brooch in which the stones make up the name *La Sonambula* — spelt with one 'n' — surmounted by a small official crest. It had originally been presented by the royal Spanish court to Emma Nevada, the American singer of the 1880s and 1890s, when she sang the role in Madrid. It was given to Sutherland by another singer and a pupil of Nevada, Louise Loring, a former diva of the Chicago Lyric Opera. She lives close to the Bonynges at Vevey in Switzerland and presented Sutherland with the treasure at a dinner party.

After a tour of the local sights and afternoon tea with the Lord Mayor it was back to the University to face an audience of 300. Sutherland was quick to point out that, being unfamiliar with such things, she was in no position to deliver a formal address about Italian opera. She admitted that it was, indeed, a subject dear to her heart, but preferred to let her husband, who was the expert and not present, talk about it. She suggested that a question-and-answer session with the audience might be the most

263

rewarding way of handling the occasion and the subsequent proceedings gave a rare insight into her thoughts about her profession.

A staff member suggested to her that Anglo-Saxon countries were often suspicious of opera, soliciting the reply, 'Well, I'm pure Anglo-Saxon and I was never suspicious'. Reference was made to Lord Chesterfield's statement in the eighteenth century describing the medium as 'essentially too absurd to mention' and Dr Johnson's description of opera as 'an exotic and irrational entertainment'. Sutherland's one-line comment was, 'And so it is...on some nights'. She elaborated, 'I think there's a great resurgence in opera, particularly amongst young people. I think they've seen small snippets or the occasional full production on television. They are then attracted to go to the theatre and see the crazy stuff on stage with a real live orchestra playing.'

She reminded the gathering that she was not a lecturer like the academics on the panel and asked that the questions be not too 'curly', admitting that she was 'rather stuck in a bit of a rut at the nineteenth century'. In spite of that, the first question from the audience was a request to comment about Benjamin Britten as an opera composer. 'You would start off with one like that!' she exclaimed. 'I'm not a contemporary music lover of any kind. I was involved in *Gloriana* and I found it fascinating to work on an opera that was being produced for the first time. I think there's a feeling of humanity in the Britten operas and a couple of the stories stand out as straight drama, but I'm afraid I prefer good old-fashioned Italian opera, I have to confess.'

'Do you find that the Italian language helps your legato line in singing?' 'I find it hard to make as legato a line in English or German because the consonants intrude too much. I think Italian is a great language to sing in, but French isn't bad either!' There was a question about singing opera in its original language.

I am in favour of opera being performed in the language it was written in because the music has been set to a specific tongue — although there is a lot to be said for opera in English under certain circumstances. The majority of the big bel canto operas, however, don't translate well into English because how can you go on saying 'Chaaaste goddess' instead of '*Casta diva*', and how can Lucia go crazy wailing Italian phrases that sound wonderful in the original but ludicrous in translation?

She added that the translations by Edward J. Dent of Mozart

opera libretti were particularly successful and there was no reason why they shouldn't be performed in English. An Italian in the audience quickly changed the mood by asking Sutherland if she liked spaghetti. To laughter, she admitted that she did, any way it was served but particularly '*alle vongole*'. The questioner added, 'I wonder because, God!, this lady can sing so beautiful!' She was requested to define bel canto and replied, 'It defines itself, it's beautiful singing, isn't it?' The woman questioner asked her to elaborate, eliciting another memorable one-liner, 'I think you need a textbook, darling — or my husband!'

Sutherland, however, did elaborate on several aspects of her career. In reply to a question about the importance of dramatic ability for a singer she replied, 'Well, I think you'd better be able to sing first'. When the laughter to that subsided she continued,

I took some vague sort of acting classes which were really deportment and we did scenes from various classical plays but I wasn't very good at it and if I'd gone by what I felt in those classes I would never have attempted to go abroad or fool myself that I could even earn a measly crust in the operatic world. But I thought I had some sort of a voice and I managed to win competitions that gave me the confidence to try my luck elsewhere. When I got to Europe I found that not many of the singers were great actresses. It is the voice that I think people go to hear rather than great dramatic performances in opera.

It was, perhaps, inevitable there would be a question about opera's élitism.

I don't think it's for the socially élite at all. I think Mozart wrote for the people, although he was a court composer; Verdi was very close to the people and wrote about them. I think it is the greatest art form because in it you have the best of everything — great dramas set to music, sets, costumes, ballet and singing — it's a marvellous blending of so many different components. I think it's for everybody, don't you?

One of the final questions at the University concerned coping with and understanding foreign languages.

I think that you have to know what you are singing about and if I don't understand the words I invariably look them up. But it can lead to some strange moments. I sang *Die Fledermaus* in San Francisco in 1973 and one of the local critics in his review stated, 'When Miss Sutherland got to the czardas she might just have well sung it in Hungarian for all we could hear'. Well, it just so happened that I did sing it in Hungarian — and I'd taken quite a long time to learn it, too! In fact, I learned my Italian from libretti and my good Italian colleagues, like Luciano Pavarotti, who were always helpful. They're not like that in France, though. The French are very uppity about their language and don't help you as much as the Italians. The Italians don't laugh at you if you try to speak their language but I'm afraid the French tend to look down their noses a bit if even your grammar gets wonky.

Bonynge, as musical director of the Australian Opera, conducts many performances in addition to Sutherland's and also records under his own contract. Sutherland attends most of the productions when he's conducting in Sydney, sitting in the centre of the auditorium fifteen rows back in the orchestra stalls. She has a continuing love of opera and is ever-interested in hearing Bonynge's performances and those of her singing colleagues. A rare occurrence for her to be in the audience with Bonynge on stage as a featured performer came in 1978 when, during a gruelling schedule of conducting, he found time to appear as solo pianist for a concert of chamber music in the 300-seat Baroque-style theatre, part of the private mansion of Vivian Chalwin in the Sydney harbourside suburb of Cremorne.

The Bonynges study a score

He was to play Mozart's Piano Quintet in G minor and Schumann's Piano Quintet opus 44 with a group made up from the Opera's orchestra. The preparations were rather hurried affairs, fitted in between opera performances and rehearsal calls,

266

usually at the Potts Point apartment. Sutherland was pleased that he wanted to do the concert. 'For so long he's been accompanying my recitals or conducting performances — whether mine or in the recording studio. But it's been such a long time since he sat down and played either as a soloist or with a group in this fashion.' The night of the concert, and Bonynge's only day off in a week of performances, attracted a capacity audience to Cremorne and brought a traffic jam of considerable entanglement to the narrow winding roads. Bonynge was apprehensive, with an anxiety about succeeding that was the result of barely adequate rehearsals and unfamiliarity with this type of performing. It was a display of nerves rarely seen in the opera house or the recording studio, and to add to it was dazzling lighting for filming the event and extra microphones to record the concert for a later broadcast. He admitted, 'I haven't played any chamber music of this type for twenty years or more. It was a great experience for me actually rehearsing with my colleagues — more than the playing because it is a bit terrifying for me to appear in front of an audience.'

Sutherland herself rarely suffers from nerves these days. There is the usual first-night tension for a new role but she knows she can cope with most unforeseen occurrences that are likely to confront her on stage because just about everything that could happen has happened to her from falling sets to forgotten lines. Occasionally, however, the irrational incident can 'throw' her. One night while performing in *La Traviata* at Melbourne's cavernous Palais Theatre she was in the middle of '*Ah! fors' è lui*', singing with the confidence that only someone who has played the role of Violetta Valéry countless times can, when she glanced out into the auditorium beyond Bonynge's baton and saw, reflected in the stage lighting spilling onto the audience, dozens of opera glasses trained on her. She was gripped with a sudden feeling of panic at this surreal sight and, although she was able to complete the aria satisfactorily, the thought of all those patrons watching her every move in extreme close-up caused an uncomfortable moment in an otherwise uneventful performance.

The concert began and Bonynge's nervousness was apparent as he made a hesitant start in the Mozart. Sutherland put on a bold face, gently smiling, being able to relax a few minutes after the start of the concert as he settled down to play with increasing assurance. She said afterwards, 'I was very excited to be in the audience because he had really worked hard at the pieces with such little time. I was very touched by the fact that he was up there performing on the stage as a pianist, which is what he set out to be as a teenager — or even before.' The performance gathered momentum and Bonynge responded to an obvious warmth generated by the audience and began to play with a fluency that gave a hint of what he might have become if his career had continued along its planned path and not deflected to opera. Sutherland thought about the times more than thirty years ago as she listened to the music. 'I first heard him play when he was about fourteen and all sorts of memories from over the years came flooding back while I was sitting there in the audience.'

Bonynge's work-load would probably preclude him from similar performances in the immediate future and yet, here he was, a musician of international stature being accepted by an enthusiastic audience and at the same time snubbed by other sections of the Sydney musical establishment. He has never conducted the Sydney Symphony Orchestra in a public concert. Ask him why it didn't happen years ago and the answer is, 'They've not asked me'. Virtually no Australian conductors have a roster of recordings and concerts with international orchestras to the extent of Bonynge's — the Los Angeles Philharmonic, the English Chamber, the Suisse Romande, the London Symphony, the London Philharmonic, Santa Cecilia Rome, Maggio Musicale Florence, the New York Philharmonic — the list goes on. And yet in Australia there often remains a grudging acceptance of his musical abilities, and even the inflight music systems of the Australian international carrier Qantas rarely, if ever, feature any of their many recordings — much to Bonynge's nationalistic chagrin — although Swissair play them regularly.

The years go by and the musical partnership shows no obvious signs of slowing down. The bookings come in for engagements several years ahead, the residences are still there — in New York, Sydney and Switzerland — and their long-standing friend Terry McEwen, as the new director of the San Francisco Opera, hopes they will spend as much time as possible there during the 1980s, continuing an association with the city that goes back almost to the start of Sutherland's starring career. The records are taped and sell in large numbers, the exclusive contracts are there for continued signing and the fans are as fervent and loyal as ever.

Donna Anna in *Don Giovanni* for television production 'Joan Sutherland: A Life on the Move'

The question of retirement is often raised by the press — as if they wanted her off the stage and out of the public eye. Sutherland usually shrugs it off with a joke,

Yes, I think about retirement every time I pack my bags and move on to the next performances. Touring becomes a bugbear. You look at the suitcases and think you've only just unpacked and now it's time to pack up and move on again. I think it's harder to travel today than it was ten years ago. Nowadays there always seem to be hordes of people at the airports, ploughing through Customs, and I really feel ill sometimes at the prospect of travelling — and yet when one's actually packed and on the plane, and a little more relaxed, I do enjoy it.

There are still personal misgivings about her public impact. 'I sometimes get anxious about the adulation. It is at the same time heartwarming and frightening because you wonder what you've done. There is a certain hysteria and sometimes it is a little frightening and puzzling.'

The time to quit will be decided, like most artistic decisions in her career, by Bonynge. 'You can't always hear yourself as others hear you', Sutherland says. 'He listens and hears things I never notice.' Bonynge says,

She has, I suppose, one of the widest repertoires of any singer who has ever lived. She's done an immense amount of eighteenth-century music — both Mozart and Handel and lesser composers. She's sung a great deal of the nineteenth-century bel canto repertoire — both the so-called lighter coloratura works up to the heavy dramatic works like *Norma*, and also repertoire like *Suor Angelica* and *Turandot*. There has also been a considerable amount of modern repertory and she must have sung twenty-five or thirty modern works, many for the first time in England during the 1950s. Where she's going now is very hard to say. She doesn't want to make any sweeping changes — perhaps to add a few more roles, both big bel canto and big nineteenth-century romantic roles, and perhaps a verismo part or two. I think probably nothing more than that.

'He thinks I'll still be at it when I'm ninety-three', Sutherland quips. 'It isn't that he wants to work me into the ground — he thinks I'd be bored in retirement — and he's probably right.'

There is little doubt that Sutherland and Bonynge will continue to work for as long as they want to call the tune. The 1960s and 1970s had begun with a similar prospect of opera, concerts, recitals and recording around the world. But when she does decide to retire the Sutherland discography will be the benchmark, the touchstone, of a long and outstanding career.

Chapter Thirteen

*I think it is marvellous to have such a splendid record of perfor-
mances to be kept either in archives or in personal libraries. At
least people in future days will be able to have some idea how we
sounded in 1950, 1960, 1970, 1980 — whenever it is.*

Of all those in the performing arts, the musicians and singers are
documented the best. On records. That most egalitarian diversion, the gramophone or phonograph, became the outstandingly
accessible and influential form of entertainment in the twentieth
century. Soon after 1900 the first records became commercially
available in increasing numbers for a widening public, and opera
singers were some of the first performers to realize the benefits.
The fame of Melba, Patti, Caruso, Tamagno and many others
increased because of records, and the history of opera this century
can be traced through the singers whose voices were captured by
the medium.

Sutherland began her recording career rather late in life but at
a significant moment in the development of the industry. In the
late 1950s the long-playing microgroove record established itself
as the new standard. It liberated the medium from its four-
minutes-a-side restraints which had been a huge deterrent to
recording all but the most popular works in their entirety.
Suddenly there were virtually no limits to what might be put onto
disc, and the rush was on to record a vast reservoir of previously
neglected music.

Unlike many of her colleagues — particularly Callas, whose
discography is huge but much of it taken from stage or broadcast
performances — Sutherland used the medium creatively. It was
now not merely for recording arias and complete operas. Under

271

Bonynge's scholarly guidance, combined with his flair for theatricality, there was a delving into all-but-forgotten repertoires of opera and operetta that could be issued in attractive and innovative ways. Sutherland's discography became unique — everything from Handel's *Messiah* and Beethoven's Ninth, through familiar and unknown opera, to operetta and musical comedy.

These days, the Bonynges visit London most frequently for recording sessions. Their performances at Covent Garden have dwindled to an appearance every two years or so, but at least twice a year, every year, they can be found at Kingsway Hall recording opera, albums of voice with orchestra, and yet more volumes of orchestral music conducted by Richard Bonynge adding to his personal discography.

Kingsway Hall, situated on one of Central London's busiest streets, is an unlikely location for one of the leading classical recording studios in the world — shared by the two giants of the industry in Britain, EMI and Decca. Not only is there a constant buzz of traffic outside, but also not far below is the Central Line Underground which adds a regular and audible rumble every few minutes as trains pass through. The hall is a former Methodist Chapel and its corridors, full of broken and discarded furniture gathering dust, suggest better days. But the hall itself, and its circular, balconied configuration give a sound quality that outweighs the disadvantages of imperfect sound-proofing, and the engineers long ago mastered traffic and underground intrusions with special 'rumble' filters. The large wooden floor space, cleared of seats, and the curving balconies culminating in a huge, wood-panelled organ loft with a stage in front, can accommodate everything from small chamber groups to the grandest opera. The bright acoustics mean that the performers — singers and musicians alike — can give something like a 'live' performance instead of battling the deadness often found in purpose-built recording studios. Beneath and behind the organ loft, in a maze of corridors and dressing-rooms, is the control room — the nerve centre of the whole operation. Its banks of faders, meters and tape recorders are the means through which the sounds generated in the hall can be channelled from microphones onto magnetic tape. A television monitor showing the hall's interior sits uneasily beside the Victorian marble plaques set into the wall, commemorating worthy pillars of Methodism, long since dead and all-but-forgotten.

To be in the hall for a session of Sutherland singing Wagner with the orchestra conducted by Bonynge makes it hard to associate the present actuality with the future product. To hear her trying to get a certain phrase correct, and on the rare occasion repeating it, and then after playbacks climbing onto the platform for another attempt muttering, 'Now I know why I gave up Wagner!', is to enter a private world far removed from the commercialism of the record shops with their glossy packaging and presentation.

Recordings have been crucial to.the Bonynges' careers. 'They make you famous, of course', says Bonynge. 'They did even in the time of Melba and Caruso.' Sutherland finds the mechanics of recording something of a strain, 'It's very hard to create the atmosphere of the theatre and I'm never convinced that it's really possible to obtain the standard of performance that happens in the theatre. There is so much technical equipment in between the voice and the recording that I find it's somewhat dehumanized.' As she records, dressed casually and comfortably, she shows every emotion, every reaction to her own performance that becomes a theatre of self-analysis. The grimaces, the hand movements, and the sudden relaxation at the end of a take, testify to the continuing difficulty of mastering the medium — and the foolishness of taking it too lightly. She can also be quick to break the tension; to joke, and even clown, where other singers are involved. Nobody can ignore the fact that, once committed to tape, the performance will be regarded as the definitive document of the artist. Striving for perfection must always be an important element of a recorded performance. 'I think we are very fortunate to be able to leave behind such a reasonably exact record of the sort of sounds we make!' She adds, 'Those in a former age were not so fortunate'.

With a recording career of more than twenty years behind her and a formidable future schedule, Sutherland now pays little attention to the finished products — except to utilize them, usually in cassette form, to re-learn a part she hasn't performed for some time. She rarely listens to records by other singers, although earlier in her career she did use recordings as a reference-point for style, being quick to add, however, that they were only for the purposes of study. 'After all, I consider it no virtue to be told that I sound like any other singer; and I am not flattered when I am called "the new Melba". To copy her or anybody else I

273

would consider to be a lack of positive ideas on my part.'

Sutherland's objectivity adds to her recorded performances. 'Of course, when you're recording it's possible to repeat things', she says. 'In a stage performance faults can creep into the production and they perhaps give it added excitement. In recording one tries to do the best, and I think we sometimes consider the music too much, instead of the musical impetus of the piece.'

A session at Kingsway Hall with the Bonynges is now a matter-of-fact affair. The orchestra, usually the National Philharmonic, exclusively a recording ensemble, is made up of the best players from London's several symphony orchestras. In their three-hour calls they are able to reach performance pitch in a short time through sheer professionalism and familiarity with the conditions. There is a minimum of fuss, both on the technical side, where microphone and cable placings have long-since been standardized, and in discipline and performance, where giving value-for-money is essential for musicians to ensure their own future bookings. As Bonynge sees it, 'The difficulty of the recording studio is that you have to emote at the press of a button and this is a very hard thing to do. But, of course, it's like everything else, it's a technique that can be learned.' The difference between a recording session and a live performance is simply the matter of reaching a high standard in a short time. Time in the studio is money; sessions can slip away all too quickly and overtime for the players is very expensive. In the opera house it can take twenty minutes, half an hour or even a complete act to warm up and get the performance flowing. 'In the studio you cannot have time to warm up', says Bonynge, 'you must be able to do it immediately, and this is one of Joan's great virtues, that she doesn't seem to require any warm-up time'.

It seems likely that Kingsway Hall will, for a long time yet, see Sutherland dominating its stage. She stands in an easy, relaxed way and yet every note, every phrase sung is reflected in her face, wincing with self-disgust or comically grimacing. She keeps a keen eye on Bonynge's conducting, and the striving for perfection shows in small movements and mannerisms. It might be pushing her slipped reading glasses back to their proper position on her nose, or thrusting one hand firmly on her hip. But during the

Opposite: Recording Wagner arias, Kingsway Hall, London 1978

274

actual takes the only movements are the delicate turning of pages of her score — delicate, so that the sensitive microphones pointing at her will not pick up the sound — and also a tendency to edge back from her position and to place her right foot forward. Regular observers of Sutherland's recording style say they can tell when she is about to unleash something special by that subtle placing of the right foot.

In the control room the producer and engineers have other considerations, other priorities. In the early 1960s, before Bonynge was established as her regular conductor, Christopher Raeburn was Decca's recording director for Sutherland's *La Traviata* which was conducted by John Pritchard. At the time he observed, 'I find she'll have learned her part thoroughly and studied it and she will be a great sport. I have never known her throw a conventional prima donna tantrum. This is in contrast to certain other foreign artists one can think of, who can be very grand at times and feel after one take that it's sufficient — and it's just too bad otherwise!'

It was a long time before the British record companies took much interest in Sutherland. Throughout the 1950s she broadcast regularly on the BBC and was being announced in recitals as 'the distinguished Australian soprano'. Neither she nor Bonynge was unfamiliar with recording for broadcasts in the studio, but her ever-growing favourable notices in concerts and opera were ignored by the companies who were recording the voice much more extensively with the increasing demand for long-play records.

Sutherland was already thirty when in May 1957 HMV invited her to sing the soprano aria *'Bereite dir, Jesu'* in Bach's Cantata No. 147 — *'Herz und Mund und Leben'* — with the orchestra conducted by Geraint Jones. The other singers were Helen Watts, Wilfred Brown and Thomas Hemsley. It was a full year before the disc was released, resulting in her first, brief record reviews, 'Joan Sutherland — making a welcome first appearance on disc — sings her aria *"Bereite dir, Jesu"* (Make ready, Lord Jesus) with beautiful tone...' — *Gramophone*, July 1958, and in *Records and Recording* of the same month there was a passing reference to 'the fluent style of Joan Sutherland'. Hearing the recording today, the voice seems to have been poorly captured when compared with some of the BBC recordings of the period. Critics noted a richness of tone in live performance, but on this recording and subsequent ones, the voice sounds younger than its thirty years and certainly not yet the unique instrument it would be called within a couple of years.

Her next session was in April 1958 — a Handel disc for Decca's associate company, Oiseau-Lyre. Ray Minshull was the producer. 'My first impression of her as a singer was that I was completely bowled over. The incredible agility and intonation. As a person she was delightfully warm-hearted, very friendly and co-operative. At the time she was not at all well, she had some trouble with her knee, which meant it was quite impossible for her to stand during the sessions.' Sutherland had to prop herself up on a high stool to ease the weight on her swollen legs and, although in considerable pain, she sang beautifully. Soon afterwards she was off to hospital for tests to discover the cause of her intense discomfort. The record of Handel arias was released in January 1959. She sang two excerpts from *Alcina* which received critical praise where her colleagues in the other pieces did not. *Music and Musicians* noted, 'The florid difficulties of the first of the two arias included here are so effortlessly surmounted that it seems churlish to complain that her Italian diction is not ideally clear'. That comment about diction was to reappear with greater frequency in records to follow. Sutherland thinks that such criticism tends to be self-generating, so that the issue of her diction became over-emphasized by constant repetition. Callas, too, when she was at her peak in the 1950s, came in for a considerable amount of attack from the critics who virtually analyzed her every note on record — and found many of them to be wanting.

Just before she left to sing in *Don Giovanni* in Vancouver, Sutherland and Bonynge recorded together for the first time in June 1958. It was on a seven-inch 45 rpm Belcanto disc — from a small independent company concerned primarily with re-issues of historic performances. Their release was announced as the first in a series by British and Commonwealth artists, and it gave for the first time an indication of how the Sutherland voice would be captured more accurately in the future, in spite of an indifferent recording which emphasized a rather tinny-sounding piano. *Gramophone* commented,

It is high time we had records of Miss Sutherland and much of this is sweet and distinguished singing of a singer with a lovely voice and a great future, no doubt... I feel sure that at her best Miss Sutherland could sing better than this. Few of the words are intelligible, but then one can't expect too much in such music, though if Callas can do it, I don't see why Miss Sutherland could not. But this is to reckon without the sweetness of prevailing tone, the excellently even development of the voice, and the fine way it is always on the breath and in basic control.

This disc from a small independent company could hardly be a big-seller, but Sutherland was being noticed by the record reviewers and that would be important for the future. In fact, the Belcanto disc demonstrated clearly the direction in which Sutherland and Bonynge had been wishing to go for the past seven or eight years, because the choice of repertoire here was obviously their own — and it was one of the most unusual collection of pieces ever brought together on such a small scale. There is the cavatina and rondo finale from Donizetti's *Emilia di Liverpool*, a song by Rossini, and an aria from Spohr's *Zemire and Azor*. Bonynge's playing gives good support in its assured authority and helps his wife's phrasing and delivery to an impressive virtuosity — particularly in the top Es of the Donizetti cabaletta.

Soon after her triumph in *Lucia di Lammermoor* and the subsequent operation on her sinuses at the London Clinic, Sutherland travelled to Paris for her first full-scale solo album. Decca was to bill the disc as 'The finest coloratura singing put on records in twenty-five years' and in technical terms they were on safe ground, for their engineers were recording the voice with a sympathetic fidelity that was the envy of the industry. The recording was made under difficult conditions and once again demonstrated the 'brink of disaster' condition in which many of Sutherland's key performances took place in the early years of her stardom. She recalled, 'I'd had a sinus operation and had been away for a holiday to recuperate, and then I caught a cold just before returning for the session, and so when I was singing I had a completely different feeling of resonance from what I should usually have'. The set-up was also unfamiliar, with the orchestra on stage and the conductor's back to her, making it difficult for the participants to communicate with each other.

The content of the disc was carefully chosen to capitalize on the *Lucia* success, and two major arias from that opera were included, together with one from Donizetti's *Linda di Chamounix*. The other showpieces for the Sutherland voice were both from Verdi operas — *Ernani* and *I Vespri Siciliani*. The recording was made with Nello Santi and the Paris Conservatoire Orchestra in April 1959 and released, more quickly than most, in August of the same year. Working with Santi, and his sometimes unsympathetic tempi in the opera house, would be a cause of concern to both Sutherland and Bonynge in the future — and already the critics noted that, although Sutherland's singing here was generally brilliant and exciting, the accompaniment from Santi and the Paris orchestra was less well recorded, suggesting a lack of preparation and rapport between the singer and conductor. But it didn't alter the fact that Sutherland was beginning to sell well and by October of 1959 many stores were noting that her recordings were in good and increasing demand.

Gramophone, in the issue of January 1960, put the Sutherland recording potential into perspective when it stated,

Joan Sutherland's Decca recital is the first serious attempt to do justice to a singer who has been transformed overnight from a valuable member of the Covent Garden company to something like a world celebrity; it is on the whole very good, so good that it deserves to be judged by the highest standards. A beautiful and intensely dramatic stage production such as *Lucia*, does not throw so revealing a light on the details of vocal execution as does a recording. Since dozens of the first and second generations of recording artists managed to pass the searching scrutiny of antique recording with honours, it is virtually certain that they must have sounded more dazzling in the theatre. How does Miss Sutherland's recital compare with the recordings of the famous coloratura sopranos of the past? Her tone in altissimo is often sweeter and rounder, her taste in phrasing and ornament sometimes more pure, than those of her predecessors. But her mastery of the mechanism of singing is not as yet so complete, or so secure, as theirs.

In the same month in a comprehensive review of the year's activities published in the *Financial Times*, the Decca company made reference to its Joan Sutherland recital album being hailed in Britain, America and many other countries as 'creating a new standard'. Sutherland was soon to be under exclusive contract with them.

Next on a recording schedule that was now gathering momentum was a complete performance, on two discs, of Handel's *Acis and Galatea*, the first dramatic work by the composer in English, with Sir Adrian Boult conducting — a musician not usually noted for his baroque style. It was the first complete recording of a version of *Acis and Galatea* that Handel had revised for a 1718 pro-

279

duction for the Earl of Carnarvon. This masque was the most popular of the composer's works in his own time. For this recording the story, about rustic love and a wicked giant, was given scrupulous attention to accuracy of performance by Julian Herbage's edition. Sutherland had already established herself in the Handelian style with *Rodelinda* at Sadler's Wells. This year, 1959, marked the bicentenary of Handel's death and there were, particularly in London, many special concerts and opera performances of his works. The record industry, too, made many versions of his music that had not been recorded before, and released them around this time, creating a Handel revival. *Music and Musicians* in March 1960, when the record was released, wrote, 'Joan Sutherland's singing as Galatea is superbly accomplished and technically well-nigh flawless, and sets a standard that the other soloists cannot equal'. They were Peter Pears, David Galliver and Owen Brannigan.

This was an intensely busy year for Sutherland, and also for Bonynge who, largely behind the scenes, spent a great amount of time preparing his wife for her many engagements and recordings. She was asked to record in Switzerland the soprano part in Beethoven's Ninth Symphony with Norma Proctor, Anton Dermota and Arnold van Mill, and Ernest Ansermet conducting the Suisse Romande Orchestra. It was speedily released in time for Christmas 1959 in mono and faced the competition of more than a dozen versions already in the catalogues. The critics thought it an average performance in the face of some of the glittering rivals, but the record did have a major advantage, for the first time the work was released on one stereo record — but that was not issued until six months later and it presented the problem of a turnover in the middle of the slow movement.

In June 1959 Sutherland was invited to take part in Sir Thomas Beecham's new recording of Handel's *Messiah* together with Monica Sinclair, Jon Vickers and Joseph Rouleau at the Walthamstow Town Hall in London. Sir Eugene Goossens's edition of the work was used, complete with full brass, a large choir, cymbals and even an anvil. There was for Sutherland something of a sentimental link with the influence Goossens had exerted on her early career in Sydney. But things went badly at the recording session and any sentimental thoughts were quickly dispelled. Beecham was at his most idiosyncratic with tempi. Sutherland found she couldn't manage the breath control for the funereal pace at which he took 'I Know That My Redeemer Liveth'. There was a clash of personalities between the eager new prima donna and the foxy old maestro which was beyond any hope of settlement, and it led to Sutherland's withdrawal from the recording. It was eventually completed with Jennifer Vyvyan, Monica Sinclair, Giorgio Tozzi and Jon Vickers. Conductor trouble would be the main source of Sutherland's rare displays of temperament.

In August and September 1959 Sutherland embarked on a much happier project — her first complete recording of a major popular opera, singing Donna Anna in Mozart's *Don Giovanni* for EMI's Columbia label. It was a very strong cast — Eberhard Waechter, Giuseppe Taddei, Gottlob Frick, Luigi Alva, Elisabeth Schwarzkopf and Graziella Sciutti, with the Philharmonia Choir and Orchestra conducted by Carlo Maria Giulini. Inexplicably the records were not released for eighteen months, by which time Sutherland had developed her role considerably in the opera house. The reviews generally praised the technical aspects of her singing but observed a lack of projected personality in her performance. Record marketing was extremely competitive by the early 1960s, and the Columbia set competed with six other versions of *Don Giovanni* already in the catalogue. In fact, a new set by RCA conducted by Leinsdorf with the Vienna Philharmonic was issued simultaneously. In more detailed analysis, *Gramophone* in February 1961 thought Sutherland's characterization was poor,

...the accuracy, poise and brightness of her top are most valuable in ensembles, where often the Donna Anna is drowning and clutching. But dramatically this Donna Anna is not, I find, strikingly enough characterized. If you follow her performance closely you will see that she has worked it all out very sensibly — that when she wilts a little, there is warrant for it, and she negotiates the tests of 'Non mi dir' like one of those lady equestrians who win medals for Britain by clearing fence after fence. But the ability to bring the character out through the music just eludes her...

The year 1960 was a significant one for Sutherland with a big advance in the use of the gramophone as a way of assembling a repertoire that could not be performed in any other way. But the first of her recordings that year was as frivolous as *Don Giovanni* had been serious. In an attempt to broaden the use of long-play discs and increase their appeal, Decca issued a complete perfor-

Recording in the mid 1960s

mance, conducted by Herbert von Karajan, of Johann Strauss's *Die Fledermaus* on three records, including a 'Gala Performance' which followed a tradition that had grown up at New York's Metropolitan Opera House of inserting an entertainment into Prince Orlovsky's party in Act II as a sort of party piece with everyone doing a favourite turn. Decca used the idea to engage its stars in unlikely numbers — Leontyne Price sang 'Summertime', Birgit Nilsson 'I Could Have Danced All Night', Giulietta Simionato and Ettore Bastianini 'Anything You Can Do', Renata Tebaldi 'Vilja' and Sutherland, Arditi's '*Il Bacio*' with orchestral accompaniment. Released in November 1960 the set was a brisk seller for Christmas that year but *Die Fledermaus* was later reissued with the Gala deleted.

In July and August of 1960 Sutherland recorded a two-disc album that was developed as an idea by Richard Bonynge and their friend, Terry McEwen of Decca. The result was to be a new direction in opera on records and demonstrated, in its originality, how the medium could be used in a unique way, and not just for capturing performances. In its simplest form, the album was an attempt to pay tribute to famous prima donnas of the past by arias associated with them being performed by the reigning prima donna of the day. The time-span extended from Mrs Billington in the late eighteenth century to Galli-Curci in the first part of the twentieth century. Bonynge said, 'It is not intended to suggest that Joan will demonstrate just how those bygone prime donne sang, or that she can sing as well as they did. The idea is to pay homage to the memory by observing their technique, or what we know of it, as scrupulously as possible.' Bonynge and McEwen did a great deal of background research before they were ready to go into the studio. They listened to as many records of singers from around 1905 as they could find — mostly those made by pupils of Aglaia Orgeni. Orgeni had herself studied with Madame Viardot-Garcia and, as such, she had transmitted to them through those early recordings something of the art and technique of Viardot-Garcia's father, the great Manuel Garcia and also her famous singer sister, Maria Malibran. By that lineage there was the possibility of transporting the spirit of the great age of bel canto through more than a century and a half for Sutherland to sing.

The sessions were in Kingsway Hall, eight of them of three hours each, including rehearsals, with Francesco Molinari-Pradelli conducting. Most of the arias were single takes. 'I would rather let an occasional error appear than have an aria recorded in pieces', said Sutherland. But one of the performances had to be done again because of the noisy intrusion of a low-flying jet plane. The engineers had no filter for that. 'I think that was the best performance I have ever given of the *Hamlet* Mad Scene. At the end, the E natural in alt came out better than I have ever sung it. And just as I took the note the jet came over. So we did it again, but it wasn't as good.' There were nearly two hours of music in the two volumes issued under the title 'The Art of the Prima Donna', and *Musical America* in February 1961 wrote about them, '...as a whole this album is an astounding and well-nigh unique achievement. No wonder that in less than a decade, Miss Sutherland has conquered all the major opera houses of the world! It is singing like this that makes audiences hysterical and impresarios rich!' In Britain, *Music and Musicians* of December 1960 commented,

Considering the repertoire covered on these records, comparison with Callas is inescapable. There is no doubt at all that Miss Sutherland's technique is much more secure — there is not a single strained or wobbly note in all the sixteen arias. When it comes to characterization Sutherland has still to acquire Callas's ability to crystallize in a single phrase a whole range of psychology and emotion... The recording gives a good idea of how Joan Sutherland's voice sounds in size and quality, from the Covent Garden stalls.

'The Art of the Prima Donna' received an Edison Award in September 1961, the highest award of the Dutch recording industry. Sutherland received the chunky, heavy bronze statuette of Edison standing by his phonograph at a reception at Decca's London headquarters. It now stands, rather forlornly, outside the Bonynges' Swiss house. That year Sutherland also received the American Grammy Award as the best classical performer of the year.

During 1961 she stepped up her recording activities with tapings in Rome. In June it was a complete *Rigoletto* and then in August the long-awaited *Lucia di Lammermoor*. *Rigoletto* had seven other recorded rivals when it was released on the British market in early 1962. *The Times* commented,

Such is Miss Sutherland's stock at the moment that it is on her performance that all ears will first be tuned. There is only one serious drawback to it. Surely the Gilda we meet in the earlier scenes of Verdi's opera is a simple girl, radiant with love, not a despairing clairvoyante already aware that men were deceivers ever? Apart from this predilection for covered, lachrymose tone and world-weary rhythm too early in the story, Miss Sutherland's performance is splendid. Her ornamentation is miraculous (Callas never comes near it) and the fullness of her tone, unimpaired by any hard edge,...helps enormously in bringing home the full, dramatic splendour of Verdi's score.

When *Lucia* was finally recorded in Rome it was already eighteen months since Sutherland's first London performance of the work and it would have been expected to have high priority on the recording schedule. But it is not so easy to assemble a cast who will not only be worthy of a work, but also be available in one place at the same time. After such a delay, Decca was able to get together one of the strongest casts available including Cesare Siepi, Robert Merrill and Renato Cioni, together with the Rome Santa Cecilia chorus and orchestra conducted by John Pritchard. The discs were on the market within three months and *Gramophone* reviewed the performance in November 1961.

Sutherland is without rival today in her command of the vocal arts — trills, scales and arpeggios, messa di voce, glissando. Her tone is beautiful, and each year becomes sweeter, rounder and fuller, in both gentle and brilliant passages. Her interpretation of *Lucia* is a fully conceived study, tremendously effective in the theatre, and a good deal of this comes over on the record. In this performance, passage after passage is melting, exquisite, dazzling, breathtaking.

There were two rival versions of the work by Callas at this time — one released in 1954 and the other in 1960. Whether Sutherland's performance was superior or not to the Callas versions was largely irrelevant. Certainly Callas's drama is more in evidence, but Sutherland's singing made her performance the most vocally exciting on record, and certainly the best recorded. Apart from a few small cuts the opera was complete on disc. John Pritchard observed Sutherland's attitudes to recording at this time:

She doesn't realize her own innate ability. She thinks she is slow musically — she is very far from that. She has an instinct. She is rarely pleased and takes a lot of convincing. For instance, in a recording when she has done a really good take, she often comes out and says, 'I don't think there's any voice there', when we are all staggered with the quality of the voice that *is* there.

Having completed the *Lucia* recording in Rome, Sutherland flew back to London to start work almost immediately on a new version of Handel's *Messiah*. This was Julian Herbage's edition with Sir Adrian Boult conducting, and there were to be none of the clashes of her abortive Beecham version of two years before — although Bonynge was not entirely in sympathy with Herbage's edition. There was a brief, painful interlude during which Ivor Griffiths attended to draining Sutherland's sinuses and eustachian tubes and then it was off to Kingsway Hall for the sessions. The record was released at the same time as a rival version at half the price. The arrival of each new *Messiah* since the days of Sir Malcolm Sargent and the Huddersfield Choral Society's overblown version on nineteen 78 rpm records, was usually marked by claims of 'authenticity' of performance. On the record sales campaign front it was Joan Sutherland versus Heather Harper, and Sir Adrian Boult and the London Symphony Orchestra against Frederick Jackson and the London Philharmonic Orchestra. In the end the Decca version with Sutherland won out, with better sound. It sold well at Christmas 1961 and remained in the catalogue until Sutherland and Bonynge recorded their own version during 1969 and 1970 which allowed Bonynge's ideas about Handelian ornamentation to be fully exploited.

By March 1962, Sutherland was a big enough record star to have a say in who would conduct her performances. Richard Bonynge had already made his conducting debut in Rome and he was known to be more familiar with her repertoire and vocal delivery than anyone else — after all, he had been mostly responsible for it. There was little doubt about his music ability, but the world was full of aspiring conductors, and few record companies were prepared to take a chance on a relatively unknown name. Decca, knowing they had a commercially successful Sutherland on contract, was now prepared to take the chance in a complete recording of Handel's *Alcina* — a role that was particularly linked with Sutherland since her 'La Stupenda' performance in Venice. But inevitably, the Bonynge-Sutherland partnership not yet widely heard in the opera house, but now to be on records, generated some criticism. Perhaps he was using his wife's acclaim to enter work areas that would, otherwise, be closed to him. Sutherland was prompted to reply to this criticism. 'Why shouldn't my husband conduct for me? He's perfectly qualified, in fact far more so than some of the people who have conducted some of my performances.' Ever the peacemaker, she hastened to add, 'But let's make it clear I have great respect for many conductors, though not as many as I would like'. A small paragraph in the magazine *Records and Recording* noted, 'Behind most of the world's great singers have been musically guiding hands. Malibran had her father, Garcia; Ponselle had Romani; Callas would hardly have been a household name without Serafin; Sutherland — Bonynge.' He, however, was in something of a dilemma. He could keep quiet and continue to conduct, hoping the comments would evaporate as the critics realized his performances were, at least, musically competent. But criticism based on bitchiness is hard to dispel. And so Bonynge felt the need to explain his position. 'I have worked with Joan for ten years and know in advance what she is going to do, and I realized that if I can learn the art of conducting the composers we love, like Bellini, Donizetti and Handel — we'd be absolutely in union with one another.' That seemed eminently reasonable. It could have been left at that, but he was prepared also to answer the main criticism. 'I know there are people who will say, "He's conducting just because his wife is famous", but that doesn't bother me. We will make beautiful music and be happy doing it. That's all I care about.'

The recording of *Alcina* was released in September 1962 and the British record critics were generally pleased with the result of their first large-scale partnership on disc. *Records* magazine stated, 'Richard Bonynge makes a distinguished debut on Decca as a conductor, obtaining pristine, lively playing from his forces, with well-judged tempi and dramatic impetus. In a way the set can be said to break new ground with the full resources of an international cast and the latest recording technique lavished on a work that has only recently begun to regain popularity.' In the *Guardian*, Edward Greenfield wrote, 'Very exciting, of course, and whatever one's incidental criticisms, this is a set to confirm how near we are to a new "Golden Age" of singing'. *Gramophone* commented, 'Whatever Sutherland's singing may lack in charm, character or dramatic impact, it is certainly phenomenal, virtuoso and often electrifying. Bonynge makes a promising debut; but *Alcina* with this cast deserves to be conducted by a master.' Ironically, as more of their records were released, there was often praise for Bonynge and his accompaniments, but continuing comment about Sutherland's poor diction and weak characterization. She refrained from commenting publicly on the diction, but she did say this about characterization,

Of course, every company wants to put out something that is as perfect as possible. Often the work is not recorded in the correct order, and is chopped up into pieces which makes it difficult to retain and create a good atmosphere. But we've been very fortunate that we've rarely recorded an opera that we have not first performed on stage, live — and that makes it easier to retain the role consistently in a recording.

During a session informality is the keynote because recording halls not noted for their facilities for either the orchestral players or the singers. It is essential to get as much done as quickly as possible in order to have a credit of time at the end of sessions for retakes. This race against the clock, and the Bonynges' other commitments, could make for an impossible tension — but that has only rarely been the case in their long recording career.

There is always a chill in the air of the windowless but drafty

Kingsway Hall — summer and winter alike — and as there are long periods of standing involved, there is usually a chair nearby on the platform. If it is a recording of solo voice with orchestra — such as in their Mozart and Wagner sessions — there is an atmosphere of deceptive calm. For a 2 o'clock call, the musicians begin to drift into the hall anything up to an hour before. Some instruments need to be carefully tuned ahead of the performance and invariably there is at least a harpist playing chords over and over again to greet the arrival of everyone else. The players wear a motley assortment of clothes reflecting the dress habits of the different generations in the orchestra — the older members with ties and jackets, the younger in skivvies and jeans. The atmosphere is one of routine.

A couple of takes will most likely be recorded and the best selected later. In addition, small sections of each aria — both vocal and orchestral — might be repeated after discussion between Bonynge and the producer, in an attempt to get as near to perfection as possible. Occasionally the producer calls Bonynge into the control room to listen to a playback in order to check the finer points of interpretation, but usually Sutherland prefers not to listen, relying on Bonynge's decision whether to retake or not. While he's listening to the tape, she will most likely chat with members of the orchestra, pull some letters out of her bag to catch up with her copious and never-ending mail, or add a little to one of the ever-growing needlepoint pieces which are scattered among friends and in their houses all over the world.

Then it's back to work and not a moment to lose. Sutherland stands again in front of her two microphones, the colour of her dress most probably clashing alarmingly with the scuffed green baize all around her on the platform and her own titian hair. Her voice blends with the sounds of the orchestra in front of her — all eighty players. Work in progress.

When an opera is recorded in the same hall, the scene is less ordered, much more confusing. With the number of people involved, it looks like a 'sitzprobe' — the early cumbersome rehearsals for stage performances. But that is deceptive. The positioning of the principals and chorus, and the movement from microphone to microphone to obtain the maximum stereo effect, is a carefully choreographed manoeuvre, needing the singers' eyes on the conductor, the stage manager and their scores all at the same time. Sutherland's composure and animated talking with her colleagues between takes, makes her 'one of the group' rather than the prima donna whose name will spearhead the record's selling prospects.

Next in her discography comes Bellini's *La Sonnambula*, recorded in Florence in September 1962 and first issued in February 1963. Once again Sutherland was capitalizing on a recent stage performance — and at the same time delving more into the bel canto repertory which she and Bonynge preferred. She said at the time,

I think that the greatest dangers to singers today are the overlarge orchestra and the insensitive, autocratic conductor who neither understands nor loves the art of song. Did Malibran or Rubini ever have to sing against an orchestra of one hundred players? Or course not! Today we are expected to sing the same operas that these people sang, but with twice or three times as much noise coming out of the pit. If we complain, we are told sarcastically that we are behaving like prime donne. I say long live the prima donna.

Sutherland has rarely spoken about critics, but in the early 1960s she wrote an article for the American *Hi Fi Stereo* magazine in which she made this comment,

...a certain critic, writing of my recent recording of Queen Marguerite's aria from Meyerbeer's *Les Huguenots*, wrote that my interpretation was not as brilliant as Melba's. I don't doubt for an instant that this may be so, but what I object to is the fact that this particular critic is younger than I am and therefore certainly never heard Dame Nellie in person, and the only memento she has left us of this aria is an ancient Mapleson cylinder recorded from the flies at the Metropolitan. I have a copy of the recording myself, and I defy anyone who hasn't read the title to even tell what aria she is singing, so scratchy, noisy and ancient is the sound.

When *La Sonnambula* was released there was, once again, comment about diction and many critics recommended the incomplete Callas set which had been recorded in 1957. All reviews were complimentary to Bonynge's conducting: '...in Bonynge we have a real dramatic conductor in the making' — *Gramophone*. 'Richard Bonynge shows himself remarkably sensitive to Bellini in his conducting...' — *Music and Musicians*. 'Mr Bonynge gets some amount of sloppy playing from the Florence Festival orchestra, but leaves no doubt that Bellini's style is at his baton's tip' — *The Times*. 'Bonynge excels particularly in his shaping of the chorus' — *Financial Times*. They were notices that could set his mind at rest about any continuing bitchiness.

Bellini himself had written, 'The actress must be playful, ingenuous and innocent, and at the same time impassioned, sensitive and loving'. His additional specifications for Amina, his heroine of *La Sonnambula*, included, 'her singing must be simple, and at the same time adorned, spontaneous, yet scrupulously controlled, perfect, yet showing no signs of study', a tall order to realize for the opera house, but virtually impossible on records. Most critics thought that Callas most closely caught the spirit of Bellini's intentions — but the new version was virtually complete and the sound was far superior; a difficult decision for a record buyer to face. It was inevitable that, in duplicating a repertoire Callas had already covered, Sutherland would be constantly compared to her, but it would not continue much longer because the Decca engineers were developing such a superior sound that the ageing Callas recordings would suffer at once in that respect.

The following month, after recording *La Sonnambula*, Sutherland, at the peak of her performing career, agreed to sing a minute part in a major recording venture, without Bonynge conducting. It was the unexpected twist in her career that separated her from her colleagues — few of whom, at the pinnacle of success, would have even considered such a small role. Decca was recording Wagner's *Ring* cycle under Georg Solti in Vienna and Sutherland was asked to sing the Woodbird in *Siegfried*. In spite of Covent Garden's early insistence that her's was a Wagner voice, she had resolutely kept away from his music ever since. For the stage, the offer would have been considered impertinent, but for recording, Sutherland readily agreed to sing the role that she had first performed eight years previously. Of course, to have the Sutherland name on the recording was a great promotional boost. The critics were not slow to miss the point when the set — the first complete recording of *Siegfried* — was released in early 1963. The *New York Times* noted, 'Joan Sutherland in something of a stunt, appears as the Forest Bird. Many lesser-known sopranos could sing this brief part satisfactorily, but the Sutherland voice gives it an extra touch of flute-like colour.' *Records and Recording* wrote,

Lastly here is the Woodbird, which Wagner wanted sung by a boy treble but which, in my experience, is invariably assigned to female sopranos. Here it is impersonated by an internationally-renowned coloratura diva, who, we were given to understand, had long foresworn Wagner and all his works in order to

290

revise the lost art of bel canto. In fact, of course, Sutherland used to sing the part at Covent Garden in pre-Stupenda days when, I suspect, she paid more attention to words than is her custom nowadays. Nevertheless, her voice flutters down from aloft to enchanting effect, and Siegfried evidently 'gets the message' — even if we do not!

A problem in recording the role, and relating directly to its clarity, is the fact that one can never really hear the Woodbird's words clearly because it is the custom for them to be sung from backstage.

Hard on the heels of the Wagner recording in Vienna, Sutherland continued her globetrotting to record *La Traviata* in Florence, conducted by John Pritchard. Most critics thought it was the best Sutherland recorded performance to date but they all make a point of mentioning yet again some unclear diction. Strangely, the six previously-issued versions of the opera were incomplete — and so her's became the first virtually complete recording, with only a few minor cuts.

With the acclaim still ringing in the cash registers for 'The Art of the Prima Donna', it was Decca's desire to present another compilation that would, as inventively, highlight the Sutherland voice. The result was 'Command Performance', another original concept, that rested firmly on extensive background research combined with brilliant singing. This time Bonynge's touch was completely in evidence, for he conducted the orchestra as well as compiling the selection and working on an extensive booklet that was issued as part of the two-disc set. The idea was to present the type of programme a famous prima donna — such as Jenny Lind, Patti or Melba — might have been commanded to perform before Queen Victoria at a royal residence such as Windsor. One of Melba's biographers, Percy Colson, described such a scene.

Her Majesty sat alone in front on a gilt chair and around her were grouped the Royal Family and Court Officials. Behind were row upon row of the élite of the aristocracy, the men in court dress or uniform, the women in their very best clothes and wearing all their family jewels. No applause was permitted unless Her Majesty gave the signal and then it was discreet, to say the least of it.

However, the disc most closely parallels the style of a Patti royal command. She sang in eighteen performances between 1861 and 1886.

Victorian ballads were mixed with operatic arias, and Bonynge accompanied at the piano as well as conducting the London

291

Symphony Orchestra and Chorus. When the records were released in early 1963 *Records and Recording* commented,

The recording is a remarkable and highly successful achievement. Enormous trouble has obviously been taken with the technical side of the recording. Miss Sutherland's voice is beautifully reproduced and the balance between voice and orchestra is excellently maintained... Naturally points of criticism suggest themselves; the question of enunciation being here the prominent one. Although Sutherland has here rid herself of most of the mannerisms that have marred many of her recent performances, the words do not come through as clearly as they should.

Gramophone noted there was no music included by Queen Victoria's favourite composer, Mr Mendelssohn, and that Mattinata, written by Leoncavallo, was composed after she died. 'The critics of Sutherland's diction will have a field day here. I can almost hear them chuckling to themselves as they reach for pen and paper.' However, Edward Greenfield, who wrote the review, thought it only a marginal defect when the text of all the songs was supplied. He thought Sutherland's tone colour to be monotonous, while praising the concept and recording of the set.

The year 1963 was also an extremely busy one in the recording studios. First came a complete recording of Bizet's *Carmen*, with Sutherland singing Micaëla, recorded in Geneva with Thomas Schippers conducting, and then the following month, in June, back to London for another compilation devoted to her particular vocal virtuosity — a two-disc set called 'The Age of Bel Canto'. American mezzo-soprano Marilyn Horne appeared on record with Sutherland for the first time and her florid technique was noted by the critics as something extraordinary when the records were released in mid-1964. Richard Bonynge was, of course, responsible for the compilation of the music and it included arias from such little-known composers as Piccini, Lampugnani and Bononcini as well as Mozart, Bellini, Donizetti and Verdi. Marilyn Horne, who sang in almost half of the twenty-three items on the recordings, had distinguished herself in performances of modern works — including Stravinsky, Berg and Webern. But here, in a much older repertoire, her voice was brilliantly used. Their partnership went on to become one of the most exciting on records, with their voices complimentary to each other, never conflicting, and their performances both on stage and in recordings formed the most impressive partnership Sutherland has shared — with the exception of the tenor Luciano Pavarotti.

292

There is not much chance, once opera stars reach the highest magnitude, to see them perform together on stage, but recordings can often bring them together.

As 1963 progressed, more recordings were on the schedule with Bellini's *I Puritani* taped in Florence, and in London excerpts from Handel's *Giulio Cesare in Egitto*. This was capitalizing on her only London appearance the previous season in the Handel Society's production of the work at Sadler's Wells Theatre. Sutherland, as Cleopatra, played three performances only, two at a decidedly un-diva-like fee and the third without payment in aid of the British Hospital for Incurables. The opera was also broadcast on the BBC Third Programme. By comparison the next year, 1964, was quieter for recording than any in the past five had been, but the one record made was significant — Bellini's *Norma*. She had first played the role, considered by her to be the most difficult, in Vancouver in October 1963 and now a few months later, with Marilyn Horne, John Alexander and Richard Cross it was recorded — and became a big seller.

Almost every singer makes a Christmas record at some time and Sutherland has been no exception. In May 1965 at Kingsway Hall she followed in the steps of other divas such as Kirsten Flagstad, Birgit Nilsson and Leontyne Price, who had all done the same. The result was a little less traditional than expected but it added Sutherland's brilliant dynamics to some new arrangements of old Yuletide favourites by fellow Australian Douglas Gamley. The idea had come some three years previously from Decca, who was keen to record as much Sutherland as possible, but both she and Bonynge were less than happy with the suggestion. At that time they thought there was a considerable repertoire to be explored on records before such sidetracks could be fruitful both in commercial and prestige terms. Also, fitting into their busy schedule a recording such as this, which needed as much care and attention lavished on it as a full-scale opera, was difficult. But by 1965 the original suggestion seemed a better idea and they went ahead.

By the end of the year with 'Joy to the World' selling briskly for the Christmas trade, Sutherland went to Vienna to record, for the second time, the soprano part in Beethoven's Ninth Symphony, six years after her first taping with Ernest Ansermet conducting. This time Hans Schmidt-Isserstedt was the conductor and the orchestra was the Vienna Philharmonic.

293

The following year, 1966, saw for Sutherland and Bonynge a recording schedule so fierce that merely describing its component parts gives an impression of its intensity. It was also a year which saw another change of direction in their repertoire on disc. January brought the complete *Semiramide*, February the full *Beatrice di Tenda*, June *Faust* and August excerpts from Graun's *Montezuma* and also another disc of excerpts from Bononcini's *Griselda*. In between these recordings they moved into musical comedy for the first time. The most impressive of the two productions was a two-record set called 'Love Live Forever', subtitled 'The Romance of Musical Comedy'. Douglas Gamley did most of the arrangements and the numbers ranged from Richard Rodgers, through Victor Herbert and back to the world of Viennese operetta. An immense amount of care and attention was lavished on the production, including a handsome booklet with illustrations from Bonynge's own collection of theatre memorabilia. The enterprise was destined, inevitably, to come under critical fire, usually along the lines of too much artistry chasing too little fine music. But Sutherland felt at home in this repertoire, as much as the more serious stuff. 'I grew up in a country that was starved of music, and one of the only chances to hear music was often musical comedy. And so you began to like it.' Some critics thought that recording thirty-two numbers of this music got in the way of the operas that Sutherland had yet to record, including many by Verdi. But Sutherland was not prepared to commit herself to one narrow repertoire. Bonynge's attitude to repertoire was, 'I'm an unashamed specialist in beautiful, cheering, joyful music. I think that music should make you happy, not miserable.'

The same attitude might have been afforded their other recording of 1966 — 'Joan Sutherland Sings the Songs of Noël Coward'. Coward was great friends with the Bonynges and they had become neighbours in Switzerland. 'I forced them to have that house ', Coward said, 'it's so important to have nice neighbours'. He was respectfully known as 'The Master' and it was in this spirit that they decided to record a collection of his songs with Coward himself voicing some of the introductions. There were, however, certain challenges to meet. Coward's songs are pitched to a different level of singing and were strongly linked to such actresses as Gertrude Lawrence. Therefore, there was the possibility of failing

The prima donna and 'The Master'

to please either the followers of Coward or, on the other hand, the devotees of Sutherland. Coward's words were meant to be perfectly clear, sung slightly tongue-in-cheek, their bite and wit standing out from their musical background. Sutherland said at the time,

It's a great joy to sing his music because I find it so operatic in quality. I think he's a great opera buff, and his music has a strong influence of Massenet and Puccini who are, I think, his favourite operatic composers. I find that to sing his music in an operatic fashion isn't easy at all, because it's not easy music. People are led astray into believing them to be marvellously simple tunes, but they're not simple to sing at all, and I find them rather wonderful.

The record gives us Coward's clipped introductions, recorded separately, followed by Sutherland's florid, operatic treatments in which the words are often blurred within the lushness of Douglas Gamley's orchestral arrangements and Bonynge's theatrically sympathetic conducting of voice, orchestra and chorus.

When the record was released at the end of 1966 one review was headed 'Bel Canto Coward'. Perhaps Coward's image, even in the later years of his life, was too indelibly established for the public to accept him as anything than a 1920s' world-weary sophisticate, clad in a silk dressing gown and languidly smoking cigarettes through a long holder whilst exuding a faintly degenerate air. The songs in this collection were originally written for the singing-actresses Peggy Wood and Yvonne Printemps and, fortunately, there is no attempt to echo their style and Sutherland goes her own operatic way.

From the mid 1960s the Sutherland/Bonynge recordings continued in a steady stream — based principally on their repertoire in the opera house, but continuing to embrace special compilations and rarities including, in 1969, a two-record album of 'Romantic French Arias'; 'The World of Joan Sutherland' — a conspectus of her career to date; and a re-cycling of previously issued pieces such as the single disc called 'The Art of Bel Canto' released in 1972 but taken largely from the 1964 two-disc set 'The Age of Bel Canto'. 'Songs My Mother Taught Me' was an original album, released in 1974, and was precisely to title — a nostalgic journey back to the Sydney of childhood for some of the songs she had heard at home sung either by her mother or played on the gramophone. The cloying sweetness of songs such as 'Homing' by Riego is tempered by the brilliance of her cuckoo coloratura in Abt's 'Der Kukkuk'. Gamley did the arrangements for the orchestral accompaniments. Another re-issued collection in 1977 was titled 'Joan Sutherland — Voice of the Century' and included highlights from her eighteen-year recording career. To this time all her recordings had been studio based, but the special concert to raise funds for the hurricane-battered Australian city of Darwin was recorded from the stage at Covent Garden and became the sole example — called 'Darwin — Song for a City' — of a Sutherland stage performance on record. She continued to sell well, with the American trade paper *Billboard* announcing that her new *Trovatore* was the top seller at the end of 1977 in the classical records list, while the newly-released collection of operatic duets with Luciano Pavarotti was placed eleventh. There were even re-recordings of complete operas with a second *Rigoletto*, an updated *Lucia di Lammermoor*, another *Don Giovanni*, *La Sonnambula* again and a new *Traviata*.

By now both Sutherland and Bonynge were comfortably at home in the recording studio — enough for Bonynge to reflect on his position in the business. 'I suppose as you get older you stop putting your ego first. When you're young you wonder, what will they write about me? Well, after they've written frightful things about you for ten years, it's no longer of paramount importance what they say.' Bonynge admits he wouldn't have got started on his conducting career if it hadn't been for his wife. But he's equally sure that many years after his conducting debut, he would be an ex-conductor if he hadn't been able to do his job. It's often overlooked by his critics that his conducting career independent of Sutherland is now extensive — particularly at the Metropolitan and in Australia — and that his own discography is extensive and ever-growing. He says he relies very much on his musical instincts. 'If I feel I want something to go one way, that's the way I'll do it, even though I may not have an intellectual reason for doing it.' He is not preoccupied with how he holds the baton, or whether he's doing something technically correct or not. 'I'm possibly doing things very incorrectly, but then so are a lot of other conductors.' Bonynge dislikes purists and would rather follow his theatrical

Richard Bonynge recording, London 1978

instincts than slavishly bow to correctness and, possibly, dullness. He says, 'I would rather hear someone sing Mozart in the style of Puccini but with great conviction and great heart, communication and warmth, than hear someone just sing it correctly'.

Occasionally, they have recorded a work that could only appear on records. One of these was *L'Oracolo*, a curiosity in which Sutherland plays a fifteen-year-old Chinese virgin in a one-act verismo role set in San Francisco's Chinatown. The composer was Franco Leoni who lived much of his life in Britain and whose work had not been staged since it was first performed in 1905. In fact, it seems likely that, along with a continuation of her active repertoire, the Sutherland discography will increasingly emphasize roles she could not perform on stage. In 1976 she stated, '*Turandot* is just another cardboard character, and I've discarded *Sonnambula* for the same reason.' At the same time Bonynge, talking about repertoire said, '*Linda di Chamounix* is a beautiful opera, perfect for Joan vocally, but the libretto is stupid — about a girl protecting her virtue. The public won't swallow that Victorian nonsense today.' But such works are ideal for recording where the sounds are predominant and the listener's credibility is not stretched beyond the limit.

The Bonynges have made little effort to retain a complete set of their records, which is surprising when the rest of their personal archive is so comprehensive. Most titles are on the shelves in the annexe to the music room at Les Avants, but some have been lent or given away and not replaced. Adam does, however, have a complete collection; a copy of each new release is lodged for him in a Swiss bank. At least, when the Sutherland recording career finally ends, there will be one complete documentation in the family.

By 1980 there were more than ninety separate recordings or albums bearing the Sutherland name and many more recorded separately by Bonynge. Many of them were in collections with other artists, but more than fifty titles — many of them three-disc sets of complete operas — testify to their immense recording activity over two decades. When the history of recording in the twentieth century is made, Sutherland will probably emerge as the most-recorded soprano in the medium, and almost certainly the one who, with her husband, used its techniques to the greatest effect.

Discography Joan Sutherland

All commercial recordings by Sutherland have been made in Europe, mainly in Britain, but also in France, Switzerland, Italy and Monaco. Apart from sessions early in her recording career for His Master's Voice, Columbia, Oiseau-Lyre, Belcantodisc and the release of the complete *Norma* originally on RCA, the majority of her output is for Decca, with whom she and Richard Bonynge are under exclusive contract. The British Decca pressings, with Decca or Ace of Clubs labels, are marketed in many parts of the world but there are variations of content in some local releases by the parent company's subsidiaries or licencees. These include the United States — on the London label, Japan — King Records, France — Société du Son, and Germany — Teldec. In Australia the records are pressed and marketed by EMI on the Decca label. In late 1979 it was announced that Decca had sold most of its record division to PolyGram, the record company jointly-owned by Philips and Siemens.

The following list is in order of original issue. Only stereo versions are noted and where re-issues have been made, the latest number is quoted. Many of the titles are now also on tapes. Decca Group releases are given only a prefix and serial numbers.

1958
Bach. Cantata No. 147, 'Herz und Mund und Leben' with Helen Watts, Wilfred Brown, Thomas Hemsley, Geraint Jones Choir and Orchestra conducted by Geraint Jones. HMV CSD 151-2

1959
Music of Handel
Alcina : Tornami a vagheggiar; Ah! Ruggiero crudel… Ombre pallide. With Philomusica of London conducted by Anthony Lewis. OISEAU-LYRE SOL 60001

Donizetti. *Emilia di Liverpool*: Cavatina and Rondo finale. Rossini. La Fioraia Fiorentina Spohr. *Zemire and Azor*: Rose, softly blooming. With Richard Bonynge (piano) BELCANTODISC B LR 1

Beethoven. Symphony No. 9 in D minor, Op 125, 'Choral' with Norma Proctor, Anton Dermota, Arnold van Mill, Chorale du

Brassus, Choeur des Jeunes de l'Eglise
National Vaudoise, Suisse Romande
Orchestra conducted by Ernest Ansermet.
SDD 108

Operatic Arias
Donizetti. *Lucia di Lammermoor*:Ancor non
giunse!... Regnava nel silenzio (with Nadine
Sautereau, soprano).
Verdi. *Ernani*: Surta è la notte... Ernani,
involami.
Verdi.'*I Vespri Siciliani*: Mercè, dilette amiche.
Donizetti. *Linda di Chamounix*: Ah! tardai
troppo... O luce di quest' anima.
Donizetti. *Lucia di Lammermoor*: Il dolce
suono... Ardon gl' incensi.
With the Paris Opera Chorus, Paris
Conservatoire Orchestra conducted by Nello
Santi. SDD 146

1960
Handel. *Acis and Galatea*:complete (Galatea)
with Peter Pears, David Galliver, Owen
Brannigan, St Anthony Singers, Philomusica
of London conducted by Sir Adrian Boult.
OISEAU-LYRE SOL 60011-2

Johann Strauss II. *Die Fledermaus*:complete.
Together with Gala Performance in which
Sutherland sings Arditi's Il Bacio with
orchestral accompaniment. SET 201-3

The Art of the Prima Donna — Volume 1
Arne. *Artaxerxes*: The soldier tir'd.
Handel. *Samson*: Let the bright seraphim.
Bellini. *Norma*: Sediziose voci...Casta diva...
Ah! bello a me.
Bellini. *I Puritani*: Son vergin vezzosa.
Rossini. *Semiramide*: Bel raggio lusinghier.
Bellini. *I Puritani*: Care, compagne, e voi...
Come per me sereno... Sovra il sen.
Gounod. *Faust*: O Dieu, que de bijoux!... Ah!
je ris.
With the Royal Opera House, Covent Garden
Chorus and Orchestra conducted by
Francesco Molinari-Pradelli. SXL 2256

The Art of the Prima Donna — Volume 2
Gounod. *Roméo et Juliette*: Je veux vivre.
Verdi. *Otello*: Mia madre aveva una povera
ancella... Piangea cantando.
Mozart. *Die Entführung aus dem Serail*:
Martern aller Arten.

Verdi. *La Travïata*: E strano... Ah! fors' è lui...
Sempre libera.
Thomas. *Hamlet*: A vos jeux, mes amis.
Delibes. *Lakmé*: Où va la jeune indoue?
Meyerbeer, *Les Huguenots*: O beau pays de la
Touraine.
Verdi. *Rigoletto*: Gualtier Maldè... Caro nome.
With the Royal Opera House, Covent Garden
Chorus and Orchestra conducted by Franco
Molinari-Pradelli. SXL 2257

1961
Mozart. *Don Giovanni*: complete (Donna Anna)
with Eberhard Waechter, Giuseppe Taddei,
Gottlob Frick, Luigi Alva, Piero Cappuccilli,
Elisabeth Schwarzkopf, Graziella Sciutti. The
Philharmonia Choir and Orchestra conducted
by Carlo Maria Giulini. COLUMBIA SAX
2369-72.

Highlights SAX 2559

Donizetti. *Lucia di Lammermoor*: complete
(Lucia) with Renato Cioni, Robert Merrill,
Cesare Siepi, Kenneth MacDonald, Rinaldo
Pelizzoni, Racquel Sartre. Accademia di
Santa Cecilia Chorus and Ochestra, Rome,
conducted by John Pritchard. GOS 663-5

Highlights SXL 2315

Handel. *Messiah*: complete with Grace Bumbry,
Kenneth McKellar, David Ward. The
London Symphony Orchestra Chorus and
the London Symphony Orchestra conducted
by Sir Adrian Boult. SET 218-20

Highlights SXL 2316

1962
Verdi. *Rigoletto*: complete (Gilda) with Cornell
MacNeil, Renato Cioni, Cesare Siepi,
Stefania Malagù. Accademia di Santa
Cecilia Chorus and Orchestra, Rome,
conducted by Francesco Molinari-Pradelli.
GOS 655-7

Highlights SXL 6008

Handel. *Alcina*: complete (Alcina) with Teresa
Berganza, Monica Sinclair, Luigi Alva,
Graziella Sciutti, Mirella Freni, Ezio
Flagello. London Symphony Orchestra
Chorus and London Symphony Orchestra
conducted by Richard Bonynge. GOS 509-11

1963

Bellini. *La Sonnambula*: complete (Amina) with Nicola Monti, Fernando Corena, Sylvia Stahlman, Margreta Elkins, Maggio Musicale Fiorentino Chorus and Orchestra conducted by Richard Bonynge. SET 239-41

Wagner. *Siegfried*: complete (Woodbird) with Wolfgang Windgassen, Birgit Nilsson, Gerhard Stolze, Gustav Neidlinger, Hans Hotter, Kurt Boehme, Marga Hoeffgen. The Vienna Philharmonic Orchestra conducted by Georg Solti. SET 242-6 RING 1-22

Verdi. *La Traviata*: complete (Violetta) with Carlo Bergonzi, Robert Merrill, Maggio Musicale Fiorentino Chorus and Orchestra conducted by John Pritchard. SET 249-51

Highlights SXL 6127

Command Performance — Volume 1
Weber. *Oberon*: Ocean! thou mighty monster.
Massenet. *Le Cid*: De cet affreux... Pleurez mes yeux.
Meyerbeer. *Dinorah*: Dieu! comme cette nuit... Ombre légère.
Leoncavallo. *I Pugliacci*: Quel fiamma aveva nelguardo.
Verdi. *I Masnadieri*: Dall'infame banchetto... Tu del mio Carlo (with John Dobson, tenor).
Verdi. *Luisa Miller*: Che! e segnar questa mano... Tu puniscimi o Signore.
Rossini. *La Cambiale di Matrimonio*: Come tacer... Vorrei spiegarvi.
Bellini. *Beatrice di Tenda*: Eccomi pronta... Deh! se un'urna.
With the London Symphony Orchestra Chorus, the Ambrosian Singers and the London Symphony Orchestra conducted by Richard Bonynge.

Command Performance — Volume 2
Benedict. The Gypsy and the Bird (with Alexander Murray, flute).
Arditi. Parla!
Ricci. *Crispino e la Comare*: Io non sono più l'Annetta.
Tosti. Ideale.
Arditi. Il bacio.
Tosti. La Serenata.
Leoncavallo. Mattinata.

Bishop. Lo! hear the gentle lark (with Alexander Murray, flute).
Flotow. *Martha*: The last rose of summer.
Wallace. *Maritana*: Scenes that are brightest.
Balfe. *The Bohemian Girl*: I dreamt I dwelt in marble halls.
Bishop. *Clari*: Home sweet home (with Tina Bonifacio, harp).
The London Symphony Orchestra Chorus and the London Symphony Orchestra conducted by Richard Bonynge. SET 247-8

Bizet. *Carmen*: complete (Micaëla) with Regina Resnik, Mario del Monaco, Tom Krause. The Grand Theatre Chorus, Geneva, and the Suisse Romande Orchestra conducted by Thomas Schippers. SET 256-8

Highlights SXL 6156

1964
The Age of Bel Canto
Piccinni. *La Buona Figliuola*: Furia di donna.
Handel. *Atalanta*: Care selve.
Lampugnani. *Meraspe*: Superbo di me stesso.
Handel. *Samson*: With plaintive note.
Handel. *Semele*: Iris hence away.
Bononcini. *Astarto*: Mio caro ben.
Arne. *Artaxerxes*: O too lovely.
Shield. *Rosina*: Light as thistledown; When William at eve.
Mozart. *Il Re Pastore*: Voi che fausti.
Mozart. *Die Zauberflöte*: O zittre nicht.
Mozart. *Die Entführung aus dem Serail*: Ich baue ganz.
Gail and Boieldieu. *Angela*: Ma Fanchette est charmante.
Rossini. *Semiramide*: Serbami ognor.
Auber. *La Muette de Portici*: Ferme tes yeux.
Weber. *Der Freichütz*: Und ob die Wolke.
Bellini. *Beatrice di Tenda*: Angiol di pace.
Donizetti. *Don Pasquale*: Tornami a dir.
Donizetti. *Lucrezia Borgia*: Il segreto.
Verdi. *Attila*: Santo di patria... allor che i forti corrono.
Bellini. *La Straniera*: Un ritrattoe?... Veggiam.
Rossini. *Il Barbiere di Siviglia*: Ecco ridente in cielo.
Arditi. Bolero
With Marilyn Horne, Richard Conrad, Hubert Dawkes (harpsichord), the London Symphony Orchestra Chorus, the London

301

Symphony Orchestra, the New Symphony Orchestra conducted by Richard Bonynge. SET 268-9

Bellini. *I Puritani*: complete (Elvira) with Pierre Duval, Renato Capecchi, Ezio Flagello, Margreta Elkins, Piero de Palma, Giovanni Foiani, Maggio Musicale Fiorentino Chorus and Orchestra conducted by Richard Bonynge. SET 587-9

Highlights SET 619

Handel. *Giulio Cesare in Egitto*: highlights (Cleopatra) with Margreta Elkins, Monica Sinclair, Richard Conrad, Marilyn Horne and the New Symphony Orchestra conducted by Richard Bonynge. SDD 213

Bellini. *Norma*: complete (Norma) with Marilyn Horne, John Alexander, Richard Cross and the London Symphony Orchestra conducted by Richard Bonynge. SET 424-6 (RCA SER 5524-5526)

Highlights SET 456

1965
Joy to the World
Handel/Watts. Joy to the World.
Willis/Sears. It came upon the midnight clear.
Adam. O holy night.
Gounod. O Divine Redeemer.
Traditional. What Child is this?
Traditional. Adeste Fideles.
Traditional. The twelve days of Christmas.
Traditional. Good King Wenceslas.
Mendelssohn. Hark! the herald angels sing.
Reger. The Virgin's slumber song.
Schubert. Ave Maria.
Traditional. The Holly and the Ivy.
Traditional. Angels we have heard on high.
Traditional. Deck the hall.
All arrangements, with the exception of the Reger, by Douglas Gamley. With Valda Aveling (harpsichord), the Ambrosian Singers, Patricia Clark (soprano) and the National Philharmonic Orchestra conducted by Richard Bonynge. SXL 6193

Beethoven. Symphony No. 9 in D minor, Op 125, 'Choral' with Marilyn Horne, James King, Martti Talvela, the Vienna State Opera Chorus and the Vienna Philharmonic

Orchestra conducted by Hans Schmidt-Isserstedt. JB 1

1966
Rossini. *Semiramide*: complete (Semiramide) with Marilyn Horne, Joseph Rouleau, Spiro Malas, John Serge, the Ambrosian Opera Chorus and the London Symphony Orchestra conducted by Richard Bonynge. SET 317-9

Highlights SET 391

Bellini. *Beatrice di Tenda*: complete (Beatrice) with Josephine Veasey, Luciano Pavarotti, Joseph Ward, Cornelius Opthof, the Ambrosian Opera Chorus and the London Symphony Orchestra conducted by Richard Bonynge. SET 320-2

Highlights SET 430

Joan Sutherland Sings the Songs of Noël Coward
Conversation Piece: I'll follow my secret heart; Never more; Melanie's aria; Charming, charming.
Bitter Sweet: I'll see you again; Zigeuner.
Operette: Dearest love; Where are the songs we sung?; Countess Mitzi.
After The Ball: I knew that you would be my love.
Pacific 1860: Bright was the day; This is a changing world.
With Noël Coward, Margreta Elkins, Elizabeth Robinson, Morag Beaton, John Wakefield, John Leach (cimbalom), chorus and orchestra conducted by Richard Bonynge. SXL 6255

Graun. *Montezuma*: excerpts (Eupaforice) with Lauris Elms, Joseph Ward, Elizabeth Harwood, Rae Woodland, Monica Sinclair, the Ambrosian Singers and the London Symphony Orchestra conducted by Richard Bonynge. SET 351

Bononcini. *Griselda*: (Ernesto) with Lauris Elms, Monica Sinclair, Margreta Elkins, Spiro Malas, the Ambrosian Singers and the London Symphony Orchestra conducted by Richard Bonynge. SET 352

1967
Love Live Forever — The Romance of Musical Comedy

302

Romberg. *The Student Prince*: Students'
Chorus; Deep in my heart dear.
Rodgers. *The Boys From Syracuse*: Falling in
love with love.
Romberg. *The Desert Song*: Desert song.
Kern. *Music In The Air*: And love was born.
Friml. *Rose Marie*: Indian love call.
Herbert. *The Only Girl*: When you're away.
Kern. *Show Boat*: Make believe.
Fraser-Simpson. *The Maid Of The Mountains*:
Love will find a way.
German. *Tom Jones*: Waltz song.
Offenbach. *La Périchole*: O mon cher amant, je
te jure; Mon Dieu! Ah! que les hommes sont
bêtes; Ah! quel dîner.
Massenet. *Chérubin*: Air de Nina.
Zeller. *Der Vogelhändler*: Schenkt man sich
Rosen in Tirol.
Millöcker. *The Dubarry*: The Dubarry.
Fall. *Die Geschiedene Frau*: Kind du kannst
tanzen; Schlafcoupé Lied.
Fall. *Die Spanische Nachtigall*: Heute Nacht.
Fall. *Die Dollarprinzess*: Dollarprinzessin.
Fall. *Madame Pompadour*: Heut könnt' einer
sein Glück.
Fall. *Der Lieber Augustin*: Und der Himmel
hängt.
Lehár. *Eva*: Wär'es auch nichts als ein Traum
von Glück.
Oscar Straus. *Der Waltzertraum*: Da draussen
im duftigen... Leise ganz leise.
Heuberger. *Der Opernball*: Im Chambre
séparée.
Johann Strauss II (arr. Benatsky). *Casanova*:
Nun's chorus.
Lehár. *The Merry Widow*: Vilja.
Kreisler. *The King Steps Out*: Stars in my eyes.
Oscar Straus. *The Chocolate Soldier*: My hero.
Posford. *Balalaika*: Cossacks' Song; At the
Balalaika.
Lehár. *Paganini*: Love live forever.
With the Ambrosian Light Opera Chorus and
the National Philharmonic Orchestra
conducted by Richard Bonynge. SET 349-50

Gounod. *Faust*: complete (Marguerite) with
Franco Corelli, Nicolai Ghiaurov, Robert
Massard, Margreta Elkins, Monica Sinclair,
the Ambrosian Opera Chorus and the
London Symphony Orchestra conducted by
Richard Bonynge. SET 327-30

Highlights SET 431

Donizetti. *La Fille du Régiment*: complete
(Marie) with Luciano Pavarotti, Spiro Malas,
Monica Sinclair, Jules Bruyère, Alan Jones,
Edith Coates, Royal Opera House, Covent
Garden Chorus and Orchestra conducted by
Richard Bonynge. SET 372-3

Highlights SET 491

Verdi. Requiem Mass with Marilyn Horne,
Luciano Pavarotti, Martti Talvela, the
Vienna State Opera Chorus and the Vienna
Philharmonic Orchestra conducted by Georg
Solti. SET 374-5

Delibes. *Lakmé*: complete (Lakmé) with Jane
Berbié, Gwenyth Annear, Josephte Clément,
Monica Sinclair, Alain Vanzo, Gabriel
Bacquier, Claude Calès, Monte-Carlo Opera
Chorus and National Orchestra conducted by
Richard Bonynge. SET 387-9

Highlights SET 488

1968
Russian Rarities
Glière. Harp Concerto, Op 74; Concerto for
Coloratura and Orchestra, Op 82.
Stravinsky. Pastorale.
Cui. Ici bas, Op 23.
Gretchaninov. Lullaby.
With Osian Ellis (harp), Richard Bonynge
(piano) and the London Symphony Orchestra
conducted by Richard Bonynge. SXL 6406

Mozart. *Don Giovanni*: complete (Donna Anna)
with Gabriel Bacquier, Werner Krenn, Pilar
Lorengar, Marilyn Horne, Donald Gramm,
Clifford Grant, Leonardo Monreale, the
Ambrosian Singers and the London
Symphony Orchestra conducted by Richard
Bonynge. SET 412-5

Highlights SET 496

1969
Handel. *Messiah*: complete with Huguette
Tourangeau, Tom Krause, Werner Krenn,
the Ambrosian Singers and the English
Chamber Orchestra conducted by Richard
Bonynge. SET 465-7

Highlights SXL 6540

Meyerbeer. *Les Huguenots*: complete
(Marguerite de Valois) with Martina Arroyo,
Gabriel Bacquier, Huguette Tourangeau,
Nicola Ghuiselev, the Ambrosian Opera
Chorus and the National Philharmonic
Orchestra conducted by Richard Bonynge.
SET 460-3

Highlights SET 513

Romantic French Arias
Offenbach. *Robinson Crusoé*: Conduisez-moi
vers celui que j'adore.
Meyerbeer. *Dinorah*: Bellah! ma chèvre chérie...
Dors, petite.
Charpentier. *Louise*: Depuis le jour.
Offenbach. *La Grande-Duchesse de Gérolstein*:
Dites-lui qu'on l'a remarqué.
Auber. *Manon Lescaut*: C'est l'histoire
amoureuse.
Auber. *Fra Diavolo*: Non temete, milord... Or
son sola.
Bizet. *Les Pêcheurs de Perles*: Me voilà seule...
Comme autrefois.
Offenbach. *Les Contes D'Hoffmann*: Les oiseaux
dans la charmille.
Massenet. *Cendrillon*: Ah! que mes soeurs sont
heureuses.
Gounod. *Mireille*: O légère hirondelle.
Offenbach. *La Grande-Duchesse de Gérolstein*:
Vous aimez le danger... Ah! que j'aime les
militaires.
Meyerbeer. *L'Etoile du Nord*: C'est bien lui que
chaque matin... La,la,la air chéri.
Gounod. *Le Tribut de Zamora*: Ce Sarrasin
disait.
Meyerbeer. *Robert le Diable*: En vain j'espère...
Idole de ma vie.
Lecocq. *Le Coeur et la Main*: Un soir Perez le
capitaine.
Massé. *Les Noces de Jeannette*: Au bord du
chemin qui passe à ma porte.
Gounod. *Faust*: Si le bonheur.
Bizet. *Carmen*: La marguerite a fermé... Ouvre
ton coeur.
Meyerbeer. *L'Etoile du Nord*: Veille sur eux...
Vaisseau que le flot balance. With the Grand
Theatre Chorus, Geneva, and the Suisse
Romande Orchestra conducted by Richard
Bonynge. SET 454-5.

1970
Donizetti. *L'Elisir d'Amore*: complete (Adina)
with Luciano Pavarotti, Dominic Cossa, Spiro
Malas, the Ambrosian Singers and the
English Chamber Orchestra conducted by
Richard Bonynge. SET 503-5

Highlights SET 564

1971
Verdi. *Rigoletto*: complete (Gilda) with Sherrill
Milnes, Luciano Pavarotti, the Ambrosian
Singers Opera Chorus and the London
Symphony Orchestra conducted by Richard
Bonynge. SET 542-4

Highlights SET 580

Donizetti. *Lucia di Lammermoor*: complete
(Lucia) with Luciano Pavarotti, Sherrill
Milnes, the Royal Opera House, Covent
Garden Chorus and Orchestra conducted by
Richard Bonynge. SET 528-30

Highlights SET 559

1972
Offenbach. *Les Contes d'Hoffmann*: complete
(Olympia, Giulietta, Antonia, Stella) with
Gabriel Bacquier, Placido Domingo, Hugues
Cuénod, Margerita Lilowa, Huguette
Tourangeau, Les Choeurs de la Radio Suisse
Romande, Pro Arte de Lausanne, Du
Brassus, and L'Orchestre de la Suisse
Romande conducted by Richard Bonynge.
SET 545-7

Highlights SET 569

1973
Puccini. *Turandot*: complete (Turandot) with
Luciano Pavarotti, Monserrat Caballé,
Nicolai Ghiaurov, Tom Krause, Peter Pears,
the John Alldis Choir, Wandsworth School
Boys' Choir and the London Philharmonic
Orchestra conducted by Zubin Mehta.
SET 561-3

Highlights SET 573

1974
Songs My Mother Taught Me
Dvorak. Songs my mother taught me.
Mendelssohn. Auf Flügein des Gesanges.

Riego. Homing.
Massenet. Oh! Si les fleurs avaient des yeux.
Gounod. Serenade — Quand tu chantes.
Nelson. Mary of Argyll.
Delibes. Le rossignol.
Forge. I came with a song.
Juncker. I was dreaming.
Hahn. Si mes vers avaient des ailes.
Massenet. Crépuscule.
Abt. Der Kukkuk.
Grieg. *Peer Gynt*: Solveig's song.
Worth. Midsummer.
Liszt. Oh! Quand je dors.
Delibes. Les filles de Cadiz.
Arrangements by Douglas Gamley. With the
    New Philharmonia Orchestra conducted by
    Richard Bonynge. SXL 6619

1975
Bellini. *I Puritani*: complete (Elvira) with
    Luciano Pavarotti, Nicolai Ghiaurov, the
    Royal Opera House, Covent Garden Chorus
    and the London Symphony Orchestra
    conducted by Richard Bonynge. SET 587-9

Highlights SET 619

Darwin — Song for a City
Recorded from the stage of the Royal Opera
    House, Covent Garden with other artists and
    the Royal Philharmonic Orchestra conducted
    by Richard Bonynge. SXL 6719

1976
Massenet. *Esclarmonde*: complete (Esclarmonde)
    with Huguette Tourangeau, Giacomo
    Aragall, Clifford Grant, Louis Quilico,
    Ryland Davies, Robert Lloyd, Ian Caley,
    Graham Clark. John Alldis Choir, Finchley
    Children's Music Group and the National
    Philharmonic Orchestra conducted by
    Richard Bonynge. SET 612-4

1977
Leoni. *L'Oracolo*: complete (Ah-Joe) with
    Richard van Allan, Tito Gobbi, Clifford
    Grant, Ryland Davies, Huguette
    Tourangeau, Ian Caley. The John Alldis
    Choir and the National Philharmonic
    Orchestra conducted by Richard Bonynge.
    D 34D2

Verdi. *Il Trovatore*: complete (Leonora) with
    Luciano Pavarotti, Marilyn Horne, Nicolai
    Ghiaurov, Norma Burrowes, Ingvar Wixell,
    the London Opera Chorus and the National
    Philharmonic Orchestra conducted by
    Richard Bonynge. D 82D3

Operatic Duets
With Luciano Pavarotti (tenor)
Verdi. *La Traviata*: Brindisi: Libiamo ne'lieti
    calici... Un di felice... Signora!... Che
    t'accadde... Parigi, o cara.
Bellini. *La Sonnambula*: Perdona, o mia
    diletta... Prendi: l'anel ti dono.
Donizetti. *Linda di Chamounix*: Da quel di che
    t'incontrai.
Verdi. *Otello*: Già nella notte densa.
Verdi. *Aida*: La fatal pietra... O terra, addio.
With Elizabeth Connell and the London Opera
    Chorus and the National Philharmonic
    Orchestra conducted by Richard Bonynge.
    SXL 6828

1978
Lehár. *The Merry Widow*: highlights (Anna
    Galwari) with Werner Krenn, Regina Resnik,
    John Brecknock, Graeme Ewer, Valerie
    Masterson, the Ambrosian Singers and the
    National Philharmonic Orchestra conducted
    by Richard Bonynge. SET 629

1979
Donizetti. *Maria Stuarda*: complete (Maria) with
    Luciano Pavarotti, Huguette Tourangeau,
    James Morris, Roger Soyer. Orchestra del
    Teatro Communale di Bologna conducted by
    Richard Bonynge. D 2D3

Donizetti. *Lucrezia Borgia*: complete (Lucrezia)
    with Marilyn Horne, Giacomo Aragall,
    Ingvar Wixell. The National Philharmonic
    Orchestra conducted by Richard Bonynge.
    D 93D3

Puccini. *Suor Angelica*: complete (Suor
    Angelica) with Christa Ludwig, Isobel
    Buchanan, Elizabeth Connell, the London
    Opera Chorus and the National
    Philharmonic Orchestra conducted by
    Richard Bonynge. SET 627

1980
Joan Sutherland sings Wagner

305

Rienzi: Gerechter Gott... In seiner Blute.
Der Fliegende Holländer: Senta's ballad.
Tannhäuser: Elisabeth's greeting... Elisabeth's prayer.
Lohengrin: Elsa's dream.
Die Walküre: Du bist der Lenz.
Die Meistersinger: O Sachs mein Freund.
Tristan und Isolde: Liebestod.
With the National Philharmonic Orchestra conducted by Richard Bonynge. SXL 6933

Joan Sutherland sings Mozart
Alleluia K.165.
Il Re Pastore: L'Amero, Saro Costante Vorroi Spiegarvi, O Dio K.418.
Le Nozze di Figaro: Voi che Sapete... Dove Sono... Deh Vieni non Tardar.
Ch'io mi Scordi di Te?... non Temer K.505 (piano obligato Richard Bonynge).
Die Zauberflöte: Ach ich Fuhls.
With the National Philharmonic Orchestra conducted by Richard Bonynge. SXL 6930

For Future Release
Massenet. *Le Roi de Lahore*: complete (Sita) with Huguette Tourangeau, Sherrill Milnes, Luis Lima, Nicolai Ghiaurov, James Morris, the London Voices and the National Philharmonic Orchestra conducted by Richard Bonynge. D 210D

Verdi. *La Traviata*: complete (Violetta) with Luciano Pavarotti, Matteo Manuguerra, the London Opera Chorus and the National Philharmonic Orchestra conducted by Richard Bonynge. D 212D

Bellini. *La Sonnambula*: complete (Amina) with Luciano Pavarotti, Isobel Buchanan, Nicolai Ghiaurov and the National Philharmonic Orchestra conducted by Richard Bonynge.

Reissues of Sutherland recordings in revised compilations include:

Joan Sutherland sings Verdi
With arias from *Ernani*, *I Masnadieri*, *Luisa Miller*, *Attila*, *Rigoletto*, *La Traviata* and *I Vespri Siciliani*. SXL 6190

Joan Sutherland sings Handel
With arias from *Alcina*, *Giulio Cesare*, *Samson*, *Messiah*. SXL 6191

Joan Sutherland sings Bellini
With arias from *Beatrice di Tenda*, *I Puritani*, *Norma*, *La Sonnambula*. SXL 6192

The World of Joan Sutherland SPA 100

Operatic Duets
With Marilyn Horne SET 456

The Art of Bel Canto SDD 317

Voice of the Century D 65D 3

La Stupenda SXL 6920

There are many other albums in which previously-issued Sutherland titles appear as part of a compilation with other artists. These include:

The Top 25 from Your Hundred Best Tunes HBT 1/1-2
The World of Italian Opera SPA 105
The World of Your Hundred Best Tunes — Top Ten SPA 112
Your Hundred Best Tunes 16-BB 223-32
The World of Sacred Music Vol. 2 SPA 297
The World of Your Hundred Best Tunes Vol. 5 SPA 299
The World of Your Hundred Best Tunes Vol. 6 SPA 316
The World of Birds in Music SPA 367
The World of Your Hundred Best Tunes Vol. 9 SPA 373
Royal Opera House Anniversary Album SET 392-3
The World of Schubert SPA 426
Festival of Sacred Music SDD-M 432-4
The World of Mendelssohn SPA 433
The World of Verdi SPA 447
The World of Handel SPA 448
The World of Opera Vol. 1 SPA 449
The World of Opera Vol. 2 SPA 450
The World of Operetta Favourites SPA 466
The World of Your Hundred Best Tunes — New Chart Vol. 2 SPA 488
The World of Opera Vol. 3 SPA 489
The World of Opera Vol. 4 SPA 490
Favourite Opera DPA 507-8
The World of Offenbach SPA 512
Favourite Operatic Duets DPA 517-8
Favourite Composers — Handel DPA 551-2

Favourite Composers — Verdi DPA 555-6
Immortal Classics DPA 615-6
Italian Opera Festival GOS-A 625-7
Grand Opera Festival GOS-B 636-8

Grand Opera Gala GOS-C 666-8
Festival of French Opera GOS-D 674-6
Festival of German Opera GOS-E 677-9
Luciano Pavarotti Sings Duets SXL 6858

Discography Richard Bonynge

1963

The Art of the Prima Ballerina
Minkus. *La Bayadère* Excerpt
Drigo. Pas de trois
Rossini. *William Tell* Ballet music. Pas de six
Adam. *Giselle* Danse des vignerons, Pas seul,
 Peasant pas de deux (Act I), Pas de deux (Act
 II)
Lóvenskjold. *La Sylphide* Pas de deux
Tchaikovsky. *Swan Lake* The Black Swan
Donizetti. *La Favorita* Ballet music
Minkus. *Don Quixote* Pas de deux. Trad. arr.
 O'Turner. Bolero 1830
Pugni. Pas de quatre
Tchaikovsky. *The Sleeping Beauty* Blue Bird pas
 de deux
Tchaikovsky. *The Nutcracker* Pas de deux (Act
 II)
The London Symphony Orchestra conducted by
 Richard Bonynge. SET 254-5

1964

Pas De Deux
Minkus. *Paquita* Pas de deux
Drigo. *Esmeralda* Pas de deux
Auber. Pas classique
Helsted. Flower Festival at Genzano. Pas de deux
Drigo. *Le Corsaire* Pas de deux.
The London Symphony Orchestra conducted by
 Richard Bonynge. SXL 6137

1965

Adam. *Le Diable à Quatre* — Ballet.
The London Symphony Orchestra conducted by
 Richard Bonynge. SXL 6188

1966

Favourite Overtures of the Nineteenth Century
Donizetti. *Roberto Devereux*

Rossini. *Torvaldo e Dorliska*
Maillart. *Les Dragons de Villars*
Offenbach. *La Fille du tambour-major*
Verdi. *Giovanna d'Arco*
Hérold. *Zampa*
Wallace. *Maritana*
The London Symphony Orchestra conducted by
 Richard Bonynge. SXL 6235
(Released as *Overtures to Forgotten Operas* in
 the U.S.A.)

1968

Handel Overtures and Sinfonias
Solomon Overture... Arrival of the Queen of
 Sheba (Sinfonia to part iii)
Berenice Overture
Teseo Overture
Ariodante Overture
Jephtha Sinfonia to part iii
Esther Overture
Rinaldo Overture... March and Battle
Sosarme Overture
Edited by Richard Bonynge. The English
 Chamber Orchestra conducted by Richard
 Bonynge. SXL 6360

1969

Music by J.C.Bach and Salieri
J.C.Bach. Sinfonia concertante in C major
Salieri. Sinfonia in D major — Veneziana
Salieri. Concerto in C major for flute and oboe
J.C Bach. Sinfonia in E flat major, Op 9, No.2
Edited by Richard Bonynge. The English
 Chamber Orchestra conducted by Richard
 Bonynge. SXL 6397

Burgmüller. *La Péri* — Ballet.
The London Symphony Orchestra conducted by
 Richard Bonynge. SXL 6407

1970

Adam. *Giselle* — Ballet complete — original orchestration. The Monte-Carlo Opera Orchestra conducted by Richard Bonynge. SET 433-4

French Opera Overtures
Auber. *Marco Spada*
Adam. *Giralda*
Lecocq. *La Fille de Madame Angot*
Thomas. *Mignon*
Planquette. *Les Cloches de Corneville*
Auber. *Lestocq*
Adam. *La Poupée de Nuremberg*
Boïeldieu. *Le Calife de Bagdad*
The New Philharmonia Orchestra conducted by Richard Bonynge. SXL 6422

A Tebaldi Festival
Verdi. *Aida* Ritorna vincitor
Puccini. *La Bohème* Quando m'en vo
Rossini arr. Gamley. *La Regata Veneziana* (3 songs)
Lara arr. Gamley. Granada
Ponce arr. Gamley. Estrellita
Cardillo arr. Gamley. Catari, Cataxi
Tosti arr. Gamley. A Vucchella
De Curtis arr. Gamley. Non ti scorda di me
Rodgers arr. Sharples. *Carousel* If I loved you.
Renata Tebaldi (soprano) with the New Philharmonia Orchestra conducted by Richard Bonynge. SET 440
Note: This is part of a two-record set SET 439-440 with SET 439 conducted by Anton Guadagno.

1971

Handel Overtures — Vol. II
Semele Sinfonia to Act II
Julius Caesar Overture and Minuet (Act I)
Faramondo Overture
Judas Maccabeus Overture
Radamisto Overture
Arminio Overture
Deidamia Overture
Scipio Overture
Belshazzar Sinfonia
Edited by Richard Bonynge. The English Chamber Orchestra conducted by Richard Bonynge. SXL 6496

Delibes. *Coppélia* — Ballet: complete.

L'Orchestre de la Suisse Romande conducted by Richard Bonynge. SET 473-4

1972

18th. Century Overtures
Kraus. *Olympie* Overture
Gassmann. *L'Amore Artigiano* Overture
Boïeldieu. *Zoraime et Zulmar* Overture
Paer. *Sargino* Overture
Grétry. *Le Magnifique* Overture
Sacchini. *La Contadina in Corte* Sinfonia
Haydn. *Orlando Paladino* Overture
Salieri. *La Fiera di Venezia* Sinfonia
The English Chamber Orchestra conducted by Richard Bonynge. SXL 6531

Arias From Forgotten Operas
Balfe arr. Gamley. *Ildegonda nel Carcere*: Sventurata Ildegonda. Chiuso nell'armi e splendido
Bizet. *Djamileh*: Ghazel (a Persian song)... Nour-Eddin, roi de Lahore
Donizetti orch. Gamley. *L'Assedio di Calais*: Al mio cuore oggetti amati
Auber. *Le Cheval de Bronze*: Ah pour un jeune coeur... O tourment de veuvage
Massenet. *Hérodiade*: C'est sa tête que je réclame
Verdi. *Oberto, Conte di San Bonifacio*: Sotto il paterno tetto
Vaccai. *Giulietta e Romeo*: Ah! se tu dormi
Maillart. *Les Dragons de Villars*: Il m'aime, espoir charmant
Huguette Tourangeau (mezzo-soprano) with L'Orchestre de la Suisse Romande conducted by Richard Bonynge. SXL 650I

Homage to Pavlova
Luigini. *Ballet Égyptienne* Op 12
Saint-Saëns. 'The Swan' (from *Carnival of the Animals*)
Massenet. *Thaïs* Meditation
Tchaikovsky. *The Seasons* Christmas
Rubinstein. *Feramors* Danses des fiancées de Cachemir
Czibulka. Love's Dream After the Ball
Kreisler arr. Gamley. The Dragonfly
Drigo. Le Réveil de Flore. Ballet in two acts
Tchaikovsky. Melody Op 42 No. 3
Assafiev. Papillons
Lincke. Gavotte Pavlova
Delibes. 'Naila' Intermezzo

309

Catalani. Danza delle Ondine
Krupinski. Polish Wedding — Mazurka
The London Symphony Orchestra conducted by
Richard Bonynge. SET 523-4

1973

Ballet Music and Entr'Actes from French Opera
Meyerbeer. *Le Prophète* Coronation march
Massenet. *La Navarraise* Nocturne
Gounod. *La Reine de Saba* Waltz (Ballet Act II)
Boïeldieu. *La Dame Blanche* Overture
Massenet. *Chérubin* Entr'acte, Act III
Bizet. *Don Procopio* Entr'acte, Act II
Massenet. *Don César de Bazan* Entr'acte,
  Sevillana
Massenet. *Le Roi de Lahore* Entr'acte, Act V,
  adagio and waltz (Ballet Act III)
Gounod. *Le Tribut de Zamora* Greek dance
Saint-Saëns. *Henry VIII* Dance of the gypsy
Massenet. *Les Erinnyés* Invocation
Delibes. *Le Roi l'a Dit* Entr'acte, Act II
Auber. *La Neige* Overture
The London Symphony Orchestra conducted by
  Richard Bonynge. SXL 6541

Serenata Tebaldi
Donizetti. Me voglio fa 'na casa
Mascagni. La tua stella
Tosti. Sogno
Rossini, L'invito — Bolero
Zandonai. L'assivolo
Cimara. Stornello
Ponchielli. Noi leggevamo insieme
Mascagni. Serenata
Pergolesi. Se tu m'ami
Paradies. M'ha prese alla sua ragna
Scarlatti. O cessate di piagarmi
Gluck. O, del mio dolce ardor
Ricci. Il carretiere del vommero
Mercadante. La sposa del marinaio
Bellini. Malinconia, Ninfa gentile
Puccini. E l'uccelino
Renata Tebaldi (soprano) with Richard Bonynge
  (piano). SXL 6579

Offenbach. *Le Papillon* — Ballet
The London Symphony Orchestra conducted by
  Richard Bonynge. SXL 6588

1974

Delibes. *Sylvia* — Ballet complete.
The New Philharmonia Orchestra conducted by
  Richard Bonynge. SXL 6635-6

Massenet. *Thérèse*
(Thérèse) Huguette Tourangeau with Ryland
  Davies, Louis Quil, Ian Caley, Alan Opie.
  The Linden Singers and the New
  Philharmonia Orchestra conducted by
  Richard Bonynge. SET 572

Pavarotti in Concert
Bononcini. *Griselda*: Per la gloria d'adorarvi
Handel. *Atalanta*: Care selve
A. Scarlatti. Già il sole dal Gange
Bellini. Ma rendi pur contento
Bellini. Dolente immagine di Fille mia
Bellini. Malinconia ninfa gentile
Bellini. Bella Nice, che d'amore
Bellini. Vanne, o rosa fortunata
Tosti. La serenata
Tosti. Luna d'estate
Tosti. Malìa
Tosti. Non t'amo più
Respighi. Nevicata
Respighi. Pioggia
Respighi. Nebbie
Rossini. La danza
Arrangements by Douglas Gamley.
Luciano Pavarotti (tenor) with Orchestra del
  Teatro Communale di Bologna conducted by
  Richard Bonynge. SXL 6650

1975

Arie Antiche
Martini. Plaisir d'amour
Sarti. Lungi dal caro bene
Bononcini. Deh più a me non v'ascondete
Handel. *Alcina*: Verdi prati
A. Scarlatti. Le violette
Gluck. *Alceste*: Divinités du Styx
Handel. *Serse*: Ombra mai fù
Paisiello. Nel cor più non mi sento
Pergolesi. *La Serva Padrona*: Stizzoso, mio
  stizzoso
Attrib. Pergolesi. Tre giorni son che Nina
Paisiello. Chi voul la zingarella
Vivaldi. Piango, gemo, sospiro
Gluck. *Paride ed Elena*: O del mio dolce ardor
Renata Tebaldi (soprano) with the New
  Philharmonia Orchestra conducted by
  Richard Bonynge. SXL 6629

Tchaikovsky. *The Nutcracker* — Ballet Op 71
  complete.
The National Philharmonic Orchestra
  conducted by Richard Bonynge. SXL 6688-9

Straussiana
J. Strauss Jnr. *Die Fledermaus* Overture
Strauss Family arr. Gamley. *Die Fledermaus*
Ballet suite
Strauss Family arr. Désormière. *Le Beau
Danube* Ballet suite
The National Philharmonic Orchestra
conducted by Richard Bonynge. SXL 6701

Auber. *Marco Spada* — Ballet (1857)
The London Symphony Orchestra conducted by
Richard Bonynge. SXL 6707

1976
Meyerbeer and Massenet
Meyerbeer orch. Lambert. *Les Patineurs* Ballet
Massenet. *Le Cid* Ballet music
Massenet. *Ariane* Lamento d'Ariane
The National Philharmonic Orchestra
conducted by Richard Bonynge. SXL 6812

1977
Tchaikovsky. *Swan Lake* — Ballet Op 71
complete
The National Philharmonic Orchestra
conducted by Richard Bonynge. D 37D3

Massenet Songs
Le sais-tu ?
On dit!
Passionnément
L'âme des fleurs
Pensée d'automne
Souvenance
Le petit Jésus
Les yeux clos
Ce que disent les cloches
La mélodie des baisers
Pitcounette
Nuit d'Espagne
L'éventail
Je t'aime!
Les amoureuses sont des folles
Printemps dernier
Roses d'octobre
Sérenade d'automne
Souhait
Elle s'en est allée
Huguette Tourangeau (mezzo-soprano) with
Richard Bonynge (piano). SXL 6765

Massenet
Scènes Alsaciennes
Scènes Dramatiques
Cendrillon Marche des Princesses
The National Philharmonic Orchestra
conducted by Richard Bonynge. SXL 6827

1978
Tchaikovsky. *The Sleeping Beauty* — Ballet Op
66 complete
The National Philharmonic Orchestra
conducted by Richard Bonynge. D 78D3

1979
Mozart Arias And Duets
The Marriage of Figaro Non più andrai...
Crudel! perché finora... Hai già vinta la
causa! Vedro mentr'io sospiro... E Susanna
non vien. Dove sono
Così fan tutte Come scoglio immoto resta...
Donne mie, la fate a tanti
Don Giovanni Là ci darem la mano... Batti,
batti, o bel Masetto... Vedrai, carino
The Magic Flute Bei Männern welche Liebe
fühlen... Ach, ich fühl's... Pa-Pa-Pa-Pa-
Papegena
Isobel Buchanan (soprano) and John Pringle
(baritone) with the Queensland Symphony
Orchestra conducted by Richard Bonynge.
A03
(Produced by the Australian Opera in
association with the Australian Broadcasting
Commission)

1980
Massenet. *La Cigale* — Ballet complete
The National Philharmonic Orchestra
conducted by Richard Bonynge. SXL 6932

For Future Release
Johann Strauss Jnr. *Aschenbrödel (Cinderella)* —
Ballet in three acts — complete.
The National Philharmonic Orchestra
conducted by Richard Bonynge.

Previously-issued titles in new compilations
include:
Great Opera Choruses   SPA 296
Favourite Opera Choruses   DPA 525-6
Immortal Classics   DPA 615-6
World Of The Great Classics — Classical
Favourites   SPA 510
The World's Best Loved Tenor Arias
(Pavarotti)   SXL 6649

311

King Of The High C's (Pavarotti)   SXL 6658
Delibes. Coppélia And Sylvia Highlights   SXL
  6776
Tchaikovsky. The Nutcracker Highlights   SXL
  6821
The Art Of Pavarotti   SXL 6839

First Performances
of Operatic Roles

VENUE	DATE	OPERA	ROLE	PRODUCER	DESIGNER	CONDUCTOR
Covent Garden	Oct. 1952	Mozart: *The Magic Flute*	First Lady	—	Oliver Messel	John Pritchard
Covent Garden	Nov. 1952	Verdi: *Aida*	A Priestess	—	Audrey Cruddas	Sir John Barbirolli
Covent Garden	Nov. 1952	Bellini: *Norma*	Clotilda	Gianfranco Enriquez	Alan Barlow	Vittorio Gui
Covent Garden	Dec. 1952	Verdi: *A Masked Ball*	Amelia	Günther Rennert	Alan Barlow	John Pritchard
Covent Garden Tour Edinburgh	Feb. 1953	Mozart: *The Marriage of Figaro*	Countess Almaviva	—	—	James Gibson
Covent Garden	May 1953	R. Strauss: *Elektra*	The Overseer	Rudolf Hartmann	Isabel Lambert	Erich Kleiber
Covent Garden Tour Bulawayo	Aug. 1953	Britten: *Gloriana*	Penelope (Lady Rich)	Basil Coleman	John Piper	Reginald Goodall
Covent Garden	Oct. 1953	Wagner: *Die Walküre*	Helmwige	—	—	Fritz Stiedry
Covent Garden	Nov. 1953	Bizet: *Carmen*	Frasquita	Anthony Asquith— Tyrone Guthrie	Wakhevitch	John Pritchard
Covent Garden	Apr. 1954	Verdi: *Aida*	Aida	—	Audrey Cruddas	Emmanuel Young
Covent Garden	May 1954	Weber: *Der Freischütz*	Agathe	Christopher West	Roger Furse	Edward Downes
Covent Garden	May 1954	Wagner: *Das Rheingold*	Woglinde	Rudolf Hartmann	Leslie Hurry	Fritz Stiedry

313

VENUE	DATE	OPERA	ROLE	PRODUCER	DESIGNER	CONDUCTOR
Covent Garden	June 1954	Wagner: *Götterdämmerung*	Rhine-maiden	Rudolf Hartmann	Leslie Hurry	Fritz Stiedry
Covent Garden	June 1954	Wagner: *Siegfried*	The Woodbird	Rudolf Hartmann	Leslie Hurry	Fritz Stiedry
Covent Garden	Nov. 1954	Offenbach: *The Tales of Hoffmann*	Antonia	Günther Rennert	Wakhevitch	Edward Downes
Covent Garden	Jan. 1955	Tippett: *The Midsummer Marriage*	Jennifer	Christopher West	Barbara Hepworth	John Pritchard
Covent Garden Tour Edinburgh	Feb. 1955	Offenbach: *The Tales of Hoffmann*	Giulietta	Günther Rennert	Wakhevitch	Edward Downes
Covent Garden	June 1955	Offenbach: *The Tales of Hoffmann*	Olympia	Günther Rennert	Wakhevitch	Edward Downes
Covent Garden	Oct. 1955	Bizet: *Carmen*	Micaëla	Anthony Asquith — Tyrone Guthrie	Wakhevitch	Edward Downes
Covent Garden	Nov. 1956	Mozart: *The Magic Flute*	Pamina	Christopher West	Wakhevitch	Rafael Kubelik
Covent Garden	Jan. 1957	Wagner: *The Mastersingers of Nuremberg*	Eva	Erich Witte	Wakhevitch	Rafael Kubelik
St Pancras Assembly Rooms, London	Mar. 1957	Handel: *Alcina*	Alcina	Anthony Besch	—	Charles Farncombe
Covent Garden	May 1957	Verdi: *Rigoletto*	Gilda	—	—	Edward Downes
Glyndebourne	June 1957	Mozart: *Der Schauspieldirektor*	Mme Herz	Anthony Besch	Peter Rice	Bryan Balkwill
Covent Garden	Dec. 1957	Verdi: *Otello*	Desdemona	Peter Potter	Wakhevitch	Edward Downes
Covent Garden	Jan. 1958	Poulenc: *The Carmelites*	Mme Lidoine	Margherita Wallmann	Wakhevitch	Rafael Kubelik
Vancouver	July 1958	Mozart: *Don Giovanni*	Donna Anna	Günther Rennert	Ita Maximova	Nicholas Goldschmidt

VENUE	DATE	OPERA	ROLE	PRODUCER	DESIGNER	CONDUCTOR
Leeds	Oct. 1958	Handel: *Samson*	An Israelite Woman	Herbert Graf	Oliver Messel	Raymond Leppard
Covent Garden	Feb. 1959	Donizetti: *Lucia di Lammermoor*	Lucia	Franco Zeffirelli	Franco Zeffirelli	Tullio Serafin
Sadler's Wells, London	June 1959	Handel: *Rodelinda*	Rodelinda	Anthony Besch	Robin Pidcock	Charles Farncombe
Covent Garden	Jan. 1960	Verdi: *La Traviata*	Violetta Valéry	—	Sophie Fedorovitch	Nello Santi
Glyndebourne	May 1960	Bellini: *I Puritani*	Elvira	Gianfranco Enriquez	Desmond Heeley	Vittorio Gui
Covent Garden	Oct. 1960	Bellini: *La Sonnambula*	Amina	Enrico Medioli	Fillipo Sanjust	Tullio Serafin
La Scala Milan	May 1961	Bellini: *Beatrice di Tenda*	Beatrice	Franco Enriquez	Nicola Benois	Antonino Votto
Covent Garden	Jan. 1962	Mozart: *Die Zauberflöte*	The Queen of Night	Otto Klemperer	Georg Eisler	Otto Klemperer
La Scala Milan	Mar. 1962	Meyerbeer: *Gli Ugonotti*	Margherita di Valois	Franco Enriquez	Nicola Benois	Gianandrea Gavazzeni
La Scala Milan	Dec. 1962	Rossini: *Semiramide*	Semiramide	Marguerite Wallmann	Nicola Benois	Gabriele Santini
Sadler's Wells, London	June 1963	Handel: *Giulio Cesare*	Cleopatra	Norman Ayrton	Michael Warre	Charles Farncombe
Vancouver	Oct. 1963	Bellini:*Norma*	Norma	Irving Guttman	Gail McCance	Richard Bonynge
Philadelphia	Mar. 1965	Gounod:*Faust*	Marguerite	Irving Guttman	—	Richard Bonynge
Covent Garden	June 1966	Donizetti: *La Fille du Régiment*	Marie	Sandro Sequi	Anna Anni – Marcel Escoffier	Richard Bonynge
Seattle	Apr. 1967	Delibes:*Lakmé*	Lakmé	Glynn Ross	—	Richard Bonynge
Vienna	May 1967	Haydn: *Orfeo ed Euridice*	Euridice	Rudolf Hartmann	Heinz Ludwig	Richard Bonynge
Seattle	Nov. 1970	Offenbach: *Les Contes d'Hoffmann*	(Olympia (Giulietta (Antonia (Stella	Bliss Hebert	Alan Charles Klein	Richard Bonynge

VENUE	DATE	OPERA	ROLE	PRODUCER	DESIGNER	CONDUCTOR
San Francisco	Nov. 1971	Donizetti: *Maria Stuarda*	Maria	Tito Capobianco	Pier Luigi Pizzi	Richard Bonynge
Vancouver	Oct. 1972	Donizetti: *Lucrezia Borgia*	Lucrezia	Irving Guttman	José Varona	Richard Bonynge
San Francisco	Sept. 1973	J. Strauss Jnr: *Die Fledermaus*	Rosalinda	Lotfi Mansouri	Oliver Smith	Richard Bonynge
San Francisco	Oct. 1974	Massenet:*Esclarmonde*	Esclarmonde	Lotfi Mansouri	Beni Montrésor	Richard Bonynge
San Francisco	Sept. 1975	Verdi: *Il Trovatore*	Leonora	Patrick Libby	Wolfram Skalicki	Richard Bonynge
Vancouver	Apr. 1976	Lehár: *The Merry Widow*	Anna	Lotfi Mansouri	José Varona	Richard Bonynge
Sydney	July 1977	Puccini: *Suor Angelica*	Suor Angelica	Moffatt Oxenbould	Desmond Digby	Richard Bonynge
Vancouver	Sept. 1977	Massenet: *Le Roi de Lahore*	Sita	Sandro Sequi	Fiorella Marianni	Richard Bonynge
Sydney	July 1979	Mozart: *Idomeneo*	Elettra	Robin Lovejoy	John Truscott	Richard Bonynge
Sydney	July 1980	Verdi: *I Masnadieri*	Amalia	Peter Beauvais	Michael Stennett	Richard Bonynge
San Diego	Sept. 1980	J. Strauss Jnr: *Die Fledermaus*	Adele	Tito Capobianco	Carl Thoms	Richard Bonynge

In addition to these performances, Sutherland sang the following roles in Sydney and London:

VENUE	DATE	OPERA	ROLE
Sydney	Aug. 1947	Purcell: *Dido and Aeneas*	Dido
Sydney	July 1950	Handel: *Samson*	Delilah and An Israelite Woman
Sydney	June 1951	Goossens: *Judith*	Judith
Royal College of Music, London	Mar. 1952	Bizet: *Carmen*	Cigarette Girl
..	May 1952	Shaw: *All At Sea*	Mrs Empson
..	July 1952	Puccini: *Il Tabarro*	Giorgietta

Selected Bibliography

Braddon, Russell. *Joan Sutherland*. Collins, London/Sydney, 1962.
Greenfield, Edward. *Joan Sutherland*. Ian Allan, London, 1972.

The following publications include references to Sutherland and her career.
Ardoin, John and Fitzgerald, Gerald. *Callas*. Holt, Reinhart and Winston, New York, 1974.
Bing, Sir Rudolf. *5000 Nights at The Opera*. Doubleday, New York, 1972.
Castle, Charles. *Noël*. W.H. Allen, London, 1972.
Chapin, Schuyler. *Musical Chairs*. Putnam, New York, 1977.
The Editors of Opera News. *The Golden Horseshoe*. Viking, New York, 1965.
Galatopolous, Stelios. *Callas: La Divina*. Dent, London, 1963.
Hallrecht, Montague. *The Quiet Showman*. Collins, London, 1975.
Jellinek, George. *Callas*. Zitt-Davis, New York, 1960.
Kolodin, Irving. *The Opera Omnibus*. E.P. Dutton, New York, 1976.
Lesley, Cole. *The Life of Noël Coward*. Jonathan Cape, London, 1976.
Mackenzie, Barbara & Findlay. *Singers of Australia from Melba to Sutherland*. Lansdowne, Melbourne, 1967.
Natan, Alex. *Prima Donna*. Basilius Press, Basel/Stuttgart, 1962.
Pleasants, Henry. *The Great Singers*. Simon & Schuster, New York, 1966.
Rosenthal, Harold F. *Great Singers of Today*. J. Calder & Boyars, London, 1966.
Rosenthal, Harold F. *Opera at Covent Garden*. Gollancz, London, 1967.
Rosenthal, Harold F. *Two Centuries of Opera at Covent Garden*. Putnam, London, 1958.
Rubin, Stephen E. *The New Met in Profile*. Macmillan, New York, 1974.
Seligman, Paul. *Debuts and Farewells*. Knopf, New York, 1972.
Sargeant, Winthrop. *Divas*. Coward, McCann & Geoghegan, New York, 1973.
Sills, Beverly. *Bubbles*. Bobbs-Merrill, Indianapolis/New York, 1976.
Steane, J.B. *The Grand Tradition*. Duckworth, London, 1974.
Tait, Viola. *A Family of Brothers*. Heinemann, Melbourne, 1971.
Tubeuf, Andre. *Le Chant Retrouvé*. Fayard, Paris, 1979.
Wayner, Robert J. (Ed.) *What Did They Sing at The Met?* Wayner Publications, New York, 1972.
Wisneski, Henry. *Maria Callas: The Art Behind The Legend*. Doubleday, New York, 1975.

The principal reviews of Sutherland's opera and concert performances are best found in the press of the city where she performed. Comprehensive reviews and information about her recordings are in the leading specialist magazines in Britain and the United States, including *Gramophone, Records and Recording, Musical America* and *High Fidelity*.

Joan Sutherland Music Editor.
Sutherland, Joan (Ed.) *Mozart.* Exsultate Jubilate K165. Augener, London.

The cantata consists of two arias for solo voice and orchestra connected by a recitative. The Alleluia ends the work. Sutherland phrases the vocal line with accents and dynamics clearly marked and the edition is obviously for an experienced singer.

Index

This index refers to people, organizations, musical works, opera houses and theatres, newspapers and journals covered by the narrative. Page numbers in **bold** type refer to illustrations.

321